Bob ZanGRando;
July 27, 2001.

The Mixed Legacy
of
Charlotte Perkins Gilman

The Mixed Legacy
of
Charlotte Perkins Gilman

Edited by
Catherine J. Golden and
Joanna Schneider Zangrando

DELAWARE

Newark: University of Delaware Press
London: Associated University Presses

Associated University Presses
440 Forsgate Drive
Cranbury, NJ 08512

Associated University Presses
16 Barter Street
London WC1A 2AH, England

Associated University Presses
P.O. Box 338, Port Credit
Mississauga, Ontario
Canada L5G 4L8

The paper used in this publication meets the requirements of the American National Standard for Permanence of Paper for Printed Library Materials Z39.48-1984.

Library of Congress Cataloging-in-Publication Data

The mixed legacy of Charlotte Perkins Gilman / edited by Catherine J. Golden and Joanna S. Zangrando.
     p. cm.
  Includes bibliographical references (p.   ) and index.
  ISBN 0-87413-688-1 (alk. paper)
  1. Gilman, Charlotte Perkins, 1860–1935—Criticism and interpretation.
  2. Women and   literature—United States—History—19th century.
  3. Women and literature—United States—History—20th century.
  4. Feminism and literature—United States—History. I. Golden,
  Catherine. II. Zangrando, Joanna S., 1939–
  PS1744.G57 Z76 2000
  818'.409 1—dc21   99-043538

To the Memory
of Elaine R. Hedges

Contents

8

Preface

THIS COLLECTION OF ESSAYS ON THE MIXED LEGACY OF CHARLOTTE
Perkins Gilman is itself the legacy of the Second International Charlotte Perkins Gilman Conference held at Skidmore College, Saratoga
Springs, New York, 26–28 July 1997. Skidmore is but one of the many
academic institutions where Charlotte Perkins Gilman lectured in the
early twentieth century. The conference itself capitalized upon the success of the First International Conference held in Liverpool, United
Kingdom, in July 1995 (designed to raise Gilman's profile in Great Britain) as well as the past thirty years of scholarship reclaiming Gilman
(evidenced by the creation of the Charlotte Perkins Gilman Society in
1990).

This Second International Conference brought together Gilman
scholars from across the United States, Germany, and the United Kingdom to share research on all aspects of Gilman's work and influence.
Panels featured eminent presenters from a range of disciplines (history,
English, American studies, sociology, women's studies, the arts) and a
new generation of Gilman scholars (graduate students and those new
to Gilman studies). Walter Stetson Chamberlin and Linda Stetson
Chamberlin, Gilman's grandson and great-granddaughter, offered
family lore, personal reflections, and an account of Gilman's extensive
lecture tours from the late-nineteenth to the early-twentieth centuries
as well as insights on Gilman's plans for dress reform. The conference
was supported by a mini-grant from the New York Council on the Humanities, the expertise of staff members of the Office of Special Programs and the Office of College Relations, Skidmore faculty members,
and the Office of the Dean of the Faculty. We are grateful to all of the
individuals who helped to make the conference a success.

Tragically, Elaine R. Hedges, a keynote presenter, died just weeks before the conference. Thus, the conference began with a tribute to
Elaine, delivered by her long-time friend and editor, Florence Howe;
editor of The Feminist Press, Florence Howe was responsible for reprinting "The Yellow Wall-Paper" with Elaine's afterword in 1973. In
the early 1970s, Elaine played a pivotal role in helping to reclaim Gilman among other overlooked American women writers. Much like the

narrator of Charlotte Perkins Gilman's "The Yellow Wall-Paper" who tears down the restricting bars of the wallpaper confining her to her patriarchal world, Elaine Hedges tore down restrictions of the literary canon in the 1970s and brought Gilman's landmark story to The Feminist Press and national attention. And in 1990, along with Shelley Fisher Fishkin, she created the Charlotte Perkins Gilman Society, serving as president until her death. A truly generous colleague, Elaine inspired and encouraged many Gilman scholars over the past three decades. It is fitting that we dedicate this collection of essays to her.

Drawing from among the excellent papers delivered at the conference, this collection focuses attention on Gilman's positive and negative characteristics. Both are integral parts of the mixed legacy of a figure still regarded as a visionary for social reform in her own time and, to an extent, our own.

There are other individuals we would like to thank for their invaluable help in bringing this project to fruition. Denise D. Knight of SUNY Cortland responded, always pleasantly and promptly, to numerous queries about Gilman's life and work. Michael Marx, too, served as a sounding board for the entire project. Nancy Osberg–Otrembiak, secretary for the American Studies Department and the Liberal Studies Program, and Ryan Kimmet, Skidmore class of '99, provided excellent assistance in a range of tasks including typing, research, and photocopying. Joosje Anderson, associate director, Graphic Design and College Relations, created the cover design for the volume. Donald Mell, chair, board of editors, University of Delaware Press, and Julien Yoseloff, director of its parent organization Associated University Presses, offered helpful assistance in all stages of this project, as did Christine A. Retz, managing editor of AUP. Kristina R. Fenelly, Skidmore class of '02, and Timothy J. Griffin contributed invaluable service at the final stage of this project. Finally, we would like to thank each of our contributors for their conscientious and prompt response to all of our requests and deadlines.

Introduction

Speaking reflectively about her childhood and her literary imagination, Charlotte Perkins Gilman (1860–1935) notes in her autobiography: "I could make a world to suit me."[1] An optimistic reformer, Gilman held on to her dream and, through her writing, aimed to "make a world" with gender equality where women would participate equally with men in performing the world's work. Gilman argued that women should receive wages for housework and be economically independent and productive members of society in occupations outside the private home—a particular target for her criticism. Some of her most visionary ideas—professional housecleaning services and community child care, for example—have become realities.

First known as a poet, Gilman—a keen critic of female subjugation—produced satirical verse "written to drive nails with."[2] Her first book of poems, *In This Our World* (1893), enjoyed a near cult following in the United States and England. At the turn of the century, Gilman enjoyed an international reputation as a writer, lecturer, and socialist, and her prodigious output on complex social and economic issues (novels, stories, poetry, lectures, journalism, theoretical works) stands as a major contribution to modern feminist thought. After her death in 1935, she was virtually forgotten, but with the revival of the women's movement in the 1960s and 1970s, Gilman was "rediscovered." In 1966, the prominent historian Carl Degler reclaimed her an important figure in women's history in his critical introduction to the reissued *Women and Economics* (1898); this work for which Gilman was best known had an enormous immediate impact on reformers and analysts of American society. In 1973, Elaine R. Hedges likewise celebrated Gilman in her afterword to "The Yellow Wall-Paper" (1892), reprinted by The Feminist Press; this publication helped to establish Gilman's place in the contemporary literary canon. Resurrected along with other works by overlooked late-nineteenth-century women writers, "The Yellow Wall-Paper" is now hailed in feminist circles, regularly included in course syllabi, and reprinted in major anthologies.

This collection emerges at an important crossroads in Gilman studies. While scholars, beginning in the 1960s, have welcomed her legacy

11

and worked to recover much of Gilman's prodigious output of fiction and nonfiction concerning important but contested social and economic issues, scholars of the late 1990s admit that the field of Gilman studies has yet sufficiently to confront evidence of repugnant racial theories, xenophobia, and ethnocentrism in her works of fiction, poetry, and theory. Nonetheless, feminists still applaud Gilman for her important analyses of women and work, the home, child care, gender relations, and women's autonomy, and interest in her life and work continues to grow in academic circles. Adding to the body of scholarship on Gilman produced during the last three decades, this collection of fourteen new essays on Gilman's mixed legacy underscores the contemporary relevance of Gilman's analysis of American society and the enduring value of her literary and theoretical work but, also, raises questions about the limitations revealed in her analyses. Consideration now of her full oeuvre embraces a complex Gilman to be sure, a very human and prolific author whose vision was both far ahead of and regrettably rooted in the biases of her own time. Doubtless, readers of the collection will find themselves trying to reconcile Gilman's, at times, reactionary perspective with her progressive evolutionist belief that human agency would achieve an equitable human world. Different from other volumes on Gilman's life and work, this collection of essays addresses Gilman's mixed legacy—her uncompromising critique of what she viewed as an unjust, inequitable society and her vision for a truly humane, egalitarian world alongside her compromising and persistent presentation of contemporary racial, ethnic, and class stereotypes. The range of essays provides scholars and students alike fresh approaches to serious critical inquiry. Examining selections from Gilman's entire oeuvre, replete with prejudice and promise, requires readers to confront her conservative, racist views as well as her progressive vision. Both are integral parts of Gilman's legacy for an audience moving from the twentieth to the twenty-first century.

A characteristic of Gilman's turn-of-the-century analyses of gender-related issues was her amazing ability to recognize, to welcome, to appropriate as her own, and to synthesize and express for a general public audience many of the cutting edge social and economic arguments of the leading critics of her era. Typically, Gilman focused her social and economic critiques on the domestic domain that traditionally defined and confined women. In doing so, Gilman the social reformer extended the contemporary association of women's reform beyond the public, political arena of the women's suffrage movement; her critiques incorporated the personal, private, and domestic arena, the impetus for her commitment to social change.

Gilman publicized and assigned public responsibility and accountability for social and economic issues generally deemed private and, therefore, the individual's responsibility. Thus, in her theoretical works, her fiction, her lectures, her poetry, her journalism—all intended for public consumption and suasion—she proposed solutions for enhancing the autonomy and self-definition of women, all of which depended upon radical changes in the nature of domestic spaces, tasks, and relationships that confined and defined women historically.

Incorporating many of the ideas current among her reformist peers, Gilman fashioned a body of foresighted reforms intended to release women from the constrictions of home and family, among them: specialized training, including the most technologically sophisticated devices, for paid housekeepers; the establishment of child care centers staffed by trained child caregivers; the creation of homes as sites of pleasant refuge for all family members; the availability of healthy, wholesome meals prepared by trained nutritionists to families in their "kitchenless homes" or to unmarried apartment dwellers; the selection of a marriage partner on the basis of mutual love and respect rather than, for women, economic necessity or, for men, ornamental service and prestige; and, importantly, the opening of professions to women, who would join with men, equally, in doing "the world's work." Admittedly, Gilman, the optimistic evolutionary, advocated solutions for ending what she called married women's "sexuoeconomic" dependent status that have yet to be fully realized; too, she addressed her solutions primarily to a middle-class audience much like herself—a mixed legacy indeed. One may well ask: what type of woman did she have in mind for professional housekeeping and child care?

Gilman's focus on gender issues reflects many of the personal experiences informing public arguments that women should achieve a good balance between a work life of economic self-sufficiency and a personal life of satisfying intimacy. For women, as well as for men, Gilman believed a sense of self could be derived from doing "the world's work." Gilman, herself, expressed hesitancy about marrying a second time unless she could, in essence, continue to write and to lecture and, thereby, pay her own way.

During her life-long crusade for gender equality and women's autonomy, Gilman necessarily undermined the traditional assumption that the site of work fitting for all women was the private, individual household. She fashioned a new presumption: the site of work appropriate for women was the community, the world, where they would join with men to create a just society. It is this insistent vision of women as public participants in the work of an evolving society that continues to inspire.

Though the work of Charlotte Perkins Gilman is still regarded as visionary for its own time, and to an extent our time, critics today are

disturbed to find evidence of problematic issues such as racism, ethnocentrism, homophobia, and classism in her vast oeuvre of fiction,
poetry, and theoretical analyses. Both her published and unpublished
writings give insufficient attention to social class, race, and ethnicity,
thereby detracting from Gilman's agenda for liberating women, a point
Susan Lanser has most forcefully addressed.[3] In her critique of "The
Yellow Wall-Paper," which she labels a "sacred feminist text," Lanser
directs attention to a side of Gilman evident in the *Forerunner* (1909–
16) and other writings that is discomfiting at best.

In the *Forerunner,* the journal Gilman single-handedly wrote, produced, and edited for seven years, she chastises the "lazy old Orientals"
who do not want to work, exhibits anti-Semitic biases, and, like some
other "nativist" intellectuals of her time, argues against the influx of
"undesirables" in favor of immigrants of a "better stock."[4] Gilman's
interest in the working class is evidenced by the gold medal she earned
from the Trades and Labor Unions of Almeda County, California, in
1893 for her essay, "The Labor Movement" (1892).[5] Too, her "adopted
mother," Helen Campbell, with whom she lived in California while they
jointly edited the *Impress* (1894–95), had earlier written about the experiences of urban, poor working-class women, whose lives she had inves-
tigated. From Campbell, Gilman doubtless gained a heightened
awareness of working class women's experiences. In the *Forerunner*
(1913), she speaks against the oppression and mistreatment of Indians,
Africans, and Mexicans. There is no denying, however, that her advocacy of racial purity via "negative eugenics" and her racial slurs, evident
throughout her writing career and particularly in her later and private
writing, reveal a darker side to Gilman. For example, in her lone detective novel *Unpunished* (written circa 1929), she refers to a "little black
Jenny," who is stereotypically a laundress. Her merciless interchanging
of rhyming Italian names for a missing servant (all names ending in
"o") is likewise evidence of stereotyping by today's standards.[6] Furthermore, Gilman's proposals for liberating women were addressed primarily to middle-class women. These biases, in part, reflect prejudices held
by some Anglo-Americans at the turn of the twentieth century and are
evident in the work of other women writers of her time, such as Virginia
Woolf. Nonetheless, for readers today, Gilman's is a mixed legacy of
prejudice and promise. Her limitations and biases—uncomfortable for
those who admire much about this multifaceted author—are addressed
in this volume by Gary Scharnhorst, Denise D. Knight, Joanne Karpinski, Ann J. Lane, Catherine J. Golden, Charlotte Margolis Goodman,
Frederick Wegener, and Shelley Fisher Fishkin.

Those familiar with the biographies of Gilman are aware that different facets of Gilman's life emerge from the perspective of each biogra-

pher, and Gilman appears anew in every biography about her as well as in her autobiography, her letters, her diaries, and her comprehensive oeuvre. For example, Ann Lane's engaging biography, *To Herland and Beyond* (1990), is decidedly personal—the chapter headings are the first names of the significant members of Gilman's family and friends. In contrast, Gary Scharnhorst's biography, *Charlotte Perkins Gilman* (1985), offers a more formal and thorough analysis of Gilman's life and accomplishments. Together, a fuller picture of Gilman emerges—at once intimate but also fully embracing her achievements and her oeuvre. Such is the intent of the first section of this book, "Five Ways of Looking at Charlotte Perkins Gilman." It brings together the views of Ann J. Lane, Joanne Karpinski, Mary A. Hill, Denise D. Knight, and Gary Scharnhorst—each of whom presents a personal perspective on Gilman's life and accomplishments.

Biographers often lament that some of their best friends are dead, and so it seems is the case for Lane. In her essay "What My Therapist, My Daughter, and Charlotte Taught Me While I Was Writing the Biography of Charlotte Perkins Gilman," Lane is clearly on a first name basis with Gilman, and her comments are as revealing about her life as Gilman's own. Writing the life of a subject is often inseparable from writing one's own life, and this has particular significance for women, as Lane contemplates: "I now believe that one of the reasons why so many feminist scholars turned to the writing of biography in the 1970s and 1980s was not only to uncover the lives and work of our forebears, an idea we all then appreciated and understood, but also as a way of dealing with our—the biographers'—own lives, sensing ourselves unworthy of writing our own stories. . . . We dealt with the silencing of our own lives by creating the lives of others" (27–28). In her essay, Lane chronicles how her own experiences rearing her two daughters as a single mother led her to connect, for example, to Gilman's feelings of inadequacy as a mother and Gilman's expression of frustration with women's responsibility for cooking in the private home presented in *Women and Economics*. While acknowledging that other biographers read Gilman differently from her, Lane also explores how Gilman as a role model, along with her therapist, helped her to succeed as a professional woman: "Coming to realize that struggle of hers gave me the inspiration and the power to forge a study of her life and to help me forge my own" (34).

In her equally personal essay "The Economic Conundrum in the Lifewriting of Charlotte Perkins Gilman," Joanne Karpinski focuses on the dichotomy between Gilman's autobiographical presentation of herself as essentially economically self-sufficient and her admission of her oftentimes economically marginal existence and dependence on gifts from others in the larger body of her lifewriting. It is this gap between "her theorizing and her personal practice" that Karpinski holds responsible for Gilman's inability to devise social solutions for the funding of philanthropic services and artistic endeavors equal to her solutions for assisting working mothers, such as professional child care. Karpinski argues that Gilman's "disinclination squarely to confront the financial ramifications of offering her life as an inspiration to other women shortchanges those she most wished to help" (42). Just what prompted Gilman to omit from her autobiography her very real dependence on loans and gifts from others at certain times throughout her life? What constrained Gilman from admitting publicly her personal, ongoing financial dependency? How useful a model for other women is a life presented for public consumption absent "warts and all?"

Mary A. Hill offers another intimate portrait of Gilman in " 'Letters Are Like Morning Prayers': The Private Work of Charlotte Perkins Gilman." Focusing on Gilman's extensive late-1890s letters to Houghton Gilman, who became in 1900 her second husband, she explores the shame and self-contempt Gilman admits to in her struggles to achieve satisfaction in her work. Hill presents here not only Gilman's struggles but her courage to confront her demons—the depths of her depression—that plagued her: "for the most part, Gilman realized that the real enemy was in herself" (48). Hill's Gilman, like the mythological Persephone, is trapped in the underworld; like Medusa, she has a "monster" within her, and she tries to work through her inner "catacombs" in her letters to Houghton Gilman. Ultimately, Hill argues, "Gilman used her letters as a source of healing and empowering" (49). Connecting her life and Gilman's readers' lives to Gilman's own, as Lane does, Hill applauds Gilman for helping women "to find the goddess in ourselves" (51).

Denise D. Knight in "On Editing Gilman's Diaries" argues that Gilman's diaries—though often a record merely of Gilman's routine daily living—give insight into *The Living of Charlotte Perkins Gilman,* as Gilman aptly named her autobiography. While the diaries contain little "confessional" writing and a large proportion of mundane events, Knight claims: "it is my contention that those daily routines—of reading, sewing, visiting, cleaning, 'trotting' about, cooking, and writing volumes of letters [as Hill witnesses]—everything, in effect, that epitomizes the cult of domesticity—were critical in the evolution of Gilman's social theories" (58). Her essay reveals tantalizing tidbits about Gilman, from the tonics she took to her literary tastes and distastes. She points to Gilman's daily recording of nineteenth-century political and historical events, as well as to how the diaries serve to document her racism, a point that Scharnhorst explores in further depth. Knight indicates how the diaries lay the foundation for her groundbreaking arguments for women's advancement, which she expands in *Women and Economics*. Instructive, too, is Knight's explanation of the various dilemmas she faced when undertaking the Gilman diary project.

Finally, Gary Scharnhorst, in "Historicizing Gilman: A Bibliographer's View," steps back from any one source or time period or topic to look at Gilman's entire oeuvre in order to focus on the uncomfortable aspects all Gilman scholars, he argues, must acknowledge:

> Gilman was at many points, especially from a modern perspective, remarkably hidebound and conventional. Her racial theories, her ethnocentrism and xenophobia, however repugnant they are to us today, were, I believe, key to many of her ideas about evolution and social motherhood. (67)

Scharnhorst notes that some of her proposals were not particularly radical; as well, she revealed a prudishness that becomes more evident in her later work. Scharnhorst offers suggestions for further research on Gilman's mixed legacy: "as scholars we should read all of her work we can find but read it critically, measuring her achievement on a historical template, situating her not only in our time but in her own" (72).

The next section, "Gilman's Literary Career and Her Contemporaries," includes essays that explore Gilman's juvenilia, her career as a writer, and her relationship to other writers of her time. Several of the essays address her biases and limitations while others call attention to her lesser-known writings and celebrate her life and achievements. In the first essay of this section, " 'When the songs are over and sung': Gilman's Childhood Writings and Writings for Children," Jill Rudd looks specifically at Gilman's juvenilia and writing for children, areas little explored to date, and contextualizes them in terms of Gilman's later theoretical writings (e.g., *Concerning Children* [1900]) in which she explores gender dynamics and adult-child relations. Rudd advances that in these writings we find "The tension lies between the lure of an apparently carefree state and the security of one bound by rules and conventions" (82). In Gilman's unfinished story "Prince Cherry," written when Gilman was but ten years old, Rudd ultimately concludes that "It is here that we find the link between the treatment of the child and of the woman in society which Gilman sought to change. For each she advocated education and information over ignorance and blind obedience" (87). Gilman's juvenilia and writing for children reveal that real freedom for children and women lies in knowledge and responsible action.

Continuing a discussion of Gilman's juvenilia in " 'Dreaming Always of Lovely Things Beyond': Living Towards *Herland,* Experiential Foregrounding," Carol Farley Kessler explores the utopian ambitions that first emerge when Gilman was ten years old; "this imagery flows like an underground stream through Gilman's life, bubbling up during the 1880s and 1890s, until it fully surfaces in the 1915 *Herland*" (89). Kessler moves from Gilman's juvenilia, to her experiences as a teen, to the letters she wrote to her daughter Katharine in which Gilman reconnects with her own childhood experiences and rediscovers her first cousin Houghton Gilman. Kessler explains how these significant junctures in Gilman's life prefigure imagery of the meeting between the male intruders and three Herlanders. Thus Kessler ultimately concludes that Gilman's juvenilia, correspondence, and *Herland* can be "understood as but fragile surfaces covering painfully-lived experience" (99).

In "Rewriting the West Cure: Charlotte Perkins Gilman, Owen Wister, and the Sexual Politics of Neurasthenia," Jennifer Tuttle uses Gilman's autobiography, *The Living of Charlotte Perkins Gilman,* to focus attention on a significant but often overlooked chapter entitled "The Breakdown." Looking not at Gilman's ideas about gender ideology and the rest cure itself, she analyzes Gilman's decision to go West, a significant theme in much of her oeuvre. Further, she examines Gilman's reference to Owen Wister's *The Virginian* (1902) and explores significant parallels between Wister's life and Gilman's own: when Wister approached S. Weir Mitchell two years before Gilman had, Mitchell advised Wister to go West, but not to rest, and this account of his time at a cattle ranch in Wyoming is fictionalized in *The Virginian.* Tuttle argues that in rejecting Mitchell's Rest Cure and his mandate never to write again, Gilman redefines the Rest Cure and goes West—as Mitchell's male patients did—to a "curative region in which she would remake herself as a public writer, speaker, and social activist" (104).

In "Caging the Beast: The Radical Treatment for 'Excessive Maleness' in Gilman's Fiction," Catherine J. Golden continues the discussion of Gilman and her contemporaries. She situates Gilman's argument for women's emancipation from patriarchy in relation to the writing of other contemporary women writers—Kate Chopin, Margaret Oliphant, Olive Schreiner, and Edith Summers Kelley—as she examines the patriarch in three Gilman texts spanning her career: her best-known "The Yellow Wall-Paper" (1892); her short story "The Widow's Might" (1911); and her lone detective novel *Unpunished* (ca. 1929), a work which, Golden argues, conveys Gilman's racism and ethnic stereotyping while still making a forceful feminist statement. These works demonstrate Gilman's increasingly violent eradication of her progressively villainous patriarchs. Golden notes: "While John, the husband/doctor of 'The Yellow Wall-Paper,' swoons at the end of the story, Mr. McPherson of 'The Widow's Might' dies of natural causes, and Wade

Vaughn of *Unpunished* ends up as a fatality of premeditated murder" (123). In her treatise *The Man-Made World* (1911), Gilman explores the negative ramifications of "excessive maleness," primal in the Victorian patriarch. Gilman suggests that in order to achieve a "human world," "It is not a question of interfering with or punishing men" (*MMW* 246–47); however, Golden argues that in her fiction, Gilman demonstrates that the patriarch must be "punished" and manhood reformulated if society is to improve.

Comparing Gilman to another literary sister whose work has also been revalued, Frederick Wegener explores "Charlotte Perkins Gilman, Edith Wharton, and the Divided Heritage of American Literary Feminism." Gilman and Wharton, though exact contemporaries, are "seldom jointly discussed" (136). Wegener proceeds to demonstrate how their literary careers parallel each other in interesting ways, but points to poignant dissimilarities, such as Gilman's devotion to overtly political writing with a "purpose" versus Wharton's dedication to writing as artistry, an aesthetic ideal. Ultimately, Wegener finds areas of conjunction—such as the attention to the economic dependence of women—between these two otherwise discordant figures whom he suggests "divide between them the legacy of American literary feminism in their time" (137).

The final paper in this section is Charlotte Margolis Goodman's "Paper Mates: The Sisterhood of Charlotte Perkins Gilman and Edith Summers Kelley." Goodman not only cites the influence of Edward Bellamy on Gilman's utopian writing, but, in this case, specifies Gilman as a possible influence on Edith Summers Kelley's novel *Weeds* (1923), a work still deserving of a wider audience. Though both Kelley and Gilman focus on the lives of women constrained in a patriarchal society, Gilman is now celebrated as a feminist writer, and Kelley regrettably remains an obscure literary figure. Comparing Gilman's poetry (e.g., "The Mother's Charge") and fiction ("The Unnatural Mother") to Kelley's *Weeds*, Goodman underscores the differences between the two authors in their respective treatment of class issues. Goodman notes, too, important parallels between the two writers who, "Believing that paper can serve a more important function than that of decorating the walls of one's house, . . . dramatized in their writing the inequities of a patriarchal society that made women economically dependent on men, confined women to the home, and prevented them from participating in the larger world as fully as men did" (169–70).

Just as the narrator of "The Yellow Wall-Paper" explores the nuances of the ever-changing wallpaper of her nursery prison, critics today continue to explore the tapestry of this richly ambiguous text, which has engendered over two dozen articles since its republication by The Feminist Press in 1973. The next section, "Re-Envisioning 'The Yellow Wall-Paper,'" offers two new readings that emphasize material aspects of Gilman's best-known and still compelling work.

Ann Heilmann, in "Overwriting Decadence: Charlotte Perkins Gilman, Oscar Wilde, and the Feminization of Art in 'The Yellow Wall-Paper,'" focuses attention not strictly on autobiographical aspects of the story but on the association of the wallpaper with fin-de-siècle decadence: Oscar Wilde, the color yellow, and a male-dominated aesthetic movement. "The Yellow Wall-Paper" is Gilman's critique, then, of an elite, male art world critical of and, generally, closed to women artists. Heilmann argues that the late-nineteenth-century aesthetic movement was male; its opposite, morality, was female. The narrator in "The Yellow Wall-Paper," then, represents the "doubly deviant" woman artist. The color and design of the wallpaper confront her as yet another version of the patriarchy from which she must free herself. Heilmann concludes that Gilman "made 'a track to the water's edge' of 'human' art by mapping the transition from male aestheticism to a new female aesthetic" (187).

In her essay "'[A] Kind of "debased Romanesque" with *delirium tremens*': Late-Victorian Wall Coverings and Charlotte Perkins Gilman's 'The Yellow Wall-Paper,'" Heather Kirk Thomas locates the narrator as a critic of particular late-nineteenth-century interior design styles. The story is a parody of the design imperatives readily available to middle-class women from the well-known promoters of taste, Charles Eastlake and William Morris. Their androgynous, serpentine designs in olive, monochromatic yellow, and khaki were the embodiment of a "debased Romanesque," in the words of Gilman's narrator. Aside from the potential health hazard the wallpaper posed for any occupant of the attic room, it presented other hazards: the male monopoly and androgynization of the decorative arts market, and the inscription of gender within domestic spaces. Kirk Thomas points out that Gilman, and not for the first time, used fiction to subvert "her culture's conventional advice to women" (189). The intrusion of male-defined aesthetic taste, in this case wallpaper, into what properly belonged to female-defined domestic space, Gilman argues, should be fought at all costs.

The final section of the book, entitled "Late Gilman: The Mixed Legacy," contains one seminal essay looking specifically at areas largely previously unexplored in Gilman's reform agenda. In "Reading Gilman in the Twenty-First Century," Shelley Fisher Fishkin asks: "How will our students read Gilman in the next millennium?" (210) Fishkin answers this question by exploring Gilman's mixed legacy. She raises issues that scholars today find uncomfortable in the work of Gilman—her racism, ethnocentrism, and class biases. Yet she also examines Gilman's illuminating gender reforms and her exceedingly modern appeals for conservation. Exploring—"How would Gilman read 'us' in 1997?" (214)—Fishkin guides an entertaining and enlightening tour of popular women's magazines, all a far cry from Gilman's *Forerunner*. She predicts Gilman's quandary in facing the mixed messages confronting women today but concludes that Gilman would take on Martha Stewart and other icons of domesticity who would return women to the kitchen while themselves escaping into mass entrepreneurial outlets.

Fishkin's essay encourages readers to ponder how Charlotte Perkins Gilman will be read in the twenty-first century. Will her messages remain relevant to a society that applauds multiculturalism and equal opportunity and expanded roles for women and for racial and ethnic minorities? As the essays of this book convey, Gilman leaves us a mixed legacy of prejudice and promise, of reactionary biases and utopian visions. As Fishkin claims: "There is still much cultural work left for [Gilman] to do" (220).

As Gilman well understood, improving the status of women promises to improve society for everyone by creating a more "human world." Many of the incisive changes she predicted for women in the twentieth century may well be realized in the new millennium. Today there remains an unrealized vision of the truly "human world" Gilman predicted a century ago. As the essays in this collection suggest, even the most astute social critics and visionaries, exemplary in their social analyses and suggestions for progressive change, may themselves embody their society's prejudices and biases. Readers of this collection are challenged to examine this phenomenon in the person of Charlotte Perkins Gilman. What would *she* make of the exercise?

NOTES

1. Charlotte Perkins Gilman, *The Living of Charlotte Perkins Gilman: An Autobiography,* with an introduction by Ann J. Lane (Madison: University of Wisconsin Press, 1990), 20.
2. Charlotte Perkins Gilman, *Topeka State Journal,* 15 June 1896, vol. 7, qtd. in Gary Scharnhorst, *Charlotte Perkins Gilman* (Boston: Twayne, 1985), 40. Gilman elaborates this point in her autobiography, *Living:* "I have never made any pretense of being literary. As far as I had any method in mind, it was to express the idea with clearness and vivacity, so that it might be apprehended with ease and pleasure" (284–85).
3. For example, there is little evidence of Gilman's attention to class issues in the Gilman papers (Arthur and Elizabeth Schlesinger Library, Radcliffe College). See Susan Lanser's article, "Feminist Criticism, 'The Yellow Wallpaper,' and the Politics of Color in America," *Feminist Studies* 15, no. 3 (Fall 1989): 415–41.
4. In her defense, Gilman does note the injustice to Jews in *Women and Economics:*

A Study of the Economic Relation Between Men and Women as a Factor in Social Evolution (Boston: Small, Maynard, 1898); reprint, edited and introduced by Carl N. Degler, New York: Harper Torchbooks, 1966; reprint, Amherst, NY: Prometheus Books, 1994, 78.

    5. Charlotte Perkins Gilman Papers, Schlesinger Library, Radcliffe College, Shelf 177, 3268.

    6. See *Unpunished,* edited and with an afterword by Catherine J. Golden and Denise D. Knight (New York: The Feminist Press, 1997), 217.

The Mixed Legacy
of
Charlotte Perkins Gilman

Part I
Five Ways of Looking at Charlotte Perkins Gilman

What My Therapist, My Daughter, and Charlotte Taught Me While I Was Writing the Biography of Charlotte Perkins Gilman

ANN J. LANE

SEVERAL YEARS AGO AT THE UNIVERSITY OF VIRGINIA, AN EMINENT FEMI-nist theorist gave a talk entitled "October 24." She began by explaining the title. When she had been invited the year before, she had no idea what she would want to talk about some months later. The one certainty was that her talk would occur on October 24—thus the title. Perhaps I should have done the same. My title is daunting in its specificity.

Let me begin with autobiography because Charlotte Perkins Gilman wrote one and because my choice of writing a biography of her carried with it a decision to write my own story as well. Everything we write is about ourselves, especially if what we have chosen is the life of another; and if both author and subject are women, the affinity is inescapable.

The act of writing an autobiography—particularly for a woman who came of age in the nineteenth century but even somewhat true for women today—challenges what a woman is supposed to be, that is, having a life worthy of being examined in a public document. Women have been carefully educated over time to deny the kind of authority that merits an autobiography. To call attention to one's special achievements is to be unwomanly.

I was aware in the 1980s that thinking about, researching, and writing Gilman's biography was inseparable from the autobiography of the biographer, that is, my story. Fifteen, twenty years ago many women were writing biographies, and we all knew then that our work was in part a study in self-representation. I was in a biography group during that time, five historians writing five biographies of five women of the past. We met regularly to talk about our work, and we also talked about ourselves in our work. I made an additional discovery. I now believe that one of the reasons why so many feminist scholars turned to the writing of biography in the 1970s and 1980s was not only to uncover the lives and work of our forebears, an idea we all then appreciated and

understood, but also as a way of dealing with our—the biographers'—
own lives, sensing ourselves unworthy to write our own stories. We did
not realize then that we may have chosen a biography in order to write
and explore our own lives. We dealt with the silencing of our own lives
by creating the lives of others. Now many women *are* writing memoirs,
a change of some significance.

I began this essay with a reference to Charlotte's published autobiography, *The Living of Charlotte Perkins Gilman,* until I become aware that
I was doing it again, that is, dealing with the designated topic, how *I*
constructed and wrote this biography and shaped her life in my work,
by talking about her—a person eminently worthy of interest and attention—and not myself. And so I will do that because I have been asked
to explore that subject and because I know how much I learned about
myself in engaging with the issues in Gilman's own work and in her life.

The great body of work that Gilman produced came almost directly
and obviously out of her continuing personal struggles. She read history and sociology, economics and ethics, philosophy and fiction in
order to make sense of her origins, to come to terms with her mother
and father, to understand the major influences in her life, and eventually how to manage love and work to her benefit. Dozens of annual
diaries preserve for us Gilman's daily activities and thoughts from her
adolescence to her decision to end her life when she was seventy-five.
We also discover in those diaries the genesis of many of the important
theories she later developed in books and essays. A two-volume selection is now available to us, thanks to the work of Denise Knight. In his
valuable work, Gary Scharnhorst makes clear how necessary it is to use
the skills of bibliographers in the effort to reconstitute a life, especially
of an author who had fallen into oblivion, as Gilman had. His uncover-
ing of vast numbers of hitherto unknown articles, essays, and poems
provides contemporary audiences access to the wide ranging and diverse audiences Gilman reached in her lifetime.

I did most of my research and much of my writing about Charlotte
Perkins Gilman—the introduction to *Herland, The Charlotte Perkins
Gilman Reader,* and a draft of the biography *To 'Herland' and Beyond:
The Life and Work of Charlotte Perkins Gilman*—during an extended and
glorious sojourn at the Bunting Institute of Radcliffe College, when I
was free of teaching and administrative responsibilities. I felt able to
apply for this grant and move way from New York because I had recently been divorced. I could have done so before, but it did not appear
to me as an option since my husband was rooted in New York. He
would not have liked my leaving home with our children, but it did not
occur to me even to raise the possibility. I made the decision to limit
myself by myself. In 1977 I was free of the commitments to a husband

and a stationary home. But I was not free of mothering two daughters, one a teenager, one about to be, in a new city. I was now mother *and* father. I bicycled back and forth from Brookline to Cambridge and spent each day in the gorgeous surroundings of the Bunting Institute with magnificent library resources, a private office equipped with an electric typewriter, splendid companions, children in school all day, happily basking in this glorious time.

Then I would go home and cook dinner and think of Gilman's *Women and Economics: A Study of The Economic Relation Between Men and Women as a Factor in Social Evolution.* Thirty women in thirty kitchens cooking thirty individual dinners and all that that entailed—planning, shopping, cooking, cleaning up—said Gilman, describing the inefficiency and social waste of cooking for individual households. In the early years of marriage, I experienced the joys of cooking, but a full-time job and family activities reduced the culinary pleasure significantly, and meals got simpler and guests for dinner virtually disappeared as an entertainment. My time at the Bunting Institute provided me for the first time with what most middle-class professional men have commonly, that is, almost full time to focus on a career. I began to see the preparation of evening meals as an interruption of my real work. Of course, I thought of Charlotte's life as wife and mother, and it was not at all like mine, with all of my stresses and complexities. I had the support—financial, psychological, professional, and cultural—denied her and women of her time who sought a life outside of domesticity, hard enough in the 1970s and 1980s, but deeply unacceptable then. I learned from reading Gilman's works, and I learned from my lived experience, that the locus of inequality for women is in the relationship between the home and the workplace. We live in traditions as exiles, as refugees, but Gilman named those traditions and incorporated them as the subject of her work because they were the subject of her life. She took the central struggles of her life and of her mother's life as the themes of her work—the political economy of home work, mothering, and marriage.

Several years after their marriage, Charlotte's mother, Mary Perkins, was abandoned by her husband, and since marriage was then the only acceptable career for women, Mary's life meant failure. Left with two infants and no way to earn a living, she became an embittered woman and a rejecting mother. As a young woman, Charlotte struggled to construct for and by herself a sense of the direction and meaning of her life that would differentiate her from the unhappy model her mother provided. The context was delineated by the nineteenth century's notion of appropriate masculine and feminine behavior. Charlotte saw herself as having to choose between the feminine path, the traditional one of husband and children, or the masculine one, which meant the use of her intellectual and creative gifts in the pursuit of a career. She tried the first, and, like her mother, she failed. Unlike Mary, she then reached for work as sustenance. And also unlike Mary, after the international success of her work, *Women and Economics,* she was able to have a long and satisfying second marriage with Houghton Gilman; that constituted a substantial personal triumph. In her work she made the "private" life the subject of public investigation, and she explored personal relations as social relations. Her analyses helped her to understand her situation, and by extension that of all women, if it did not always make it easier for her to live each day.

I also had the advantage of feminist scholarship to help me understand Gilman and me; especially helpful was *Life/Lines: Theorizing Women's Autobiography,* edited by Della Brodzki and Celeste Schenck in the late 1980s. Mary Mason, in her essay in that collection, "The Other Voice: Autobiographies of Women Writers," tells us that the Western "obsession with Self" is not ordinarily the central theme of women's autobiographical writing. On the contrary: the self-discovery of female identity seems to be linked to the identification of some "other." The recognition of an other seems to enable women to write openly about themselves. The other in Gilman, I realized, came as a projection of her private consciousness and self-definition onto a collective consciousness. Her definition of the self was formed in collaboration with an abstract, but nonetheless historical and very real female community.

In Gail Twersky Reimer's essay in Brodzki and Schenck's collection, I learned about the tension between procreativity as a theme in a genre dedicated to the exploration of creativity—that is, mothers can write, but are they permitted to record their struggles as mothers? Gilman did that. It was that pioneering assertion that I originally underestimated in its boldness and its originality. She wrote most obviously and clearly about the world, past, present, and, in the utopian fiction, future, but she wrote acutely and intensely, if obliquely (with the exception of "The Yellow Wall-Paper"), about her personal life, particularly her failure and her feelings of inadequacy as a mother.

The assumption of traditional autobiography is that the life being written and being read is exemplary, noteworthy. But women who achieve eminence are thereby unwomanly and unrepresentative of any but a few women. That tension between the public definition of legitimate male place and private domain assigned to women—the tension between representative and exceptional—is exactly the central issue of Gilman's life and her work. From her unusual, exceptional life she was trying to cull insights about how any woman might live in a world in which such an exceptional life as hers could be made accessible to all women. I use "exceptional" to mean positive. The life-long depressions from which she suffered and her immediate collapse after the birth of Katharine were also part of her life, and of many women's lives, then and now. Not a deeply psychological or introspective person, Gilman saw those debilities as essentially social and cultural in origin, suggesting that the world she wished to create would inevitably eliminate such misfortunes. And maybe she is right. Mary Hill makes clear the courage Charlotte needed to confront the dark times and to wait them out until she was able to act and to work again.

In the process of writing her life, I found in my life, sometimes to my astonishment, many of the issues with which she struggled. I love my children. I love being a mother, and I chose to become a mother, an option not available in the same way to Charlotte. I chose to become a mother at the age of thirty-three, a very advanced age in my generation. An incredible distance separates me and my problems from Gilman and hers. I do not minimize the challenges I faced or the resentments I felt at what we now call the double shift, but they were/are nothing like those she confronted. Despite the differences in our circumstances, her struggles reverberated in mine. Those echoes allowed me a method with which to grasp her life.

I did not collapse into a serious depression when I gave birth as Charlotte did. But I almost collapsed under the pressure of the adolescence of one daughter, whose struggle to become herself apart from me almost did us both in. Writing Charlotte's life at that moment helped me enormously to write her story and to understand mine. We both gave our daughters away. More accurately, we both lost our daughters, although differently and with different endings. She gave her child to Grace Ellery Channing Stetson. My daughter left home, only temporarily I am happy to say, and I tried to accept it and deal with it in a positive way to keep us together, learning from Charlotte and from my therapist what to do. My daughter moved in with other families, ultimately nine of them, all but one observant Jewish, which I am not, all of them intact, which our family was then not, and all of them with a mother who, if she worked, had a job, not a career—pretty clear messages. I learned in those many months what it was like to feel in a new and incredibly painful way how inadequate a mother I was, although I had not until then seen myself as such a failure. Charlotte and my therapist got me through.

Charlotte did it by offering herself as a model. She never broke the relationship with Katharine, even though she did not live with her consistently until Katharine was an adult and then only briefly. But Charlotte wrote to her daughter frequently, probably over-much, and she visited as often as she could. They lived on opposite coasts, and neither was affluent, but whenever Charlotte could manage a lecture engagement near Pasadena, Katharine's home, they saw each other. Charlotte suffered a good deal from the absence of her child, but she kept that anguish from her letters. Indeed, the letters reflect an artificial cheerfulness, which was probably not the best strategy for creating a candid relationship, especially as Katharine matured, but it was what Charlotte believed was best. Charlotte had no difficulty expressing affection for Grace, because she felt it sincerely, and she worked at maintaining cordial relations with Walter. Grace was clearly the better choice as a mother, but Katharine grew up, nevertheless, to the end of her long life resenting her mother and feeling abandoned by her. How could she not? Charlotte was labeled an "unnatural mother" in newspaper editorials because of her decision when Katharine was a child to relinquish her to her father and new step-mother for rearing. Katharine as an adult was able to sustain a long and seemingly strong marriage. She was a kind and loving and loved mother, suggesting that she had freed herself from repeating with her own children the strained relationship she and her mother had. She was an artist who worked at her art for much of her life. She must have learned some of that from Charlotte in spite of her unresolved anger that plagued her.

Grace was the better model as a mother, but she gave up aspiration for a career to rear Katharine. Charlotte could not be Grace and do what Grace did, but Charlotte did what she could, and her decisions seemed to have worked for her and for her child. Grace was self-effacing, and so we do not know how she would assess her life choices. Long before I encountered Charlotte Perkins Gilman, I had committed myself to a life that included full-time work and children, but her efforts strengthened my resolve at critical moments and provided useful clues into the nature of the connection between work and home.

I am luckier with my daughter than Charlotte was with hers, mostly, I think, because we lived in different times and I was judged less harshly for my ambitions. My daughter and I did reconcile. We are close friends now. But I had help, and I had a culture that gave me considerably more maneuvering room than Charlotte had.

It was not until years after my divorce that I "suddenly" realized that I had separated from my husband soon after I received tenure. It did not occur to me at the time that I was unwilling to separate before I was sufficiently secure financially to care for my children, that I would not put myself in the same unprotected position that Mary Perkins had occupied. Many, many years later Anita Hill was willing to come forward to identify the sexual harassment she suffered from Clarence Thomas the year after she received tenure at the University of Oklahoma. I thought about writing to her, but never did, in case she, too, had difficulty realizing the obvious.

Charlotte suffered with debilitating depressions most of her life, a state of mind that made her feel helpless, powerless, and enervated. I never had that kind of difficulty, and it was troubling because I was not able to appreciate adequately the grimness and terror of those recurrent crises. Then I fell into the hands of the Harvard medical establishment, and those doctors almost destroyed me. It took several operations to correct the error of the original one, and I suffered repercussions from those medical procedures for a long time. The only gain from that miserable experience was the emotional sensitivity I developed to what it felt like to be helpless in the hands of doctors who give you bad advice and bad treatment.

The conversation that took place among my various different voices—our biography group, colleagues at the Bunting Institute, my therapist, and Charlotte herself through her published work, diaries, letters—all contributed to the shaping of the book. I knew from various sources, as Carol Gilligan and Nancy Chodorow later put it in their famous books, that as women we are inclined to see ourselves relationally. The aspect of the biography that I am most satisfied with is the structuring of the narrative through the major relationships in Charlotte's life, beginning with mother and ending with daughter.

Those varied and frequent conversations occurred at my typewriter but in therapy as well. I used one particularly important insight to great advantage in the writing of the book and in the managing of my life. The problems one has with a child, especially if the child is the first born and of the same sex, are frequently the problems that have remained unresolved with one's own mother—with Charlotte it meant Katharine, and with me, my older daughter.

One of the pleasures of the Bunting Institute was the daily lunch with the other scholars and artists there, and I frequently shared with them the wisdom I had achieved in therapy. I remember with delight how many Bunting colleagues offered to contribute to my mental health expenses, so much did they benefit from my sessions. That particular observation about unresolved tensions with the same sex parent spilling over to the same sex child kept us all going in conversation for weeks.

Of all of Gilman's books, *His Religion and Hers: A Study of the Faith of Our Fathers and the Work of Our Mothers,* published in 1923, spoke most directly to my own beliefs. The disapproval to which I have been subjected on and off for decades about my negative views of religion and its destructive impact through the centuries made me appreciate the courage that Gilman showed in the writing of that book half a century before. She was sixty-three years old when she wrote it, and she

34 ANN J. LANE

chose to sum up her life's work with a study of ideology. Except for her autobiography, it is Gilman's last published book. (Elizabeth Cady Stanton, too, twenty-five years before, put together her controversial book, *The Woman's Bible,* as her last major published work; it also is a critique of organized religion.)

In *Women and Economics,* which appeared in 1898, Gilman turned Aunt Catherine Beecher on her head by challenging the prevailing ideology of domesticity. With the book on religion she turned the entire Beecher clan on their collective heads by asserting that religion, the defining characteristic of the lives of her ancestors, with its emphasis on faith and obedience and subordination of women, has done more disservice to humanity than any other institution. Although this book is not well known, it completed the intellectual journey that began when she, as a young woman, shook her fist at the universe, demanding recognition of her place in it. Male-created religions, she proclaimed, center on death. If religion had come to us through women, she shouted, then birth, not death, would have been the central question. Instead, we are burdened with what she called the "posthumous egotism" of man the hunter—what will happen to me after I die?—rather than the "immediate altruism" of woman the nurturer—what must be done for the child who is just born? We cannot improve a dead man, she said; we can, a baby.

Gilman took the nineteenth-century notion of maternal service and made it the foundation of an ethical system and a guide for social conduct. In my study of her, I tried to answer for her the question she asked, indirectly, all her life. How shall a woman live? She did not have the habit of living well or loving well to call upon from her early years. She learned how to do it. She taught herself, and not always successfully. Joanne Karpinski grapples imaginatively and intelligently with some of the self-deceptions to which Charlotte was susceptible.

Mary Hill and I hang on to the heroic image of Charlotte Perkins Gilman, without, I think, overlooking her serious deficiencies. More recent, younger Gilman scholars, not surprisingly, focus more sharply on those flaws, particularly the racism, anti-Semitism, and ethnocentrism, so prevalent as to be almost commonplace in her day, and so offensive in ours, although certainly not eliminated. She was able to reject and deny so many prejudices that we are impatient and unforgiving when she did not repudiate others.

Despite her failings, and different critics assess them differently, Gilman flew in a world that conspired to deny her flight. She could not undo her past, but she learned to live with it and around it. Coming to realize that struggle of hers gave me the inspiration and the power to forge a study of her life and to help me forge my own.

The Economic Conundrum in the Lifewriting of Charlotte Perkins Gilman

JOANNE B. KARPINSKI

WHEN I FINISHED THE MANUSCRIPT OF *CRITICAL ESSAYS ON CHARLOTTE Perkins Gilman* (New York: G.K. Hall, 1991), I dedicated it to my husband who, I said, " 'got it' more than Walter ever did." Two years later he departed to marry a woman who made him laugh, a woman he did not have to treat as a partner, a woman with whom he did not have to negotiate. As I continued to study the body of Gilman's writing, I came to see similarities between her situation at the end of the nineteenth century and my own at the end of the twentieth. While Tolstoy was surely right in saying that "each unhappy family is unhappy in its own way," it seems to me that the similarities in our circumstances nearly a century apart point to intractable problems in the progress of women toward gender equity, problems which Gilman did not address adequately in her theoretical writing because she was unable to work through them in the arena of her own experience.

Elsewhere in this book, Ann Lane says of Gilman that "she took the central struggles of her life as the subject for her life's work . . . she made the 'private' life the subject of public investigation," yet when evaluating Gilman's autobiography in *To Herland and Beyond,* Lane states that "she did not want to make herself, her personal life, her subject, a trait she shared with many public figures of her generation."[1] How can these statements be reconciled? I believe that Gilman's theorizing was powerfully grounded in her own experiences, but with the exception of her autobiography, her public presentations were not directly self-referential. And the autobiographical voice that spoke to posterity in the first person was a model of circumspection compared to the voice that laughed and cried in hundreds of letters to Houghton Gilman that were not composed with publication in view. Had she participated in the less reticent, indeed compulsively revelatory climate of contemporary public discourse, Gilman might have been less inclined to construct her life narrative as a female *Pilgrim's Progress* and more apt to bring to the surface elements of her own story that challenged the optimistic and rationalistic assumptions of her social analysis.

In *Women and Economics,* Gilman made it clear that hard work is not in itself a guarantor of economic independence:

> For the woman there is, first, no free production allowed, and second, no relation maintained between what she does produce and what she consumes. . . . Her industry is not the natural output of creative energy, not the work she does because she has the inner power and strength to do it, nor is her industry even the measure of her gain.[2]

In contrast, *The Living of Charlotte Perkins Gilman* suggests that Gilman's hard work outside the home did produce financial independence, if not lavish reward. Gilman was ingenious at stretching her slender means. Before her second marriage, she kept a boarding house. She raised much of her own produce and remade donated garments into current style. She was literally able to maintain herself and saw herself as financially independent.

Ann Lane writes in *To Herland and Beyond* that even though "there was no family money behind her and no wealthy husband to provide a cushion, she supported herself and others even down through the 1920s and 1930s, when she was out of fashion and when lecturing was a genre that had faded in popularity." Lane further states that it was "more important that she was able to support herself than that her income was on the meager side" (Lane 342). Since she was accustomed to genteel poverty from her early childhood, a meager income may well not have fazed her. The major premise of self-support, however, is not sustained by other areas of Gilman's lifewriting.

Why does it matter that Gilman was not financially independent when she believed herself to be? Because she specifically intended her autobiography to inspire young women to emulate her choices. "One girl reads this, and takes fire! I write for her," proclaims one often-quoted passage of her work.[3] As Denise Knight's essay in this volume points out, even the title of the autobiography—*The LIVING of Charlotte Perkins Gilman* (emphasis added)—seems to refer to the idea of *making* a living. If this living is only sustainable through unacknowledged assistance, the proffered life model winds up conforming to rather than breaking away from the patriarchal paradigm that she attacked in *Women and Economics.*

I would like to suggest three possible reasons why Gilman was unable to recognize, let alone forthrightly to acknowledge in her autobiography, the financial ramifications to her choice of life's work. First, Gilman's theorizing does not equate work with wage-earning. On the one hand, this made it possible for her to bring to light the enormous contributions to social and economic progress made by women's unpaid domestic labor; on the other, it placed her own work—largely produced without reference to its marketability—in a problematic zone. Second and more significantly, she thought exclusively in terms of gender about the kinds of intellectual, artistic, and philanthropic work that often proves equally unremunerative when men undertake it. Finally, her choice of vocation represents an irreconcilable jointure of Comtean cooperativism in its subject matter and entrepreneurial individualism in its medium of communication.

As the passage from *Women and Economics* quoted above suggests, Gilman did not automatically connect working to earning a wage—to employment. Indeed economic historian Michael Katz points out that

> Unemployment is a modern concept. It assumes the transmutation of work into employment; presupposes the reorganization of production into a collection of jobs that mediate the relation between labor and subsistence; and requires the intervention of a market in which work becomes a prerogative contingent on the sale of labor.[4]

In addition, because Gilman sympathized with Nationalism and Fabian socialism, she regretted the inevitable connection of producing to selling that characterizes capitalist economics:

> Where do you get money? It does not grow on trees. You must get it from other people. How can you get it? By giving them something for it. Suppose you have nothing to give for it? Go work for them, give them your time and labor—be their slave. Suppose they do not want your time and labor—they have enough? Then you are not even a slave—you are a criminal—or a dead man.[5]

Moving from theory to praxis, it is noteworthy that Gilman's habit of chronically supplementing earned income with loans was widespread among the working poor of the nineteenth century. The combination of seasonal layoffs, periodic depressions, and the paucity of both public funds and private charity in the last quarter of the nineteenth century caused both male and female unemployed to rely on relatives for relief.[6] In this context, the practice of accepting loans and gifts might not have impinged on Gilman's overall sense of self-sufficiency (although she did keep careful end-of-year accounts of what she owed to whom—at least until about 1900; the diaries do not reconcile these debts to earnings).

However she justified it to herself in private if not in print, Gilman's letters and diaries show that throughout her life she required the assistance of loans and gifts to make ends meet. Her autobiography consistently overlooks the lifelong contributions of money, food, lodging, and clothes that supplemented her own efforts and that in a number of years exceeded the amount she recorded as being paid for her work.[7] As one might expect, the particularly lean years were clustered at the beginning and the end of her professional life, before her reputation was well established, or after it had begun to decline. But even at the height of her powers, Gilman understood that her viewpoints could not be made commercially successful even as she consistently overestimated what she could earn through her writing.

Although her father was an indifferent provider during her childhood, in adult life he managed to give her a small allowance until her mother's death (*Diaries* 540). When she separated from Walter Stetson and began her independent life in California, she financed the move by the sale of property in Hartford that an aunt had left her (*Diaries* 408). She received periodic loans from the family of Grace Ellery Channing, the lifelong friend who married the husband Gilman divorced, and from her uncle Edward Everett Hale. Other friends—especially Harriet Howe—pitched in at moments of crisis. As her mother had done before her, she occasionally attempted to raise money on personal property— several diary entries in 1891 record her frustration at being unable to get someone to loan her fifty dollars on the security of seventy-five dollars worth of lace (*Diaries* 471).

When she decided to move to Oakland, she got the money for the trip from the journalist Adeline Knapp, with whom she formed an intense personal relationship. Over the course of the two and a half years that the two women lived together, Gilman amassed a debt of eight hundred dollars, which she was unable to repay until 1900 (*Diaries* 472–546 *passim*, 805). The need to provide skilled nursing care during her mother's last illness greatly overstrained Gilman's slender resources in 1893; by the time her mother died on March 3 of that year, Gilman owed the nurse $120, more than her recorded earnings for the previous twelve months (*Diaries* 520).

During the period in which she edited the *Impress*, Gilman lived with her co-editor, Helen Campbell. Financing the production of this magazine was a constant struggle; despite enormous efforts, Gilman repeatedly needed assistance to meet printing costs. When it became clear that subscription revenues alone would not support the journal, Gilman and several friends incorporated a joint stock company to finance it. Unfortunately, the depression of 1893 had drastically diminished investment resources; the enterprise folded after twenty months, and she was left with a debt of several thousand dollars.[8]

Not surprisingly, the pressures that accumulated following the decree of her divorce and as a result of managing the *Impress* brought about the suspension of Gilman's diary entries from September 1894 to January 1896. After the journal's collapse, she became a full-time itinerant lecturer without a permanent address "to which to send 'the remains' in case of accident."⁹ When diary entries begin again, it becomes clear that the hospitality provided during her extended speaking tours sustained her as much as the cash income generated by them.

For a time after the publication of *Women and Economics* in 1898, Gilman achieved the self-sufficiency she had long sought. In 1900, Small and Maynard took her second book, *Concerning Children,* on very advantageous terms (*Diaries* 794). As a result, she was able to arrange repayment of her California debts.¹⁰ She also hired an agent to schedule lectures for her; if the $135 she paid Mrs. Laura Davitz Pelham in November 1900 represents a percentage or commission on earnings, her lecture fees had risen substantially since her first tour (*Diaries* 799–801). Unfortunately, this period of prosperity was brief. McClure, Phillips agreed to publish both *The Home* (1903) and *Human Work* (1904), but Gilman was disappointed that the positive if not enthusiastic reviews of these books did not generate better sales (*Living* 286). Accordingly, Gilman and her second husband Houghton formed the Charlton Publishing company in 1909 in order to bring before the public ideas which commercial presses did not foresee as profitable.

Gilman realized that her unorthodox views were not destined for commercial success. As she wrote in the final issue of the *Forerunner* (November 1916): "Many have asked why this matter was not presented through the medium of established publications.* * * Why did not John Wesley preach in the established church?"¹¹ Despite this awareness, she believed that the magazine could reach the subscribership of three thousand that it needed to become self-sustaining. Unfortunately, the magazine earned only half its production costs, and she had to borrow money from Houghton Gilman to keep it going (Ceplair 190).

After 1920, Houghton Gilman's small income from his legal practice largely sustained them both, and he left her a small legacy at his death (Lane 350). Gilman became a homeowner when Houghton's aunt left him a half share in her residence. In the last months of her life she dined three times a week with her daughter's family, although Katharine was herself in financial straits at the time (Lane 350). It would not have been possible for her to maintain a home or leave even a small legacy without this assistance, yet characteristically, she underestimated it. When Houghton Gilman's father died, she wrote to her daughter that "Houghton is richer by two heavy overcoats . . . and several pair of old shoes," although he had actually left his son six thousand dollars, a fairly substantial sum at that period (Lane 337). Perhaps Gilman neglected to mention the more substantive bequest from her father-in-law because he had disapproved of her. This behavior is consistent with her underestimation of the assistance she received from such male mentors as William Dean Howells in furthering her literary career.[12] She was even capable of resentment when the aid she sought was not as generous as she had hoped; after receiving two hundred dollars from Mrs. Sargent to help pay for the *Impress* in the summer of 1894, she was surprised when Mr. Sargent reacted in an "utterly cold and haughty" manner to her request for a further advance (*Diaries* 591–92).

There is certainly nothing culpable in any of these practices, which are undertaken by many women—and men—when need arises. It is unfortunate for Gilman's readers, however, that she chose to share her triumphs alone, without acknowledging the tribulations she could not overcome on the way to her achievements. In general, the practical financial history of women is so poorly documented that every generation of women is apt to think that both the obstacles and opportunities presented to it are unique, whereas the few longitudinal studies available tend to demonstrate that this is not the case.[13] Paradoxically, Gilman could have left an even stronger legacy if she had been able to critique the potential weaknesses of her advocated positions.

Gilman's marginal financial status was not novel in her family; indeed, she contributed to the support of her brother and her daughter even when she had to borrow money to do so. The reasons for her relatives' financial difficulties are instructive because they are not gender-specific, but rather point to the absence of a social welfare safety net for Americans facing hard times or making unconventional career choices in the early part of the twentieth century. The efforts of Gilman's father to live the life of the mind made him an ineffectual breadwinner. He left the family he could not support when Charlotte was nine; when he remarried, his second wife supported him by running a boarding house (Lane 186). Her brother Tom suffered from chronic health problems complicated by alcohol and so was periodically unable to work (Lane 322, *Diaries* 834, 853 inter alia). Gilman's first husband, Walter Stetson, achieved more esteem than income through his creative efforts, a problem that also faced his son-in-law Frank Chamberlin. Stetson's father, an itinerant preacher, found his vocation unremunerative and eked out a living for his family by selling patent medicines (Lane 81). Even Gilman's famous great aunt Harriet Beecher Stowe had embarked on her literary career in order to supplement the slender income generated by her husband's ministerial activities. Gilman sought only to maintain herself, not a whole household—before she married Houghton Gilman she was careful to demonstrate to them both that she would not have to depend on him financially (although her calculations proved overly optimistic).[14] Nevertheless, her family history might have warned her that generating an income in the field of good works might be a tough row to hoe.

Gilman turned to speaking and writing with mixed motives: a sense of calling combined with determination to earn her own way. In addition, as Stowe's precedent indicated, she would have seen that writing was an appropriately genteel means by which a middle-class woman could seek an income (another early option occasionally undertaken by Gilman was designing greeting cards; the advertising inserts she created for Soapine laundry detergent demonstrate both graphic skill and wit). Perhaps Stowe's smashing success in the field of publication led Gilman to disregard the less rewarding outcomes of her other relatives' efforts to prosper by intellectual, artistic, or philanthropic labor. Undoubtedly Gilman's financial woes were complicated by the fact that she was a middle-class woman who shouldn't have needed to be paid for her work. She had difficulty insisting on payment for her poems and lectures, turning to self-publication for her later books because getting her message to an audience was a more urgent concern than reaping profits. Moreover, she was attempting to cultivate a financially unyielding field by aiming to educate rather than cater to prevailing tastes. Last, but not least, it should be taken into account that her primary intended audience of middle-class women had little independent disposable income. Repeatedly in her diaries, Gilman notes with disappointment that the house was full but the collection meager.

Had Gilman attempted to analyze the apparent contradiction between her economic theorizing and her personal practice, she might have arrived at the kind of prescient solution to the problem of funding philanthropic service or artistic endeavor that she proposed for providing child care and food service to working mothers. Early on, she imaginatively foresaw something like the National Endowment for the Humanities, reassuring a hypothetical individualist that a Fabian socialist society would include a "public fund, kept to encourage and promote all progress—scientific, artistic, or mechanical";[15] on the whole, however, she did not envision the state as a surrogate for the community. Ironically, in this regard she more closely resembled black social reformers—from whom she was separated by the ingrained racism noted in Denise Knight's essay on editing the diaries—than the elite white sisterhood with whom she interacted despite the economic gulf between them.[16] According to welfare historian Linda Gordon, white female reformers active between 1890 and 1935 appealed for state or federal social welfare intervention because they had more to gain from it than blacks, who were consistently denied civic benefits. Black reformers in this period tended to organize on the local community level; nationally, of course, the National Association for the Advancement of

Colored People (NAACP) and the National Urban League (NUL) focused on achieving basic civil rights for African Americans. Other important similarities between Gilman's thinking on improving the condition of women and that of her black contemporaries focus on institutional changes in education and child care practices that would allow women to assume significant jobs outside the home. Gordon's research into the lives of female welfare reformers demonstrates that Gilman's black women contemporaries, accustomed to working outside the home out of economic necessity, sought to develop social structures that supported women workers. Meanwhile, white women reformers largely subscribed to plans that supported the traditional family model of male breadwinner/female homemaker.

Had Gilman more systematically connected her theorizing and her personal practice, she might have envisioned a system for supporting creative work that could be developed by the private sector, as child care centers and take-out restaurants have to some extent satisfied (although some might argue that they have travestied) her call for baby-gardens and kitchenless homes. Her disinclination squarely to confront the financial ramifications of offering her life as an inspiration to other women shortchanges those she most wished to help.

The central thesis of *Women and Economics* posits that in the human species the sexual relationship has become an economic relationship and that the resulting overcommitment to competitive individualism by both men and women impedes equitable social development. This dilemma seems to achieve a clear-cut resolution in Gilman's autobiography, while the total body of her lifewriting presents a more complex picture. Gilman successfully resolved her personal dilemma of being economically and emotionally dependent on a spouse who, while himself an idealist and an indifferent provider, resisted his wife's efforts to bring in extra income or to dedicate herself to some great work; she resolved it by terminating their legal relationship. In so doing, however, she displaced the larger social problem onto another woman. Gilman's good friend Grace Ellery Channing also had literary aspirations (indeed, she and Gilman collaborated on some playscripts). When she became Walter Stetson's second wife, however, she left her editorial office to work at home, where she attempted to portion out household tasks to her husband and stepdaughter in order to set aside some time each day to write (Lane 317). One might argue that Channing simply didn't want success as much as Gilman did, but such an argument relies on a survival-of-the fittest model that Gilman's own reform Darwinism had sought to mitigate. Had Gilman more scrupulously examined the role of competitive individualism in her own life, she might not have been so surprised and disheartened that, after the achievement of suffrage, the struggle for women's rights came increasingly to include the professional aspirations of individual women rather than self-sacrificially pursuing their common good.

I was struck by Ann Lane's observation that at age thirty-five Gilman had never lived without dependence upon a family, by birth, marriage, or adoption (Lane 181). In five years she had married again, so the period of her emancipation was relatively limited and, as we have seen, financially incomplete. After my divorce I realized that I had never lived alone, either; there had always been parents, a sibling, roommates, a spouse, children. Unlike Gilman, I am unwilling to relinquish my children in order to devote myself wholly to my work and test my independence; moreover, I realized from the outset that my daughters and I could not live at our former standard on my income alone. I am fortunate among single mothers in that I do receive adequate and regular maintenance. I occasionally feel (as I did when married to a man who earned seven times what I did) like a kept woman, but I find myself unwilling to change careers in order to earn more on my own (my former husband wanted to send me to law school in lieu of paying maintenance). Like Gilman, I have a sense of the work I am meant to do, but I harbor no illusions about my financial prospects. I suspect she protested so much in order to avoid the feeling of being beholden. If she had acknowledged all her benefactors, she would have had to eat the sometimes crusty bread of gratitude, while I can grouse about an economic system that values CEOs more highly than college professors, male *or* female.

In her published writing, Gilman foresaw evolutionary social progress unfolding as both men and women came to realize that it was in the rational best interests of both genders for women to fulfill the complete range of their potential. Her autobiography consistently takes a tone of rational optimism toward events that might well have called forth powerful negative emotions. Thus, in recalling that her mother would never offer affection to her children unless she thought they were asleep, Gilman's autobiographical voice focuses not on the pain of "the child" (Not even a personal pronoun is permitted about this painful memory!) but on the protective rationale of her mother (*Living* 10–11). Here Gilman may be unconsciously illustrating the Freudian principle of repression, but she is also expressing a conviction that all human passions and drives can be understood and so ultimately harmonized with the common good.

Without citing specific influences, Gilman, nonetheless, echoes the preceding generation of women's rights advocates who blended "a Comtian faith in science with Hegelian conceptions of duty and service."[17] Mary Putnam Jacobi, a pioneer female physician whom Gilman admired, wrote about her belief in positivism that it "derives from consciousness of social welfare, and from the cultivated habits of subordinating immediate personal impulses to higher sentiments of honor, of sympathy. . . . Interdependence of functions . . . means the sacrifice of one part to another or to the welfare of the whole" (Leach 208). The paradox inherent in declaring one's independence in order to subordinate it was addressed by education reform advocate Anna Brackett, who argued that a justly organized division of labor requires "renunciation of a certain roundness and perfection in the individual . . . the attainment of many minor faculties"; but she found compensation for this self-sacrifice in the conviction that "by yielding up his will to the good of the whole, he is served in turn by the will of every individual in the organized state" (Leach 208). In contrast, the nineteenth-century women's rights historian Paulina Wright Davis argued that "a statement of women's rights which ignores the right of self-ownership as the first of all rights is insufficient to enlist enthusiasm and even the common interest of the most intelligent portion of the community" (Leach 191).

Half a century later, Gilman was urging women to move away from domestic service into world service, but the principle of implicitly sacrificial focus on the common good remained central to her vision. She did not succeed in resolving the conflict between Brackett and Wright Davis's positions because she didn't address it analytically. To the end of her life, Gilman chose to deal with her internal tensions between individual achievement and dedicated service by striving to strengthen her character so as to combat negative feelings.[18] Like many nineteenth-century feminists, Gilman did not wholly abandon Christian philosophy as a personal conviction even though she criticized the androcentricity of Christian churches. Role models like Mary Putnam Jacobi had consistently played down the atheistic underpinnings of Comtean positivism (Leach 153). Comte's belief that reason could discover social laws that mirrored scientific laws in their order and precision led reformers influenced by him to use metaphors of sickness rather than of sin to describe states of disorder; "Not sin but sickness became the required conversion experience, the enforced meditative interlude through which one passed to sanity and well-being in a democratic and capitalist society" (Leach 20). According to this model, Gilman's recurring bouts of debilitating depression could be understood not as psychosomatic events but as periodically necessary organic adjustments to a disordered social environment. Gilman never referred specifically to Comte as an influence on her own thought, but then she rarely cited influences or precedents of any kind.

A potential influence which she specifically rejected was Freudian-ism. As Gary Scharnhorst's essay points out, Gilman feared that the Freudian-inspired liberation of sexual mores in the 1920s merely increased the chances that women would be exploited. Consequently, she had little incentive to discover how Freud's exploration of conflicted desire might have enhanced her self-understanding or applied to her general analysis of women's roles. While Mary Hill's essay rightly lauds Gilman for maintaining a healthy distance from academia, I think that Gilman's posterity pays the price for her lack of systematic education. Her own contemporaries, of whom a much smaller percentage received a higher education and a much larger percentage were exposed to her ideas through her lectures rather than her writing, were better positioned to feel the thrust of her arguments when they were unburdened by scholarly apparatus.

Gilman's expurgation of the negative from her autobiographical voice ultimately impinged on her social analysis in several ways. It did not occur to her that women might find it more advantageous to emulate rather than transform male workplace behaviors as they entered the work force, and she underestimated the degree to which cultural traditions of male dominance would continue to shape the attitudes of both men and women in the work environment. Finally, because she believed that acquired social traits could be transmitted between generations, she failed to anticipate that her own hard-won knowledge would not replicate itself in each new generation of women to approach the threshold of opportunity. She did not foresee that her own daughter, let alone the daughters of immigrants or racial minorities, might become enmeshed in the same network of gender role expectations that she had found intolerable. She did not want to know that the individual and the institutional psyche would prove so resistant to change, and neither do my first-year students, who cherish the illusion that their foremothers have won the battles, leveled the ground, and made straight the road on which they will march into the new millennium.

NOTES

1. Ann Lane, *To Herland* and Beyond: The Life and Work of Charlotte Perkins Gilman (New York: Pantheon, 1990), 354.

2. Charlotte Perkins Gilman, *Women and Economics* (Boston: Small & Maynard, 1898), 118.

3. Charlotte Perkins Gilman, "Thoughts and Figgerings," quoted in *The Diaries of Charlotte Perkins Gilman,* ed. Denise Knight (Charlottesville: University Press of Virginia, 1994), 855.

4. Michael Katz, *In the Shadow of the Poorhouse: A Social History of Welfare in America* (New York: Basic Books, 1986), 195.

5. Charlotte Perkins Gilman, "Human Nature," a lecture presented to the Pasadena Nationalist Club on 5 June 1890, reprinted in Larry Ceplair, ed., *Charlotte Perkins Gilman: A Nonfiction Reader* (New York: Columbia University Press, 1991), pp. 52–53.

6. Katz, *Shadow,* 147.

7. In 1891, for example, the diary registers loans of $100 and receipt of $49 in fees. While her diaries may not document every receipt and expenditure for a given year, the predominance of recorded loans over recorded earnings is significant.

8. Ceplair, *Nonfiction,* 41. It isn't clear from the diaries that the arrears are this substantial.

9. Charlotte Perkins Gilman, *The Living of Charlotte Perkins Gilman* (New York: Appleton Century, 1935), 181.

10. In 1899, Gilman's lecture tour took her westward. When she arrived in California in December, she made a round of calls to pay debts in person. Her former dentist felt she had overpaid, while her Oakland landlady was "paralyzed with astonishment" to receive $160 for back rent and gas bills (Diaries 804). Despite these accomplishments, her "Notes for 1900" still include the resolution to "pay all debts if possible" (Diaries 807).

11. Charlotte Perkins Gilman, "Summing Up," *Forerunner,* 7 (November 1916), 286.

12. Joanne B. Karpinski, "When the Marriage of True Minds Admits Impediments," in *Patrons and Protégées: Gender, Friendship and Writing in Nineteenth Century America,* ed. Shirley Marchalonis (New Brunswick: Rutgers University Press, 1989).

13. Claudia Goldin, *Understanding the Gender Gap: An Economic History of American Women* (New York: Oxford University Press, 1990), vii. See also Mimi Abramowitz, *Regulating the Lives of Women: Social Welfare Policy from Colonial Times to the Present* (Boston: South End Press, 1988) 1–2; and Walter Trattner, *From Poor Law to Welfare State: A History of Social Welfare in America* (New York: The Free Press, 1974), ix.

14. *Diaries,* 808 and 837 are illustrative of the contrast. On 1 January 1900, Gilman wrote that she hoped to earn $4,000 in that year, but 1923 starts with "nothing in bank but $75 Houghton put in for me!"

15. Charlotte Perkins Gilman, "First Class in Sociology, First Lesson," *American Fabian,* 3 (May 1897): 9, reprinted in Ceplair, *Nonfiction,* 83.

16. Linda Gordon, "Black and White Visions of Welfare: Women's Welfare Activism, 1890–1945," *The Journal of American History,* 97 (February 1992): 19–51.

17. William Leach, *True Love and Perfect Union: The Feminist Reform of Sex and Society* (New York: Basic Books, 1980), 208. Gilman probably never read Comte or Hegel, but absorbed their ideas through association with other reformers, like Jacobi, whose convictions were grounded in these currents of philosophy.

18. See, for example, her "Thoughts and Figgerings" for 25 April 1929 (quoted in Knight, *Diaries,* 853). At age sixty-nine she is still telling herself, "Come come!—As for the past—drop it!"

"Letters Are Like Morning Prayers":
The Private Work of Charlotte Perkins Gilman

MARY A. HILL

CHARLOTTE PERKINS GILMAN LEFT US AN ENORMOUS LEGACY—RICH, complex, diverse—as is reflected in the diversity of papers in this collection. It is almost as though we are celebrating on ever deeper levels Gilman's stature as a hero, or heroine—and presumably for a lot of different reasons. One of them, and *only* one, of course, is the courage she showed in confronting contradictions in herself, the courage of her personal journey, a heroic journey in my view, a journey to explore some of the deepest layers of sexism, internalized within herself. The problem, as she put it in *Women and Economics,* is that "We ourselves, by maintaining this artificial diversity between the sexes, . . . have preserved in our own characters the confusion and contradiction which is our greatest difficulty in life."[1] My sense of Gilman as a heroine is that she confronted that reality. She explored deeply, as heroines often do, by going into dangerous terrain—terrifying for us all—surviving the process, and then returning with a wisdom that enabled her to be our teacher, our healer, our friend.

As most of us know, Gilman worked on several different levels. Publicly, she was on the national and international lecture circuit. Well respected as a writer, she was enormously successful in making a rich contribution to many women's lives. But privately she had to war against what she called her "poignant grief and shame."[2] In her late-1890s letters to her second husband Houghton Gilman, she described a "compelling desire . . . to complain—to whimper . . . and seek for sympathy which don't do me any good if I get it."[3] She wanted satisfying work, but apologized for needing it. She wanted an intimate love relationship, but felt "shamelessly wicked," "unreasonable," "absurd." "I don't wholly like to be held—and yet I do!" "Makes me kind of angry too. Seems a weakness. To be so tangled up in another person." "O Houghton—I am so *tired* of all this restless doubt and hope and fear and flickering joy . . . I've got to the place I wanted. I can write what I please and say what I please and the world is ready to listen.

And here I am floundering helplessly among my own affairs . . . It is shameful—shameful."[4]

One question some might ask, of course, is why? Why the shame and self-contempt? Was it because of a hereditary inclination? Or a chemical imbalance? Or a deserting father? Or an impoverished and depressed mother? Or an environment in which, as she later believed, she had been told so many times that she was "no good" that she believed it? Was it an individual phenomenon, as some might argue? Or on a more sociopolitical level, were there complex deeper causes: a patriarchy which devalues and objectifies women economically, politically, sexually, intellectually, and psychologically. As Gilman put it, when we say *"men, man, manly, manhood,"* we mean the "world and all its activities," but when "we say *Women,* we think *Female,* the sex."[5]

Whatever the causes of Gilman's suffering, however, what impresses me is her courage to confront it. She could have lashed out at other people—her parents, Walter, Houghton Gilman—which actually and understandably she did at times, for we certainly now know that abused people often become abusers. Instead, however, for the most part, Gilman realized that the real enemy was in herself. As she put it in one letter, she was like the "old campaigner" in a "seventy year's war. Sometimes bitterly depressed, often defeated, long imprisoned, scarred and wounded beyond recognition but not crippled past all usefulness."[6] And yet it was almost as though, like Persephone, Gilman was willing, in fact she was uncompromisingly determined, to explore the length and depth of her depression. Self-indulgent, some might call it, but courageous in my view, was her determination to travel to the underworld, to take Houghton to her "catacombs."[7] "Blind" and "creeping," she kept moving forward, kept turning up old "gravestones" or "trapdoor-stones" and finding "all these buried things, dead and alive." She would experience an "awful landslide," severing her "way down to the bones." She was the Medusa, the "monster" threatening to swallow or destroy her lover and thus needing to be crushed, shattered, or drowned.[8]

Helene Cixous, as well as many other writers, also talks about traveling to the underworld and seeing the laugh of Medusa. "You only have to look at the Medusa straight on to see her," Cixous writes; and "she's not deadly. She's beautiful and she's laughing," and her "Dark Continent is neither dark nor unexplorable."[9] Understandably we've been taught to fear Medusa. As women we have been taught *to be afraid.* As Cixous queries, where is the woman who has not been ashamed of her strength, her beauty, her vitality? Where is the woman who has not accused herself of being a monster—sick, neurotic, self-absorbed? Of course, women are defined as "sick" and travel to the dark side fearfully: Inanna stripped of her accomplishment, her attributes, her identity; Persephone exiled to the underworld. But the more we read and write and hear each other's stories, the more our understanding changes. The more subversive it becomes, the more outrageous, more healing, perhaps moving to the rhythms of the inevitable Life/Death/Life cycle, night into day, dark into light, spiraling toward wholeness, whole making, and, therefore, holy: to face the shadow and thereby learn to touch the soul; to confront the dark side; to cease projecting hates and fears on others; to expose the death-dealing forces in our culture; to combat the *outside* monsters; to confront the monsters in ourselves. One has to lose oneself to find oneself. It takes a death to find the gold inside ourselves.

So what we find in Gilman's 1890s letters is a courageous exploration of "dangerous" and "threatening" emotions and a process of learning to respect and then disarm them. Her letters were her "morning prayers," she explained to Houghton. Confronting and then working through her "monster" feelings, Gilman began to move from metaphors of violence to images of birthing, of spiritual awakening, of reaffirming her own power. "It doesn't feel like quicksand anymore," but like rowing on the "open ocean . . .—the oars dripping or not dripping as the waves may rise—. . . and withal the tremendous elation of that very power beneath—the vast rise and swell." Or again, it is as if "some system of irrigation were gradually spreading in a desert country, reclaiming more ground daily, and making the wilderness to blossom as the rose." "I feel as if I had been only playing—before—that *this* is life and I am but just born!"[10]

Proudly but surreptitiously, Gilman used her letters as a source of healing and empowering. Enthusiastically she could describe the satisfactions of her work commitments: the sense of "constructive power," "rich and sweet with the response of hungry hearts." And increasingly she could delight also in a "mended strengthened re-born feeling," a sense of "heavenly wonder, so utterly unknown, undreamed of in my life."[11]

With Houghton Gilman standing as her lover, friend, and witness, increasingly Gilman was "ceaselessly hungry" for life, a "voracious comet," a "wild floating soul":[12]

well, sometimes I feel like a "heathen goddess come again"—a wonderful struggling mixed feeling . . .—to most people's knowledge a stern cold thinker . . . a widow—a celibate, a solitary—and inside—Ashtoreth![13]

Ashtoreth was the fertility goddess: in ancient cultures she was worshipped as the queen of heaven; in Palestine she dates back to the time of the earliest Semitic occupation. Solomon built a shrine to her near Jerusalem. And in Babylonia and Assyria, Ishtar was her name.

Although an absolute delight to Gilman, Ashtoreth was not so pleasing to most writers of her time. To Professor George Barton, writing in 1891, for instance, Ashtoreth was a goddess who, "measured by our standards," was a "demon of impropriety." She was a threat to "the very basis of family life and social purity." Her behavior was "in some details [so] disgustingly obscene" that as cultures became more "civilized," they necessarily had to "root out" her "excessive impurity" and impress "a higher moral standard" on the people. After all, this biblical scholar continues, they needed obedience to Yahweh that was "as absolute and whole-hearted as a wife should render to her husband" before the conflict with heathenism, with Ashtoreth and her allied cults, could finally be replaced with moral purity and religious truth.[14]

In contrast, Gilman dreamed about the goddess Medusa with terror. It's almost as though her dream images anticipated later understandings: that Medusa had been laughing as she took her to the underworld, but that she was beautiful instead of ugly; that the serpent goddess in ancient Libya, her head surrounded by serpent hair, was the revered symbol of divine female wisdom.

Ashtoreth, the fertility goddess, Medusa—the life-giving and death-giving goddess with the magic moon blood—these archetypes served Gilman's generation, and our own as well, to combat destructive patriarchal images and to celebrate women's creativity, beauty, and power. Gilman recognized, as we do, the need for myth as well as reason, the need to see patriarchy itself as myth, and to allow Cassandra, silenced for centuries, finally to be heard.

In conclusion, I would like to give Charlotte Perkins Gilman a rather hearty word of thanks for her several very special gifts:

First, for using her intellect to probe the complexity and depth of women's issues.

Second, for taking bold interdisciplinary perspectives; for daring to probe the fields of biology, history, anthropology, economics, sociology, psychology, and as a consequence to roam out through galactic space, to use Mary Daly's words.

Third, for maintaining a healthy distance from academia. Even though Gilman wished that she were more "credentialed," and even though she teased from time to time about her lack of "xyz" scholarly degrees, the result, I think, was that she kept her creativity intact. Unshackled from the sacred canon, she focused on her own priorities and on the realities of her own and other women's lives. She achieved healthy exile, James Joyce might say.

Fourth, for plunging down into the underworld—depressing and debilitating as that clearly was—and saving the record of that journey. Never yielding to the monsters of addiction that could have sapped her strength and offered cheap solutions, she confronted the Medusa she had been taught to fear and the Ashtoreth whom she grew to love within herself.

Fifth, for taking the soul journey instead of just the ego trip. Joseph Campbell notes the striking difference between the celebrity who seeks fame and recognition and the hero who returns as messenger, as healer, or, in Gilman's case, as woman-empowering-woman.[15]

That is not to say that I admire *everything* about Gilman. Like some other Gilman scholars, I recognize that Gilman, like most people, had her even darker side, her racism, her ethnocentricity, her homophobia—all of which deserve attention. But she, nonetheless, was an impressive mentor, a delightful humorist, a spiritual leader, a radical critic of patriarchal structure, and a proud, forceful woman who urged us to find the goddess in ourselves.

NOTES

1. Charlotte Perkins Gilman, *Women and Economics* (New York: Harper Torchbooks, 1966), 331.

2. Charlotte Perkins Stetson to George Houghton Gilman, 14 November 1899, Arthur and Elizabeth Schlesinger Library, Radcliffe, College (AESL).

3. Charlotte Perkins Stetson to George Houghton Gilman, 3 November 1897, AESL.

4. Charlotte Perkins Stetson to George Houghton Gilman, 16 May 1899; 6 November 1899; 28 July 1899; 26 July 1899, AESL.

5. Charlotte Perkins Gilman, *Herland,* serialized in *Forerunner* 6 (1915), 321.

6. Charlotte Perkins Stetson to George Houghton Gilman, 1 October 1897, AESL. The use of violent metaphors is not unusual in women's writings. Consider Kate Chopin's *The Awakening,* for instance, or George Eliot's *The Mill on the Floss.* See also the work of Sandra M. Gilbert and Susan Gubar, *Madwoman in the Attic* (New Haven and London: Yale University Press, 1979), for example. Moreover, it was not only fictional women who lost their lives in the battle. Virginia Woolf, Anne Sexton, and Sylvia Plath are but a few more contemporary examples of tough courageous women who ended their own lives. As Carolyn Heilbrun puts it, "suicide became a part of life, so violent was the action necessary for rebirth and truth" (Carolyn Heilbrun, *Writing a Woman's Life* (New York: W. W. Norton, 1988), 70.

7. Charlotte Perkins Stetson to George Houghton Gilman, 8 November 1897, AESL. Although the traditional myth suggest that Persephone was raped by Hades and then was taken forcefully to the underworld, a more feminist version of the story envisions her as traveling voluntarily, purposefully, and autonomously. See, for example, Charlene Spretnak, "The Myth of Demeter and Persephone," in *Weaving the Visions: New Patterns in Feminist Spirituality,* ed. Judith Plaskow and Carol Christ (San Francisco: Harper & Row, 1989), 72–74.

8. According to conventional narratives, white middle-class women were expected

to experience the "erotic impulse." But if they also experienced the "impulse to power," almost always they "suffered individual guilt, each supposing herself a monster when she did not fit the acceptable narrative of a female life." Heilbrun, *Writing a Woman's Life*, 45.

9. Helene Cixous, "The Laugh of the Medusa," in Pat C. Hoy II, Esther H. Schor, and Robert DiYanni, *Women's Voices: Visions and Perspectives* (New York: McGraw Hill, 1990), 488.

10. Charlotte Perkins Stetson to George Houghton Gilman, 22 April 1898; 21 April 1898; 10 March 1899; 17 May 1900; 20 February 1898, AESL.

11. Charlotte Perkins Stetson to George Houghton Gilman, 5 October 1898; 8 May 1898; 21 May 1898; 20 February 1898, AESL.

12. Charlotte Perkins Stetson to George Houghton Gilman, 29 November 1898; 4 May 1897; 28 December 1898; 2 April 1898; 12 March 1899; 18 December 1898, AESL.

13. Charlotte Perkins Stetson to George Houghton Gilman, 18 December 1898, AESL. In Greek mythology, Ashtoreth was a ruler of the universe, a charioteer trying to live her life with authority, with self-mastery, trying to keep her balance while moving at high speeds.

14. George A. Barton, "Ashtoreth and Her Influence in the Old Testament," *Journal of Biblical Literature*, Tenth Year, 1891, part 2, 73–91. Contemporary scholars—for example, Marija Gimbutas, Gerda Lerner, and Helene Cixous—are probing pre-patriarchal history and discovering distortions—shall we call them lies?—that patriarchal writers used to crush women's power. See Marija Gimbutas, *The Goddesses and Gods of Old Europe, 6500–3500 B.C.: Myth and Cult Images* (London: Thames & Hudson, 1982); Gerda Lerner, *The Creation of Patriarchy* (New York: Oxford University Press, 1986).

15. Joseph Campbell, *The Power of Myth*, with Bill Moyers, ed. Betty Sue Flowers (New York: Anchor Doubleday, 1988), 151–52.

On Editing Gilman's Diaries

DENISE D. KNIGHT

THE ENGLISH DIARY HISTORIAN ARTHUR PONSOBY ONCE WROTE THAT "No editor can be trusted not to spoil a diary."[1] While Ponsoby is right, of course, that the edited product can never substitute for the original diary, measures can be taken to preserve the textual integrity of a published edition. Still, there are any number of decisions for an editor to make, challenges to overcome, and problems to address in transforming a diary from manuscript to published text. When I decided some years ago to edit the diaries, after published excerpts in the Gilman biographies piqued my interest in what remained in manuscript, the challenges I encountered included establishing the scope of the project, addressing the criticisms of outside readers, resolving discrepancies that appeared between the original diaries and previously published excerpts, preserving both textual purity and historical accuracy, and transcribing illegible and mutilated text.

The Diaries of Charlotte Perkins Gilman document a range of experiences in Gilman's life—oftentimes routine, occasionally humorous, sometimes dramatic. Yet they are but one small piece of a greater whole. The diaries should be viewed, therefore, as a complement to other biographical sources by Mary A. Hill, Ann J. Lane, and Gary Scharnhorst; they add yet another dimension to the complex portrait of Gilman that has gradually emerged over the past three decades.

Defining appropriate parameters became the first significant challenge I faced when I began this project. The extant diaries begin on 1 January 1876, when Gilman was fifteen years old, and continue uninterrupted until 19 April 1887, the day before she traveled to a Philadelphia sanitarium to seek treatment for neurasthenia and was forbidden to engage in writing of any kind. They resume on 1 January 1890 and continue, with occasional breaks, until 3 May 1903, when Gilman was forty-two, at which point they abruptly end. Collectively, they cover approximately twenty-four years of Gilman's life. From the start, the length of the diaries was a concern, yet I was reluctant to edit a "selected edition," for all of the obvious reasons, most notably that doing so would compromise textual purity. Yet, I was aware that Gilman's

53

diaries were not likely to command the same audience as would those of a more prominent figure, and since the project would be undeniably expensive for a press to undertake, some kind of compromise would be necessary.

The juvenile diaries in particular posed some unique problems in editing. Several of the entries written by Gilman between the ages of fifteen and eighteen were recorded in shorthand for the purpose of thwarting any attempts by family members who might be inclined to read them. The shorthand Gilman used, however, was not the commonly taught Gregg shorthand still in use today; rather it appeared to be based on a now-obsolete form of an earlier method of shorthand, popular in the nineteenth century. The likelihood of locating an expert who could offer an accurate transcription was extremely remote, particularly since Gilman apparently devised her own abbreviated forms of some of the standard shorthand symbols. In addition to passages recorded in shorthand, the majority of the early entries, although written in longhand, tend to focus on repetitive themes. Gilman's teenaged infatuation with a young Rhode Island actor, for example, consumes much of the diary for 1876, as do her accounts of altercations with her brother, Thomas, and power struggles with her mother, Mary Perkins. Likewise, the later diaries, those written after Gilman's second marriage in 1900, provide little variation in theme and little insight into her interior world; rather, they record Gilman's financial transactions, appointments, speaking engagements, travel plans, and shopping lists. Only occasionally after 1900 did Gilman include remarks that are biographically noteworthy. I then made the rather difficult editorial decision to excerpt what I deemed to be the most illuminating selections from the juvenile journals and from the late diaries and to include them, respectively, in a prologue and epilogue. I chose to include in their entirety the extant diaries written in the twenty-year period between 1880 and 1900 (from the time Gilman was twenty to shortly before her fortieth birthday), when she first made her mark on the world. These years best illustrate Gilman's development from a restless, high-spirited, and opinionated young woman to a middle-aged internationally known author and lecturer.

After transcribing the diaries from microfiche, verifying the transcription against the original diaries at Radcliffe College, and writing chapter introductions and textual and explanatory notes, I began the process of locating a university press that would be willing to publish a 1,700-page manuscript. After a rather protracted review process, one university press declined on the basis of cost but asked me to consider editing an abridged version that would be less expensive to publish. The press's own reader, however, had argued in the reader's report about the drawbacks of a streamlined edition. The problem with a " 'selected edition,' " the reader wrote, "is that one loses the scholarly 'purity' of the complete edition, loses the fabric and texture of daily life."[2] And of course, that objection is valid: in Gilman's case, the collective diaries document a series of experiences in her life that are often disjointed or fragmented; they are interwoven through the fabric of many years.[3] Together, these analectic threads chronicle the experiences of nearly twenty years of her life. To reduce by half that which I had carefully constructed was not an attractive option.

I next queried the University Press of Virginia and was invited to submit the manuscript for consideration. Another protracted review process followed, but eventually, the press's reader, who identified herself only as one of Gilman's biographers, prepared a five-page, single-spaced report reproaching me for failing to provide an indepth *psychological* study of Gilman both in my general introduction and in the thirty-six chapter introductions that I had written. The reader eventually concluded, however, that she would be "delighted" to see the diaries published, provided, of course, that I accede to the revisions she suggested. Her recommendations for changes presented somewhat of a dilemma, since I had defined my editorial methodology in my "Note on the Text," explaining that as a textual editor, my role was to be less interpretive than objective, and that I had attempted, in the chapter introductions, to retain a fair degree of neutrality while still providing as background an appropriate amount of historical and biographical contextualization. I also suggested that readers wishing to have a fuller psychological profile of Gilman should consult one of the full-length biographies. The problem became how to address the reader's concerns without compromising my own editorial integrity. It was my intention from the beginning of the project to facilitate additional research into Gilman's life and not to draw any hard and fast conclusions about her psyche. In the end, I decided to add a fuller account of Gilman's biography, including the various psychological dramas in her life, to the general introduction and to leave the chapter introductions as they were. This compromise satisfied the press.

A more delicate problem was how to address the numerous discrepancies that emerged when comparing Gilman's original diaries to the published excerpts included in *The Living of Charlotte Perkins Gilman*. Gilman relied heavily on the diaries in reconstructing events included in her autobiography, most of which she penned at the age of sixty-six. Although she was fairly faithful in preserving the historical accuracy of the numerous diary passages that she quoted, she occasionally invented passages that did not actually exist, or she altered the excerpts in a significant way. These alterations of truth—including the citation of diary entries that don't actually exist—served a variety of purposes: to elicit sympathy on the part of the reader, to transform mundane events into something more sensational, and to fill in gaps in experiences that Gilman could no longer clearly recall.

Certainly many of Gilman's minor alterations of text can be attributed to her simple desire to tidy up her prose to enhance its readability—transforming, in effect, sections of her private journal into a public document—acknowledging Benjamin Franklin's dictum that "one does not dress for private company as for a publick ball."[4] Indeed, Gilman's diaries provide an unselfconscious and often unpolished record of daily events. In the more substantial autobiographical alterations, however—the deliberate invention or omission of text—Gilman engaged in a form of mythmaking, attempting to perpetuate the image of herself as a woman who was brave, strong, and invariably self-sufficient. The actual diary entries, however, often present a strikingly different scenario.

One example of Gilman's falsification of fact is in her autobiographical description of her first visit to England in 1896, where she attended the International Socialist and Labor Congress. In her autobiography, Gilman "quotes" her diary as stating that she had only ten dollars when the ship set sail. The diary entry that Gilman is allegedly citing, however, clearly states that Gilman had in her possession not just ten dollars, but one hundred dollars.[5] While even one hundred dollars was a dangerously insufficient sum for a person embarking on a four-and-a-half-month trip abroad in 1896, Gilman seems to have been intentionally distorting the truth to make her struggle with chronic poverty—and her subsequent contributions to society—seem even more heroic. Her rewriting of her history in this instance magnifies the often untenable circumstances resulting from her financially precarious condition. It also reinforces her image as a survivor who was able to overcome seemingly insurmountable obstacles.

Another example of Gilman's distortion of the truth occurs midway through the autobiography when she relates the events surrounding the murder in 1893 of a casual acquaintance—one Mrs. Griffes of San Francisco. The woman's husband asked Gilman to deliver the eulogy at her funeral, and Gilman agreed. In the autobiographical version of the funeral, Gilman remarks that "there were no mourners [in attendance except] the husband" (*Living* 175). In her diary, however, Gilman clearly states that there were about twenty people present. Furthermore, the autobiography describes the funeral service as "pathetic," "painful," "dreadful," "gloomy," and "ghastly," while the *diary* entry cheerfully proclaims, "[it was] the pleasantest funeral I ever attended," with plenty of "noble spirit" (*Diaries* 539). Initially, one might wonder why Gilman includes an account of this particular funeral in the autobiography in the first place. The circumstances of this one, however—a grisly murder in a low saloon—made it unique, and in this instance, Gilman's rewriting of history serves a specific purpose. Her autobiographical report of "no mourners" being in attendance elevates the importance of her own presence at the funeral and allows her to appear to be more compassionate, more caring, more benevolent perhaps than she really was toward this casual acquaintance. Moreover, the episode adds a splash of sensationalism to the "San Francisco" chapter of the autobiography, which is not particularly riveting.

These various distortions of truth—the discrepancy between events described and documented in the diaries and the subsequent embellishment of episodes in the autobiography—are more biographically interesting than Gilman's simple revision of diary passages. While my preference was to append to the published diaries a corrigenda—a list correcting all substantive errant transcriptions of passages in the diaries that had been previously published—the press preferred that I simply include a sentence in the "Note on the Text" informing readers that I had silently restored accuracy to previously mistranscribed diary passages.

The physical condition of some of the diaries posed yet another problem. Before the Schlesinger Library acquired them in 1970–71, Gilman's daughter, Katharine Beecher Stetson Chamberlin, had stored the papers in a garage for nearly thirty-six years. Three of the extant diaries were badly damaged along the spine and appear to have been chewed either by rodents or termites and required a fair amount of textual reconstruction. In cases where parts of words were missing because of damaged or mutilated text, I attempted to reconstruct the passage based on the partial word. Where there was any question, however, as to the content of the text, I inserted the somewhat intrusive abbreviation, "msm" (manuscript mutilated), in brackets. This was a particularly important though somewhat cumbersome task since the editorial method I used was a highly conservative one: my purpose throughout the project was to reproduce Gilman's original text, rather than to "improve" it through editorial emendations, thereby preserving the integrity of the text.

Contextualizing Gilman's diaries, both within the genre of women's personal writings in general and within her own body of writing in particular, was another difficult task. Most notably, as numerous contemporary critics have argued, the ideological constructs of gender have caused the personal writings about women's lives, especially those dating back to the nineteenth century or earlier, to be viewed with quite a different lens and in a different context from those written by men.[6] With respect to diary writing in particular, Mary Jane Moffat has ob-

served that "the central conflict expressed by the female diarist is that
between Love (the family, self-abnegation, reproduction) and Work
(the outside world, self-affirmation, production)."[7] Thus, "torn between writing their lives and living their lives as women, women's diaries frequently become uninteresting (from a canonic male point of
view) because . . . the banal elements of everyday life" tend to dominate
(Raoul 61). Indeed, the domestic scenes around which Gilman framed
many of her entries would likely be deemed too marginal for inclusion
in a man's journal.

Consequently, when I applied for a grant to fund part of my research
on the diaries at the Schlesinger Library in 1991, one anonymous external reviewer recommended against funding the project because, "I am
afraid that in my opinion there simply is not enough diary material to
make the project worth her while. . . . Most of Gilman's diaries are little
more than date books. . . . They record her appointments, the places
she has been, the people she has met; but they will not, in my opinion,
provide sufficient data for a book."[8] Conversely, another anonymous
reviewer wrote of the same grant proposal, "I well know how valuable
and useful such a project would be. The diaries are extraordinary documents for those examining the late 19th- early 20th century."[9] The former viewpoint, that there was "not enough . . . material" to justify the
project, reflects the often negative value judgment about the relative importance—or lack thereof—of material commonly found in women's
diaries.

In any event, readers looking for intimate details of Gilman's life will
be disappointed. The diaries contain little confessional writing and a
disproportionately large record of mundane daily events. But it is my
contention that those daily routines—of reading, sewing, visiting,
cleaning, "trotting" about, cooking, and writing volumes of letters—
everything, in effect, that epitomizes the cult of domesticity—were critical in the evolution of Gilman's social theories. Indeed, the places she
went, the people she met, the appointments she kept, were instrumental
in shaping the ideological views that eventually emerged. For better or
worse, it was in the domestic arena that much of Gilman's "living" took
place. As Margo Culley notes, "Keeping a diary . . . always begins with
a sense of self-worth, a conviction that one's individual experience is
somehow *remarkable*. Even the most self-deprecating of women's diaries were grounded in some sense of the importance of making a record
of the life" (8). Significantly, and after much deliberation, Gilman titled
her autobiography *The* Living *of Charlotte Perkins Gilman* [emphasis
added], using the active verbal "living" rather than a passive noun—
"life"—which would imply a form of stasis. From the inception of this
project, then, it was my objective to document the daily *living,* trivial

events included, and to encourage students and scholars to use the published diaries as a tool to facilitate their own research.

So what *do* the diaries tell us about Gilman? About the cultural climate in late nineteenth-century America? And why are they important?

Despite the fact that the diaries are characterized by emotional understatement—events are often presented in a flat and factual manner—they reveal a great deal. They provide both a larger framework for Gilman's life, as well as more intricate details about her personal quest. They chronicle her journey from adolescence to maturity, from obscurity to international fame. They take the reader through painful periods of severe depression, loss, and longing, but they also reveal Gilman's perseverance, growth, and success as a social reformer. There are entries, too, that tell us much about late-nineteenth-century domestic life, social history, and material culture.

For example, in reading the diaries, we learn about nineteenth-century medicinal treatments: remedies consisting of beef teas, raspberry phosphates, coca elixers, potassium bromides, and tropical fruit laxatives were prescribed to treat everything from congestion of the liver, to sciatic rheumatism, to insomnia, to various discomforts stemming from pregnancy. Strictnine pills were prescribed to treat weak eye muscles (*Diaries* 750), while "two doctor ladies" provided gelsemium to Gilman for "brain fatigue" (802). Gilman found "hot water and whiskey" an effective remedy for symptoms of seasickness (776), while a bit of "sherry with water, sugar, and nutmeg" helped quell morning sickness (302). "Blackberry Cordial and boiled milk" was the treatment of choice for indigestion (726). "Fellow's Compound Syrup of Hypophosphates" relieved chronic fatigue, but an "over dose of acid phosphate" could cause "*terror,*" Gilman discovered in 1890, after ingesting too much of it (418). After receiving electric shock therapy to treat her "brain trouble" (819), Gilman still felt "very badly," but the doctor's prescription of "phospho-glycerates in wine" was "fine stuff" that made Gilman "feel better" (820). The diaries written through 1903 also reveal that while Gilman would not hesitate to seek advice from male physicians, she preferred that women doctors perform examinations that required disrobing.

The diaries reveal much about Gilman's literary tastes and distastes; she dismissed Shakespeare's *Titus Andronicus* as "poor stuff"; didn't "think much of" Emerson's essay, "Compensation"; and condemned Walter Besant's narrative, *St. Katharine by the Tower,* as "a most miserable book" and "utterly without excuse for being" (486). She also opined that Ambrose Bierce, in his role as a journalist, "ought not to go unwhipped" (590) for his disparaging remarks about women writers. She found Charles Dickens, however, "a permanent satisfaction" and read Longfellow, whom she described as "The perfect poet," to "revive [her] spirits" (550). Of women writers, she declared both Margaret Fuller's book *Woman in the Nineteenth Century* and Blanche Willis Howard's novel *Guenn* to be "fine" works of literature (293, 371), while Olive Schreiner's "Heaven" made her "cry like a child" (443). On the other hand, she dismissed Charlotte Yonge's *Womankind* as a "weak book" (375) and characterized Ouida's "article on Female Suffrage" as "a *contemptible* piece of writing, bad in aim and execution" (346).

Gilman was no less opinionated when it came to characterizing public figures whom she met. Writer Joaquin Miller was a "dirty person," who received Gilman and other visitors "in bed" and whose floors were littered with "cigar ashes" (554); Governor Lucius Hubbard of Minnesota was "A Bombastic egotistical long winded fat man" (625), and Dr. Mary Walker, both a physician and a women's rights activist, was "old fashioned," possessed "no feeling for beauty in costume," and sported "short hair of course" (355). But Gilman was perfectly capable of being objective, as well. While she found one Colonel Fairman, "an artist, dramatist, poet, soldier, teacher, etc. etc." to be a "stupendous dogmatist—bigoted and belligerent to an intense degree" (446), she could still appreciate his artistic talent by acknowledging that his paintings were "very fine and impressive" (448). She became impatient with people who failed to use reason and intellect; she denounced the son of an acquaintance as "the most disagreeable young man I ever met . . . harsh and haughty criticism of every idea you dare offer—offering none himself" (484). And after an uninspired audience response to a "powerful" lecture she had delivered on economics, she exclaimed in her diary, with unconcealed disgust, "Such paltry people! Such feeble minds! Such ignorance!" (523) After attending a lecture delivered by one Cyrus Feed, she complained that he was "an ordinary person, unimpressive, illogical. How pitifully it speaks to our unhappy condition that we are so ready to hear such persons!" (516) On the other hand, we witness her apparent pleasure when one enthusiastic audience member compared Gilman's lecture style to that of her great uncle, Henry Ward Beecher (828), who was renowned for his powerful rhetoric.

Allusions to popular culture in the nineteenth century also appear throughout the diaries. Among the fads that Gilman mentions, and to which she ascribes varying degrees of credibility, were palmistry, hypnosis, and phrenology. While she found palm reading to be "a dirty-handed cheap fraud!" (650), a demonstration of hypnosis was "very jolly" (667). Her experience with phrenology, a popular practice which alleged that one's character could be analyzed by an examination of the contours of the skull, was pleasant and the reading "very satisfactory" (544). Her attendance at a stereoptican show, a popular form of nineteenth-century entertainment using magic lanterns, was "immensely" enjoyable and provided "one continuous giggle" (24).

Gilman also recorded first-hand accounts of late-nineteenth-century political and historical events. When President James Garfield was assassinated in 1881, for example, Gilman's simple observation that there was "more black than there was for Lincoln" (82) reveals much about her assessment of its impact on the nation. Similarly, when President William McKinley was murdered twenty years later, Gilman reports that New York City, where she was then living, was "in mourning," the "stores [were all] closed" and the "cars all stop[ped] at 3:30" (818) out of respect for the fallen leader.

The subtleties of late-nineteenth-century class and race issues are also reflected in the diaries, a topic about which Scharnhorst elaborates in his essay in this collection. Gilman documents her own struggle against chronic poverty; the receipt of seventy cents, for example, in 1879, elicited a simple comment: "It goeth to squench our hunger" (6). In 1892, when she was struggling to make ends meet in California, she received with good humor a Christmas Eve visit by a fellow socialist who came "to offer assistance" since "he had heard that I was 'destitute' " (506). The diaries record numerous occasions when Gilman was down to her last dollar, her last quarter, or in one case, her last eight cents (10). But in addition to her own economic difficulties, Gilman occasionally records her observations about human suffering in others. In 1897, for example, she expressed dismay that "the streets [are] full of . . . beggars—little boys mostly—a pity—in America!" (701) And her description of a visit to an almshouse in 1891 is both graphic and chilling as she takes us inside its very walls: "800 paupers in that asylum. All was neat and well-kept, every reasonable measure taken, but O———! a man without legs, . . . an idiot girl of thirteen helpless as [an] infant, an old woman dying alone in a 'ward' unconscious, and with no one even to brush the flies from her face; a girl blind, dumb, deaf . . . a parchment-faced old man, tied in a chair and moaning endlessly" (447).

The diaries also document Gilman's racism, particularly with respect to African Americans. When, for example, in 1881, she and her mother moved out of a racially mixed neighborhood in Providence, she bid a contemptuous farewell to "ungraded 'Coonville' " (52). She made other insensitive remarks as well, referring, for example, to a black neighbor as "Topsy," the mischievous and untutored slave girl in her great-aunt Harriet Beecher Stowe's *Uncle Tom's Cabin* (294). She also makes occasional comments, usually derogatory, about various "darkies" she has encountered in her travels (217, 352). She could also be charitable and compassionate, however, as in her account of her visit to "Mrs. Williams, the colored woman our [Sunday school] class [is] going to help. She is partially paralyzed, and has a little 9 year old boy. Lives in two little *holes* in an attic, & pays $4.00 a month for them! . . . [I] Leave her 67 cts." (236). A month later, Gilman organized a church collection that was "$3.00 over the regular contribution to get [a] Xmas present for [the] little Williams boy" (241). On Christmas Eve, in weather approaching ten below zero, Gilman ventured out to "call on Mrs. Williams to ascertain what her little boy needs most" (241). In subzero temperatures, she traveled back down town, purchased two sets of underclothes and "a pound of 20 ct. candy," and presented the gifts to Mrs. Williams, leaving an additional "five cents for [the boy]" and money to cover a month's rent (241).

On a lighter note, Gilman's love of the theater is also reflected throughout the diaries. Her opinion of the famous French actress, Sarah Bernhardt, whom she saw perform in *Cleopatra* in 1891, was highly favorable: "Am much impressed with the power of the great actress, and surprised by her appearance of youth, and the *cleanness* of her acting. It gave me the impression of a singlehearted deep and ardent love—more love than passion in our disparted sense" (452). The Majestic Theatre at Columbia Circle was "A *beautiful* theatre—very rich and noble . . . most satisfying" (831), and *The Wizard of Oz,* which she saw performed there, was "funny & amusing, [and] also a rich spectacular" (831). Gilman found *Mice and Men,* however, starring American actress Annie Russell, to be "The most painful play I ever saw—I sit and suffer and snivel & come [home] very tired" (832). The next day, in fact, found her still "weary & sad from that weepful play" (832).

We learn, too, that Gilman experimented with chloroform, the compound she used in 1935 to take her own life, as early as age seventeen, when she tried to euthanize Brinnle, her cat, who managed to escape, but she successfully euthanized other cats with chloroform in 1883 and again in 1925.[10] We are also treated to Gilman's droll, and often self-deprecating, sense of humor. At the age of eighteen, for example, and with comic exaggeration, she writes, "I am blessed with a cold sore of such amazing size and hideous aspect as to strike terror to all beholders. Oh it is grievous" (13). When she was plagued by another particularly bad cold in 1881, she casually remarked, with no small degree of hyperbole, that her enormous sneeze caused a fellow passenger in a horse car to "kindly lend me [a handkerchief after] I desecrate mine, my gloves, dress, car step, and the surrounding county" (64). She is humorously self-critical when she commented, with only modest enthusiasm, that she had learned to play the piano, but, unfortunately, "to the dire distress of [her] friends" (63). We also witness her love of puns when she writes that she had spent a busy morning writing "Iowa" letters ("I owe a letter") to various correspondents (667).

Some of the diary entries lay the groundwork for issues and theories upon which Gilman would expound at length in later years. There is little question, for example, that her proposal to Walter Stetson in 1884, just one week after their wedding, that "he pay me for my services" (280) would inform her theory vis-à-vis domestic subservience years later in *Women and Economics*. And we recognize the formal genesis of that ground-breaking work in her simple comment, "Get hold of a new branch of my theory on . . . [the] economic basis of the [woman] question" (682). We are also treated to pearls of wisdom that Gilman dropped onto the pages of her journals—such gems as, "A person who has a good creed and does not follow it is a weak fool" (10). "A steady struggle, if never wilfully [*sic*] relaxed, is invincible" (8). And finally, we delight in her witty assertion that "Egotism, in a journal, should be excused" (9).

The Gilman diaries are evidence of the capacity for the human spirit to overcome illness and adversity, and they are a testament to human growth and development. Moreover, they bear the distinct imprint of Gilman's "self" (or selves). Despite the fact that they don't always provide riveting reading and lack the coherence and unity of more traditional narrative forms, the diaries, nevertheless, contribute much to our understanding about the daily life—and *living*—of a remarkable figure in our cultural and literary history.

NOTES

1. Quoted in Margo Culley's *A Day at a Time: The Diary Literature of American Women from 1764 to the Present* (New York: The Feminist Press, 1985), 15.

2. Anonymous. Reader's Report of "The Diaries of Charlotte Perkins Gilman," University of Wisconsin Press, 19 October 1992.

3. An abridged edition of the Gilman diaries was published only after the two-volume edition was made available. See *The Abridged Diaries of Charlotte Perkins Gilman*, ed. Denise D. Knight (Charlottesville: University Press of Virginia, 1998).

4. Benjamin Franklin, *Autobiography of Benjamin Franklin* (New York: John B. Alden, 1892), 13.

5. See *The Living of Charlotte Perkins Gilman: An Autobiography* (New York: Appleton-Century, 1935; reprint, Madison: University of Wisconsin Press, 1990), 199. Hereafter, *Living* in the text. See also *The Diaries of Charlotte Perkins Gilman*, ed. Denise D. Knight (Charlottesville: University Press of Virginia, 1994), 629. Hereafter, *Diaries*. Subsequent page numbers in the text refer to this edition.

6. In addition to Culley, see also Carolyn G. Heilbrun's *Writing a Woman's Life* (New York: W. W. Norton, 1988); Nancy K. Miller's *Subject to Change: Reading Feminist Writing* (New York: Columbia University Press, 1988); and Sidonie Smith's *A Poetic*

of Women's Autobiography: Marginality and the Fictions of Self-Representation (Bloomington: Indiana University Press, 1987).

7. Quoted in Valerie Raoul, "Women and Diaries: Gender and Genre," *Mosaic* 23, no. 3 (1989): 57–65.

8. Anonymous. Review of SUNY Cortland Faculty Research Program Grant Application for "The Diaries of Charlotte Perkins Gilman," ed. Denise D. Knight, 11 February 1991.

9. Anonymous. Review of SUNY Cortland Faculty Research Program Grant Application for "The Diaries of Charlotte Perkins Gilman," ed. Denise D. Knight, 26 February 1991.

10. Gilman "murdered" a number of cats over the years, beginning at age seventeen with her attempt on Brinnle's life. See diary entries for 18 July 1877; 20 July 1877; 11 August 1883; and 29 July 1925.

Historicizing Gilman: A Bibliographer's View

GARY SCHARNHORST

BIBLIOGRAPHERS ARE NORMALLY CONSIGNED IN THE HIERARCHY OF
scholarship to footnote hell. Like carp, they are scorned as bottom-
feeders, only rarely appreciated for their unique and distinctive taste.
Let me plead the case here, however, if only in passing, for the continuing relevance of basic bibliographical research in the present climate of
literary studies. Though we are in the midst of a reformation whose
most radical protestants decry the very notion of a canon and proclaim
"the death of the author," the ongoing recovery of such neglected or
marginalized writers as Charlotte Perkins Gilman underscores the need
for such basic research. Establishing a reliable record of what exactly
Gilman wrote and when and where she published it is certainly no less
and perhaps a good deal more important than reading it through the
lens of theory.

A case in point: Gilman began her long public career in 1890 as a
foot-soldier in the Nationalist army inspired by Edward Bellamy's utopian romance *Looking Backward,* and she contributed regularly over the
next three years to the Boston *Nationalist* and *New Nation, California
Nationalist,* and *Weekly Nationalist.*[1] Though she wrote both publicly in
her autobiography and privately in her diary about her participation in
the Nationalist movement in California, the extent of her involvement
cannot be fully gauged without tracing her various writings and lectures
on behalf of the movement in Nationalist papers. Bellamy himself described her as "the poet of nationalism,"[2] and indeed the most lasting
legacy of the movement may have been the utopian impulse it galva-
nized in Gilman, who apparently modeled parts of *Herland* on *Looking
Backward* and who repeatedly referred to Bellamy throughout her life,
even in her last book, *His Religion and Hers* (1923).[3]

Similarly, I believe the extent to which Gilman found an audience for
her ideas should be inferred not only from the most familiar of her writings (e.g., "The Yellow Wall-Paper," *Women and Economics,* or the volumes of the *Forerunner*) but from the wide variety of venues in which
she published. Her work appeared not only in the pages of *Harper's
Bazar,* the *Woman's Journal,* and *Cosmopolitan,* after all, but in such

ephemeral or forgotten magazines as *Kate Field's Washington,* the Chicago *Social Democrat,* and the Ruskin, Tennessee, *Coming Nation.* Her most obscure publications survive today only in single original copies of such periodicals as the *California Nationalist,* the San Francisco *Wasp,* and the *Kansas Suffrage Reveille* (Scharnhorst 8–9, 76–77, 99). Sad to say, some of her published writings are apparently lost, such as a piece about Ambrose Bierce printed in the San Francisco *Star* in 1894.[4] At least one essay survives only in German translation and only in a single original copy in the Austrian National Library in Vienna, entitled "Fortschritte der Frauen in Amerika" (or "Women's Progress in America) and published in *Neues Frauenleben* in 1903 (Scharnhorst 107). Much of her early work survives only because she saved it: the only complete extant file of the *Impress,* for example, is the one Gilman preserved, which remained in her daughter's garage in Pasadena until 1971.

All of this prompts me to suggest some potential projects I hope Gilman researchers will soon undertake. We need an annotated edition of the dozens of lectures Gilman delivered over the years, most of them in manuscript in the Schlesinger Library at Radcliffe, others lost to scholarship which will need to be recreated if possible from newspaper reports. We need both a complete modern edition of her writings for the *Impress* and a collection of the hundreds of daily columns she contributed to the *New York Tribune* syndicate in 1919–20. We need a scholarly edition of Gilman's letters, at least a few hundred of the most significant ones, selected from the many hundred that are extant in the Schlesinger Library and elsewhere. We know almost nothing about Gilman's friendship with the popular writer Eugene Manlove Rhodes, though they probably met no later than 1912 and certainly were acquainted in 1926, when Rhodes inscribed a copy of his latest book to Gilman.[5] Above all, we need to know more than we do about Adeline Knapp, Gilman's companion in 1891–92. Virtually all we know about her is what Gilman records in her diary and autobiography, though she is a fascinating and, ironically enough, a neglected figure in her own right. A working reporter for the San Francisco *Morning Call* in the 1890s, Knapp was a target of Bierce's satire almost as often as Gilman. In the mid-1890s, she was also a regular contributor of fiction to the Sunday supplement of the *Call,* though no one so far as I know has tracked down and read these stories.[6] Before her death at age forty-nine in 1909, she published some poetry, juvenile fiction, and a popular story collection entitled *The Well in the Desert.* A line-drawing of her which accompanies a *San Francisco Chronicle* report about the Pacific Coast Women's Press Association convention in 1892 is only one of two images of her I have seen.[7] I doubt whether the letters Gilman sent her—

the letters she feared would surface and embarrass her in later life—will ever turn up, but in reclaiming Knapp from the margins it is at least possible we will also recover some additional information about their relationship. I should add here, too, that as a bibliographer I've also come to expect serendipitous discovery, such as early in my Gilman research when I withdrew the single copy of *In This Our World* from the stacks of Fondren Library at Southern Methodist University (SMU) in Dallas and learned from an inscription on the flyleaf that in 1898 Gilman presented it to Lester Ward. This volume, which includes Ward's marginal glosses, is now located in the special collections department at SMU.

And how might this shift in focus to her less-familiar or neglected writings affect perceptions of Gilman? Frankly, I suspect that many of these writings will either delight or offend. On the one hand, Gilman analyzed the problems associated with the economic dependence of women repeatedly and in nuanced detail during the course of her long career. She was perhaps most systematic in her social diagnosis in *Women and Economics,* but she continued to call for the economic independence of women in articles printed in magazines such as *Success* and *Pictorial Review* to the very end of her life. On the other hand, however, Gilman was at many points, especially from a modern perspective, remarkably hidebound and conventional. Her racial theories, her ethnocentrism and xenophobia, however repugnant they are to us today, were, I believe, key to many of her ideas about evolution and social motherhood. Gilman's defenders, while certainly acknowledging her racism, seem to regard it as a discordant note or a minor strain in her thought that can somehow be isolated like a virus and set aside. Mary A. Hill, for example, devotes only three pages to the subject in her Gilman biography, according to its index; Ann J. Lane, who pays even less attention to the topic, refers vaguely to "the racism that spilled out periodically in Gilman's work," "most apparent in her private writings," "particularly as she aged"; and Carol Farley Kessler suggests "this flaw in her thinking" should not obscure "her better-known work."[8] In effect, Hill, Lane, Kessler, and others argue that Gilman's racism was based on assumptions common in the intellectual climate at the turn of the century, and so it was. But Gilman, who challenged conventional ideas about gender roles and patriarchal marriage, should not be so easily let off the hook. Certainly, Gilman often expressed her racist views privately, a point Denise D. Knight makes in her essay in this collection. In fact, as many of her lesser-known writings attest, her racism was deep-woven into the fabric of her social thought, as inextricable from it as a Gordian knot. Far from a note she struck more often privately than publicly or an unfortunate welter of biases that "spilled out periodically," her assumptions of "Aryan" superiority colored much of what she published after the turn of the century, when she was widely regarded as "the leading intellectual in the woman's movement in the United States."[9]

Consider her argument for professional childcare or the "baby garden," most fully developed in her book *Concerning Children* (1900), the first book she published after *Women and Economics* (1898). It is the only one of Gilman's books never to have been reissued in a modern edition, for obvious reasons: Gilman based her argument on the essentially obsolete, pre-Darwinian or Lamarckian idea that parents transmit acquired characteristics to their children. She resisted or ignored the more modern view that children inherit genetic traits. As Gilman insisted, "The way to make people better is to make them born better. The way to have them born better is to make all possible improvement in the individual before parentage." By this logic, a child born into an "advanced" civilization is by nature superior to a child born into a "backward" culture. Or as Gilman explained in the book, "If you were buying babies, investing in young human stock as you would in colts or calves, for the value of the beast, a sturdy English baby would be worth more than an equally vigorous young Fuegian. With the same training and care, you could develop higher faculties in the English specimen than in the Fuegian specimen, because it was better bred."[10] Gilman argued, on the basis of discredited science, that professional childcare was instrumental to social evolution, moreso in "advanced" cultures than in "savage" ones. Lest her ignorance of modern science on this point seem a mere aberration, Gilman suggested as late as 1915, in chapter 7 of *Herland,* that acquired traits may be transmitted by parents to offspring.[11] However commendable her plea for the professionalization of childcare in *Concerning Children* and elsewhere may have been, it was rooted in her ignorance of science and her assumption of Anglo-Saxon racial superiority. She was right about the benefits of professional childcare, but for the wrong reasons.

Many of Gilman's other reform proposals were flawed for the same wrong reason. For example, in her 1908 essay "A Suggestion on the Negro Problem" in the *American Journal of Sociology,* she argued for the forced conscription or draft of black Americans into an "industrial army" reminiscent of the one Bellamy had described in *Looking Backward.* "We have to consider," according to Gilman, "the unavoidable presence of a large body of aliens, of a race widely dissimilar and in many respects inferior, whose present status is to us a social injury." The "proposed organization" would not be a form of "enslavement," she insisted, but a compulsory "enlistment"—a humane "system" that "should involve fullest understanding of the special characteristics of the negro; should be full of light and color; of rhythm and music."[12] Predictably, Gilman also favored restricting immigration of non-whites, those "alien" races and ethnicities she thought could be assimilated only with difficulty. She pondered in an essay for *Forum* magazine in 1923 entitled "Is America Too Hospitable?" the "cheerful willingness with which the American people are giving up their country to other people, so rapidly that they are already reduced to a scant half of the population. No one is to blame but ourselves."[13] She was especially haunted by the specter of miscegenation or "mongrelization." Even before the turn of the century, in *Women and Economics* (1898), she bemoaned the birth of "pitiful" racial "hybrids," the products of "moral miscegenation": "Marry a civilized man to a primitive savage, and their child will naturally have a dual nature. Marry an Anglo-Saxon to an African or Oriental, and their child has a dual nature."[14] A quarter-century later, Gilman was more explicit: some races "combine well, making a good blend," she asserted, but "some do not. We are perfectly familiar in this country with the various blends of black and white, and the wisest of both races prefer the pure stock. The Eurasian mixture is generally considered unfortunate by most observers." In her argument, she compared breeds of dogs to races of people: dogs, like people,

> can interbreed practically without limit. But if you want a watch-dog you do not mate an Italian greyhound with a hairless pup from Mexico. If dogs are left to themselves . . . they are cheerfully promiscuous, but do not produce a super-dog. On the contrary they tend to revert to the "yaller dog," the jackal type.

Like the most rabid nativist, Gilman urged those who wish to "mix all racial ingredients into a smooth paste" to "select an uninhabited island for their experiment."[15]

Not surprisingly, too, given her reactionary racial assumptions, Gilman endorsed in spirit many of the proposals of the early twentieth-century eugenics movement, including compulsory sterilization of the "unfit," whom she once defined as "admitted defectives living on our taxes."[16] Even the "Aryan" women of Herland practice "negative eugenics" or selective birth control; that is, "the lowest types" or "those held unfit are not allowed" to reproduce.[17] Of course, Gilman also purged her utopia of all racial difference. As she noted in her autobiography, mostly written by 1922 though published posthumously, such "defective" types were less likely to be white than people of color. She averred that "insanity had increased greatly among the Negroes since they were freed, probably owing to the strain of having to look out for themselves in a civilization far beyond them."[18] If, in 1900, Gilman had been right about the need for professional childcare, albeit for the wrong reasons, a few years later she was no longer right about a variety of issues related to race, even for the wrong reasons. She was, quite simply, wrong.

Her expressions of concern about "race-mixing" may be related, too, to her repeated condemnation of sexual promiscuity and the cult of Freud. She was, in fact, no advocate of sexual freedoms for women any more than for men. A proponent of the Social Purity movement in the 1890s, she was horrified by the phenomenon of the "flapper" and the bohemian "Greenwich Villager," by the unexpected (by her) conse- quences of safer and more efficient birth control and the modest sexual liberation of the 1920s, which she feared only increased the chances of "race suicide" and the exploitation of women. In essays written near the end of her life, she seemed petulant and prudish, scarcely a progres- sive at all. In a 1927 essay for the *North American Review,* she argued, for example, that birth rates of "many races" should be restricted for reasons of "sheer economic and political necessity," even as "there is at the same time a need for a definite increase in some stocks unless they wish to vanish from the earth."[19] "The basic use of sex," she in- sisted, was procreation, "the conscious improvement of the species."[20] She was explicitly critical of those "who call themselves feminists" who "seem quite largely to have adopted the theory that the purpose of sex is recreation."[21] She complained in her 1923 essay "The New Genera- tion of Women" that birth control, rather than simply protecting poor mothers from "enforced childbearing," had become "a free ticket for selfish and fruitless indulgence, and an aid in the lamentable misbehav- ior of our times."[22] As she wrote the next year in an essay for the *Nation,* "Just as women have imitated the drug-habits of men, without the faintest excuse or reason, merely to show that they can, so are they imi- tating men's sex habits, in large measure."[23] Or, as she declared in her essay "Feminism and Social Progress" (1929), "we must disabuse our minds of that mire of psycho-sexual theory which is directly responsible for so much of present day perversion."[24] She regarded the "pitifully narrow and morbid philosophy" of Freud as nothing more than a "re- surgence of phallic worship."[25]

Gilman's racism, ethnocentrism, and class bias are also implicit in her proposal to abolish the traditional home, which she regarded as little more than an inefficient sweatshop, and to "out-source" most of the labor by centralizing domestic services. She was best known among her contemporaries for her ideal of the "kitchenless home," a model of domestic efficiency she tirelessly pitched throughout her career in doz- ens of articles in such magazines as *Puritan* and *Delineator.* Upton Sin- clair mentioned her by name and praised her ideas in chapter 31 of *The*

Jungle: "All of these things" one needs to know about reorganizing the home "you may find in the books of Mrs. Gilman."[26] To quote Jake Barnes, isn't it pretty to think so. As in much of Gilman's writing, there was a yawning discrepancy between theory and practice. While she claimed in her autobiography that she and her new husband moved into a "home without a kitchen" in New York City soon after their marriage in 1900, for example, her diary reveals that they rented a standard apartment and simply boarded at a local restaurant.[27] The very idea of a "home without a kitchen" was far from a radical idea, moreover. As Dolores Hayden concluded nearly twenty years ago, Gilman's *idée fixe* was a "belated and conservative" response to "the consequences of industrialization and urbanization" upon the middle class, in one sense little more than a *petit-bourgeois* solution to the "servant problem."[28] And who would actually perform the domestic labor displaced from the traditional home? By "those who like to do such work," she suggested in *Women and Economics,* and more tellingly in her book *The Home,* by those "best fitted for" it.[29]

More to the point, Gilman envisioned how professional domestic services might be provided in her novel *What Diantha Did* (1910), which betrays her racial and class prejudices. Sponsored by a maternalistic capitalist, Gilman's middle-class, entrepreneurial white heroine Diantha Bell contracts to provide customers with such housekeeping services as cleaning and cooking. She hires employees who are exclusively lower-class ethnic and racial types, among them "a melancholy Dane" who runs her laundry, her brain-damaged, "docile, quiet, and endlessly strong" husband who does the mental "heavier work," and a "misanthropic" black woman who runs the kitchen.[30] In effect, that is, Gilman envisioned a scheme that merely transferred the drudgery of the traditional home to other shoulders, to those of dull-witted brutes and lower-class women, particularly women of color. According to Hayden, Gilman "failed to develop a sufficiently complex analysis of the ways in which class position modified women's experience of domestic work." In fact, Hayden adds, she was hardly the Fabian socialist she professed to be but "a romantic advocate of benevolent capitalism."[31] She was opposed to barter exchange and cooperative housekeeping, even to the Pure Food and Drug Act on the grounds that professional buyers and middle-management types such as Diantha Bell were likely to be more expert at detecting adulterated foods than government inspectors. Her progressivism was more asserted than proved.

In short, many of Gilman's ideas, more stale than fresh, simply do not translate well. Rather than read her writings selectively, rather than appropriate from them only those ideas we can adapt to our purposes, rather than remake Gilman into some kind of femme ideal or role model, I believe that as scholars we should read all of her work we can find but read it critically, measuring her achievement on a historical template, situating her not only in our time but in her own.

NOTES

1. Gary Scharnhorst, *Charlotte Perkins Gilman: A Bibliography* (Metuchen, NJ, and London: Scarecrow Press, 1985), 3–11. Subsequent references are cited parenthetically in the text.
2. Edward Bellamy, "Rich Men Not at Fault But the System That Makes Rich Men," *New Nation* (24 June 1893): 315.
3. Charlotte Perkins Gilman, *His Religion and Hers* (New York: Century, 1923), 27.
4. Gilman, *The Diaries of Charlotte Perkins Gilman,* ed. Denise D. Knight (Charlottesville and London: University Press of Virginia, 1994), 2: 591. See also Lawrence J. Oliver and Gary Scharnhorst, "Charlotte Perkins Gilman v. Ambrose Bierce: The Literary Politics of Gender in *Fin-de-Siècle* California," *Journal of the West,* 32 (July 1993): 58.
5. Gary Scharnhorst and Denise D. Knight, "Charlotte Perkins Gilman's Library: A Reconstruction," *Resources for American Literary Study,* 23 (Fall 1997): 48.
6. Knapp's stories appeared in the following Sunday editions of the *Call*: 7 July 1895, p. 22; 14 July 1895, p. 22; 21 July 1895, p. 22; 28 July 1895, p. 24; 11 August 1895, p. 13; 1 September 1895, p. 16; and 1 March 1896, p. 16. I have discussed Knapp's story, "The Ways That Are Dark," in the Sunday *Call* for 18 August 1895, in " 'Ways That Are Dark': Appropriations of Bret Harte's 'Plain Language from Truthful James,' " *Nineteenth-Century Literature,* 51 (December 1996): 396–98. Knapp also published a number of essays and stories during the last fifteen years of her life in *Outlook, Arena, St. Nicholas, Overland, Critic, McClure's, Sunset,* and *Century.*
7. "Women of the Press," *San Francisco Chronicle,* 23 September 1892, p. 12. The other image of Knapp appears in *Bookman,* 27 (August 1908): 546.
8. Mary A. Hill, *Charlotte Perkins Gilman: The Making of a Radical Feminist, 1860–1896* (Philadelphia: Temple University Press, 1980), 172–74; Ann J. Lane, *To Herland and Beyond: The Life and Work of Charlotte Perkins Gilman* (New York: Pantheon, 1990), 255–56; Carol Farley Kessler, *Charlotte Perkins Gilman: Her Progress Toward Utopia* (Syracuse: Syracuse University Press, 1995), 47. Gilman's apologists also repeatedly mention her opposition at a suffrage meeting in 1903 to a literacy requirement for the vote (Hill, 279; Lane, 256; Kessler, 39).
9. Carl Degler, Introduction to *Women and Economics* by Gilman (New York: Harper, 1966), xiii.
10. Charlotte Perkins Gilman, *Concerning Children* (Boston: Small & Maynard, 1900), 4, 9–14.
11. Gilman, *Herland* (New York: Pantheon, 1979), 78.
12. Gilman, "A Suggestion on the Negro Problem," *American Journal of Sociology,* 14 (July 1908): 78, 83.
13. Gilman, "Is America Too Hospitable?" *Forum,* 70 (October 1923): 1983.
14. Gilman, *Women and Economics* (1898; reprint, New York: Harper, 1966), 339, 332.
15. Gilman, "Is America Too Hospitable?" 1985. Similarly, in "Sex and Race Progress" in *Sex in Civilization,* ed. V. F. Calverton and Samuel D. Schmalhausen (New

York: Macaulay, 1929), 111, Gilman noted that "no one refuses to recognize the difference between a *dachshund* and a great Dane."

16. Gilman, "Birth Control, Religion, and the Unfit," *Nation* (27 January 1932): 108. See also Gilman, "Sex and Race Progress," 122: "The elimination of the unfit is . . . necessary[,] already approached in some places by enforced sterilization of grossly injurious types."

17. Gilman, *Herland,* 69, 82.

18. Gilman, *The Living of Charlotte Perkins Gilman* (New York: Appleton-Century, 1935), 245. See also *Diaries,* 2: 726.

19. Gilman, "Progress Through Birth Control," *North American Review,* 224 (December 1927): 629.

20. Gilman, "Sex and Race Progress," 122.

21. Gilman, "Parasitism and Civilized Vice," in *Woman's Coming of Age,* ed. Samuel D. Schmalhausen and V. F. Calverton (New York: Liveright, 1931), 125. See also Gilman, "Vanguard, Rear-Guard, and Mud-Guard," *Century,* 104 (July 1922): 351: "It is not 'suppressed desire,' but indulged desire, that writes the foulest chapter in human history."

22. Gilman, "The New Generation of Women," *Current History,* 18 (August 1923): 736.

23. Gilman, "Toward Monogamy," *Nation* (11 June 1924), 672.

24. Gilman, "Feminism and Social Progress," in *Problems of Civilization,* ed. Baker Brownell (New York: D. Van Nostrand, 1929), 131–32. See also Gilman, "The New Generation of Women," 736: "the solemn philosophical sex-mania of Sigmund Freud, now widely poisoning the world."

25. Gilman, "Parasitism and Civilized Vice," 123.

26. Upton Sinclair, *The Jungle* (New York: Signet, n.d.), 336.

27. See Gilman's diary entries for 13 October 1900 (vol. 42) and 19 September 1901 (vol. 43), Gilman Papers, Schlesinger Library, Radcliffe College.

28. Hayden, "Charlotte Perkins Gilman and the Kitchenless House," *Radical History Review,* 21 (Fall 1979): 225.

29. Gilman, *Women and Economics,* 247; *The Home: Its Work and Influence* (New York: McClure, Phillips & Co., 1903), 319.

30. "What Diantha Did," *Forerunner,* 1 (August 1910): 13.

31. Hayden, "Kitchenless," 241, 230.

Part II
Gilman's Literary Career and Her Contemporaries

"When the songs are over and sung": Gilman's Childhood Writings and Writings for Children

JILL RUDD

In 1870–71, WHEN SHE WAS TEN AND ELEVEN, CHARLOTTE PERKINS COM-
piled a collection of stories and poems, some her own, others pieces
by George MacDonald and Robert Louis Stevenson, and called it *The
Literary and Artistic Vurks of Princess Charlotte.*[1] Underneath this title,
on what serves for a title page in the simple exercise book she used, is
a quick sketch of a very circular face, with lines of straggly hair and
impish grin, under which is written, "This is the Princess." In 1890,
when she was thirty and when she and Walter Stetson finally separated,
Charlotte Stetson sent off to the publishers, E. E. Hole, a book of her
verse written for children, entitled *Mer-songs and Others.*[2] Each of these
two volumes could be described as children's literature, though more
accurately the first is juvenilia and the second verse for children. Nonetheless, bringing them together under the heading of children's literature allows us to draw comparisons between the two and in particular
to see how the idealized childhood world created by the adult voice is
challenged by elements which are latent in the later verses, but more
explicit in the juvenilia.

Carol Farley Kessler touches on *The Vurks* in her book *Charlotte Perkins Gilman, Her Progress Toward Utopia,*[3] and also in her contribution
to this volume, finding traces of motifs which reappear in Gilman's
later fiction. My approach here is rather different; I wish to show how
certain themes, in particular that of freedom from constraining rules,
are surrounded by an unease which has its roots in the contrary desire
for rules and secure knowledge of right and wrong evidenced in her own
childhood writings. In each case the text is underpinned by a sense of
the consequences of choices and actions and an acknowledgment that
those consequences may not always be welcome ones.

Gilman's *Mer-songs* is a collection of poetry which might easily fit
the description of children's literature that Jacqueline Rose provides in
her book *The Case of Peter Pan or the Impossibility of Children's Fiction*:
"Children's fiction rests on the idea that there is a child who is simply

there to be addressed and that speaking to it might be simple." Further, "Children's fiction draws in the child, it secures, places, and frames the child."[4] Drawing on the ideas of Locke and Rousseau, who associated the child with the presumed simplicity and purity of nature and advocated nurturing children in rural surroundings, almost like plants (an association continued in our use of the term "nursery"), Rose argues that children's literature is posited on the idea of:

> [a] primitive or lost state to which the child has special access. The child is, if you like, something of a pioneer who restores these worlds to us, and gives them back to us with a facility or directness which ensures that our own relationship to them is, finally, safe. (9)

She further links the idea of the child-innocent, as created and held within children's texts, with a desire for an innocence of language in which meaning is transparent and subtext absent. Such language may itself be controlled and organized and so seen to have a comprehensible and tractable coherence, which can be trained into desired forms (to continue the horticulture analogy).

Compare these descriptions to one Julia Briggs offers in her chapter "Women Writers: Sarah Fielding to E. Nesbit" where she says: "Children's books are not written by children for children, but by adults for adults, since it is adults who provide the money to buy the books." A picture of a carefully controlled arena is beginning to emerge, which is further reinforced when Briggs goes on, "While a book's popularity (or lack of it) may depend on how strongly it appeals to its child readers, the whole process of reading is initiated and controlled by adults.[5] Interestingly, bearing in mind that Gilman is the subject here, Briggs further points out, "By writing for and about children, however, and by emphasizing the importance of education, they [women] demonstrated that their interests were still firmly focused upon the house and their natural functions as child bearers and raisers" (223).

Adding some more generally received notions about children's literature contributes to a conglomerate of presuppositions that provides a useful entry point for analyzing Gilman's juvenilia and children's fiction. Among such generalities would be ones of broad subject matter such as elements of the surreal or fantastic (through adventure, magic, or nonsense); simplicity of time; surface clarity; and often some form of moral or educational direction. It is also usual to have a child protagonist, and a happy ending is more or less required. Thus, we are accustomed to a pattern of safe returns home, felicitous discovery of loving relations or successful and stoical bearing of trials, duly rewarded.

These prevalent views of children's literature promulgate the notion that children's stories are in some way utopian if not indeed edenic. The texts are presented as alternative but enclosed worlds in which, free from the constraints of the external world, the child may safely explore or even subvert reality. Meanwhile, through the child, the adult reader also feels able to partake of this freedom for a while. The adult investment in this version of children's literature is huge, for it perpetrates the idea that childhood itself is a kind of paradise, inevitably lost to the adult and unappreciated by the child. It is this view of children's literature that Kessler broadly reflects when she terms "The Literary and Artistic Vurks of the Princess Charlotte" "a child's utopia."[6]

The adult Gilman's poems for children at first appear to exemplify many of these attitudes. The poem "The Little Mer-Girls," one of the Mer-songs of 1890, provides an example:

THE LITTLE MER-GIRLS

Said the little mer-girls to the big mermaid
"We want to be big like you!
With longer tails, and shinier scales,
And hair more wavy and blue!"

Said the little mer-girls to the big mermaid,
"We want to have golden combs!
And waver and swing and float and sing,
Where the shore-wave breaks and foams!"

Said the little mer-girls to the big mermaid,
"We want to have mirrors too!
And sing to the sailors, the fishers and whalers,
And carry them down like you!"

Said the big mermaid to the little mer-girls,
"O dear little sisters—be young!
For we weary of foam, of glass and of comb,
And the sailors are drowned when we carry them home
—When the songs are over and sung!"

In this rather saccharin poem, the respective spheres of adulthood and childhood are reflected in the magical mirror of mer-life. The expected wish of the young to be grown up and supposedly self-determining is simultaneously recognized and reinforced, if not, in fact, inculcated, through the use of deliberately childlike diction—"We want to be big like you"—and also through the faintly humorous use of precise physical details which remind us that we have entered the world of myth in which mermaids abound. In this world, full adulthood is signalled by the possession of full-length tails and scales that doubtless require a full beauty routine to maintain maximum shine and hair that is not only desirably and aquatically wavy, but also blue. Most obvious is the mutual desire of each party for the opposite state; the older mermaid's exhortation to the "dear little sisters" to be young inevitably acts more as a signal of her regret at being no longer a girl herself than as any kind of useful advice to the mer-girls. After all, they have no choice but to be young, and an integral part of that youthfulness is a desire to be adult. So, too, it is tacitly assumed that one of the marks of being adult is a habit of viewing childhood as a desirable though now unobtainable state. Indeed, the fact that it is unrecoverable in its original, supposedly innocent, form is what renders it so attractive.[7]

It is also worth noting some of the more latent aspects of Gilman's poem. It was written in 1890, the year of her lecture "Human Nature" in which Gilman asserts unambiguously, "I wish to assert that Human Nature is the *result of Social Conditions* far more than the conditions are a result of nature!" yet "The Little Mer-Girls" serves to reinforce some of these conditions.[8] The markers of mermaid-hood are fully gendered by both girls and maid: the glass and comb figure strongly, and the life of a mermaid is generally accepted to consist of singing songs designed to lure seamen to their deaths. The adulthood so desired is thus clearly that of the femme fatale, but what is interesting is that only the young in this poem actually enjoy the pastime of drowning sailors. Significantly, they are not yet practitioners of this art, and they ignore, or are ignorant of, the fatal consequences their defining occupation has for the men upon whom it is practiced.

The mermaid's version of events, with its world-weary tone and extra line, allows for some recognition of the fact that if mermaids are trapped in a social role whereby they ensnare and subsequently drown their victims, the sailors, fishers, and whalers are equally trapped by their roles into being legitimate prey. Thus, the figure of the mermaid, which is alluring as an idea, is finally shown to embody a fatal attraction, but here (as opposed to in her lecture and indeed throughout *Women and Economics*) one to which there is no alternative. It is from this standpoint that the world of childhood can be presented as utopian; the mer-girls are as yet without mirrors or combs and have yet to enter the social economics of the adult world. But the poem fails to make childhood fully desirable. Gilman neglects to mention how these youngsters do pass their time when they are not observing and interrogating their elders. We associate happy childhood with games and excitement, things for adults to recall wistfully in later life as they wish they could simply "be young." Yet whatever these mer-girls do is clearly neither stimulating for them (or why yearn to grow old?) nor enticing enough in retrospect for the mermaid to mention. In other words, even in the playful world of this mer-song, there is a careful silence about the actual state of childhood and a recommendation instead of the uns-pecified but apparently ideal state of "being young."

In the same volume, the poem "The Mer-Baby and the Land-Baby" contains some hints as to what childhood actually entails. While the poem ostensibly suggests that the childhood of the mer-baby, with its apparent freedom, is to be preferred to that of the land-baby, the poem as a whole promotes, almost schizophrenically, the dual ideals of a carefree and unrestrained "natural" childhood and one in which the child is protected and guarded by an ever-attentive nurse. Once again, analysis of this seemingly simple verse reveals a conflict of ideals.

THE MER-BABY AND THE LAND-BABY

> The little land-baby she sat on the land,
>   The mer-baby sat on the sea,
> The little land-baby was dusty with sand,
> And the mer-baby, on the other hand,
>   Was as wet as wet could be!
>
> The little land-baby was thoroughly dressed
>   From her shoes to her well-brushed hair;
> She had ribbons and ruffles and all the rest,
> And delicate petticoats starched and pressed,
>   But the little mer-baby was bare!
>
> The little land-baby she mustn't do this,
>   And alas she mustn't do that!
> She had care and comfort and many a kiss,
> But she was as thin as a "hankerfiss,"
>   And the little mer-baby was fat!
>
> The land-baby's nurse came and carried her home,
>   Away from the shining sea;
> But the little mer-baby could wriggle and roam
> And frolic and splash in the soft sea foam—
>   Now which would you rather be!

A couple of things are immediately striking. The complete division between sea and land and the utter lack of communication between them is remarkable. Even more than "The Little Mer-Girls," this poem enacts the process described by Jacqueline Rose, whereby it "draws in the child, it secures, places, frames the child" or, as she also puts it, "children's fiction sets up the child as an outsider to its own process and then aims, unashamedly to take the child *in*" (2).

In this poem, and perhaps generally too, I would argue that the deception practiced on the child (most frequently, that of telling it how desirable a state childhood is) is also and indeed primarily a willing self-deception on the part of the adult. There is a desire to delude in order to be able to create this presumed state of idyllic childhood. But there are inevitably fissures, cracks in the façade, or points where desired aspects conflict, and this little poem contains several.

In the first place, both adult and child readers are being credited with the power to judge between two contrasting states, while simultaneously being directed strongly about which state to prefer. The playful last line—"Now which would you rather be!"—may theoretically allow us to go against the grain and declare in favor of the land, but, in fact, it presupposes a vote for the sea. Of course, part of the basis for that preference is that the sea state is unobtainable. It is assumed that readers will recognize aspects of their own existence in the brief and comic picture of the land-baby and that those aspects will be ones they deemed objectionable at the time or that now (either in adulthood or upon reading this poem) they feel they ought to have regarded as objectionable. For, like the land-baby in the poem, the chances are that they were not in a position to object at the time. Similarly, readers of this poem are not actually given an opportunity for dissent, for that final line is not, in fact, a question, but an exclamation. Readers are not expected to answer, nor even offered the fiction of having their opinion asked. Instead, they are swept up with the strength of that exclamation, much as the land baby is swept up by its nurse.

And the effect may be much the same; the presumed preference for naked and frolicking freedom is in some ways a safe ground, familiar in its escapism and mild humor and one which allows us to overlook other elements which might conceivably have a bearing on the desirability of this seemingly edenic state. Regarding the poem as a piece of harmless doggerel written to amuse children allows us to leave unscrutinized some of the assumptions which underpin this kind of sentimentality—a sentimentality which ought to disturb us as readers of Gilman.

The seemingly safe waters of this poem are, in fact, more troubled than they appear. The tension lies between the lure of an apparently carefree state and the security of one bound by rules and conventions. The mer-baby is clearly the figure of freedom, unburdened by conventions, responsibilities, ideas of right conduct, and even clothes; its place in this text is analogous to that held by the idea of the child-innocent in literature generally. The land-baby thus represents those bound to the real world and takes up the textual position of adult, placed in opposition to the mer-baby, but strangely distant from it. There is no suggestion of any interaction between these two babies, not even the dimmest awareness of each other's presence. Rather, the reader, outside the text and seeing both babies, draws likenesses or makes connections. Yet this is done with a strong presumption of innocence; not only is there no room for cynical comment (isn't an unwatched mer-baby in danger of being beached?), but there is also such a willingness to collude with the fantasy of the text that other potential readings are ignored.

For instance, if the sea is the desired place, at the very least the land-baby would rather be left to look at it than be carried off by its nurse. Yet it would be possible to see in this image a figure of the attentive adult world, which offers some sense of comfort, security, and identity. The existence of the world represented by the nurse makes it possible to regard the idea of the world inhabited by the mer-baby as desirable. The fun lies precisely in its being an idea, and it is all the more firmly placed in the realms of the impossible by the use of a mythological figure. Furthermore, it might be noted that the existence of mer-babies is an extrapolation from mermaids which itself reveals a compulsion to superimpose the field of human relations upon all others. The very fact that we easily accept the existence of mer-babies and by implication of mermen (who figure in other poems in the collection) is a testimony to the power of our normative habits of thought.

So, in the poem the mer-baby represents the poem itself as each is an emblem of an idealized escapist world—a site of innocence which is attractive because it is unobtainable. Hence that strange lack of exchange between the two babies of the poem: the divide between the two worlds seems absolute, much as it is in "The Little Mer-Girls," where, although inhabitants from the land-world are brought into the mer-world, they are killed by it. If we regard children's literature, then, as a place for adults' imagination as well as children's, a more disconcerting picture begins to emerge. For these texts are not after all the happy-go-lucky innocent places they seem. Rather, they contain within them recognition of the fact that to enter fully into these worlds, or to stay there too long, proves fatal. It is possible to see in these texts a trace of the unease expressed by the adult Gilman in a letter to Houghton Gilman on 6 November 1899 in which she says: "Seems a weakness. To be so tangled up in another person."[9] That word "tangled" echoes the imagery associated with mermaids whereby the entanglement may be not only physical, as in fishing nets or seductively long hair, but also emotional as the mermaid is traditionally all but irresistible to the unfortunate sailor-victim.

Such darker elements are, of course, part of the world of fairy tale and children's literature, as reading George MacDonald or Robert Louis Stevenson, as Gilman did, would remind us. Many of these texts enact a battle between the often suppressed knowledge of the unidyllic experience of childhood and the overt desire to make the notion of childhood something magical. This desire grew through the nineteenth century, and Gilman herself partook of it with her ready espousal of the kindergarten movement and declarations about the best way to raise children. Gilman recalls her own wish for imagined and imaginative freedom in her autobiography at the very point she records being required to give it up. Simultaneously, she attributes her desire to create happiness for others in her stories to her own personal lack of happiness (*Living* 23–24). But there she is an adult rewriting her childhood for an adult audience and creating, through this attribution of such an accessible motive, the fiction of the child's imaginary world as one of harmony and due reward. Her childhood writings themselves encompass and sometimes hinge upon darker, even punitive elements, which may more accurately reveal the conflicting fears and desires of the childish imagination. For balancing the desire for freedom is a wish for security, which may take the form of strict adherence to dictates of right and wrong and the assurance that all actions have consequences. The frightening, disconcerting, or emotionally hurtful aspects of life may thus be safely contained by strictures and frameworks, either of moral codes or of plot. The adult Gilman meets this need by providing the nurse who collects the land-baby, or the older and wiser mermaid who instructs the young. The young Gilman, however, was less easily satisfied, as the juvenilia reveals.

Several of the original stories contained within "The Literary and Artistic Vurks of Princess Charlotte" are unfinished. One, "A Fairy Story," is not so much explicitly dark or punitive as simply a tale which loses its courage. In many ways it is a typical girl's escapist fairytale: the heroine, Araphenia, becomes the savior of herself and her father by disguising herself, leading an army, and vanquishing the enemy which besieges her father, thus earning his respect and the reward of a trip to the country of her newly found friend and ally, the fairy Elmondine. The escapism is obvious in the tomboyish element as much as in the removal to a different world. In this new world, Araphenia proves her worth by rejecting worldly goods in favor of friendship at which point the story takes an awkward dive into another secondary tale of the rescue of a distressed damsel. This second story, for which Araphenia is the audience rather than one of the protagonists, functions in some way as Araphenia's reward. Through it she is able to transpose herself into the damsel of this tale and so take part in a fantasy version of her own life, much as the created child reader and even the author of "A Fairy

Story" may enter the imagined world Gilman created. In this tale-within-a-tale, the damsel, the only daughter of a baron, was lost, but returns to the baron's care, described in a haunting sentence which ends this unfinished story:

> I comforted her and took her back to her father; we met him half way searching for her.[10]

Here lies the vein latent in her adult writings: escape and freedom have their allure, but there is something very powerful about the notion of being looked for and looked after. Yet the breaking off of the tale at this point suggests to me not, as Kessler puts it elsewhere in this volume, that the arrival of the longed-for father figure provides a resolution needed to complete the story, but that this "fairy tale" plot resolution is profoundly lacking. It is simply inadequate. Despite being recognized in the tale as a fantasy, the story of the lost and found princess is no more a reward for Araphenia than a consolation for the young Gilman. Such awareness of not only the realities of life, but also the uses of fiction is evident in other of the *Vurks,* too, but it is a voice the adult Gilman sought to silence when she came to write for children.

The issue of the uses of obedience furnishes a useful example. In "The Story of Mr. & Mrs. Rabbit," another of the Princess Charlotte's literary or artistic works, the moral is clear. Nibbles is one of the many children of Mrs. Rabbit and her husband. He is habitually disobedient and always in trouble, often as a result of ignoring explicit warnings. It comes as absolutely no surprise, then, when he falls foul of a snare, nor is it the occasion of much grief. The tale ends with comic swiftness, which allows no dissent from its moral message:

> They called and searched the forest round but no Nibbles was there. But after a while Mrs. Rabbit had some more children but they never could not forget (sic) poor Nibbles, whose fate was a warning to all future children always to obey their parents and never to disobey them.
> The End.

"The End" indeed—there is not a shred of ambiguity concerning the dire effects of disobedience. Here there is no suggestion that poor Nibbles might have benefited from being reared differently. In later life, however, Gilman cautioned against inculcating habits of blind obedience into children, as she saw that teaching unquestioning obedience led to trouble. In "Concerning Children" (1900) she writes,

> Obedience is defended, first, as being necessary to the protection of the child, and second, as developing desirable qualities in the adult. But the

child can be far better protected by removing all danger, which our present civilization is quite competent to do; and "the habit of obedience" develops very undesirable qualities. On what characteristics does our human pre-eminence rest? On our breath and accuracy of judgment and force of will. (Ceplair 117)

This paragraph rather intriguingly overlooks matters which "The Story of Mr. and Mrs. Rabbit" recognizes. First, it assumes that the adult has the power to remove all danger, whereas the snares set for the rabbit are beyond the power of Mr. or Mrs. Rabbit to remove. In terms of our individual experience, I would suggest that we all feel ourselves far more often in the position of Mr. and Mrs. Rabbit than that of the implied omnipotent adult so optimistically and sweepingly described in "Concerning Children." On the matter of developing judgment, Gilman does have a point. Nibbles epitomizes the reaction to frequent admonishment that Gilman terms "the injurious reaction from obedience, . . . namely, that fierce rebellious desire to do exactly the opposite of what one is told, which is no nearer to calm judgment than the other [unquestioning obedience]" (Ceplair 117).

Nibbles encounters his fatal snare when dashing through a tempting shortcut in the forest, the very thing he has been warned against, but which he does to prove his independence, flair, and defiance. Yet while such blind flouting of rules is clearly as undesirable as mindless concurrence, there is a disturbing third path which the young Gilman herself confronted in the unfinished story "Prince Cherry," which also forms part of the "Vurks." For, while Nibbles could be seen to deserve his fate, the same can hardly be said of the unfortunately named Cherry. This tale begins recognizably in the tradition of a reward story, but stops abruptly at the point where Cherry must either take on the mantle of the unrepentant villain or become a martyr to the cause of enforced good behavior and the stringent rules of fairies.

This fragment of a tale is itself short: Cherry's father proves himself worthy of his soubriquet "The Good King" by rescuing a white rabbit who is being hunted and turns out to be the Fairy Candide in disguise. Naturally, his reward is a granted wish, and his desire is that the Fairy extend "whatever kindly feeling" she has toward the King to Cherry. Candide's reply smacks of a blueprint for parenthood:

I cannot make him good: he must do that himself. I can only change his external fortunes; for his personal character, the utmost I can promise is to give him good counsel, reprove him for his faults, and even punish him, if he will not punish himself. You mortals can do the same with your children.

When it comes to it, though, Candide does not seem to follow her own methods. Rather than offering constant advice, she simply presents him with a ring and due warning: "whenever you do ill it [the ring] will prick your finger. If, after that warning you still continue in evil, you will lose my friendship and I shall become your direst enemy." This is not the blissful, carefree ignorance of the innocent child text, where lapses into wrongdoing are to be gently corrected, and the child is assumed to be good by nature. It is an aware world wherein reproof and punishment are active and moral responsibility high on the agenda. It refutes the notion that ignorance, under the guise of innocence, is a virtue and particularly refutes that notion for the young.

It is here that we find the link between the treatment of the child and of the woman in society which Gilman sought to change. For each she advocated education and information over ignorance and blind obedience. To quote Ann Lane, "to Gilman, innocence is the first chain women must discard if they are to be free."[11] Innocence is thus akin to freedom, and neither is the carefree, irresponsible state we often want to think it. Yet Gilman's juvenilia reminds us that the whimsical world of the carefree, amoral mer-baby is not one which is either created by, nor, in the end, lastingly appeals to the child any more than the position of uneducated domestic ornament is presented as satisfying for women. The mer-babies long to grow up, and the land-baby seems content enough to be taken home. It is only the romanticizing adult who assumes otherwise and seeks to overwrite the persistently questioning child voice. In the end, Gilman's children's poetry cannot be comfortable for any reader. The awareness shown in her juvenile stories, which we know she kept and remembered (as Carol Kessler notes in this volume), undermines the happy world she ostensibly seeks to create and surfaces in the recognition that if we aspire to be mermaids, we must drown the sailors "when the songs are over and sung."

NOTES

1. "The Literary and Artistic Vurks of the Princess Charlotte," folder 336, volume 12, Arthur and Elizabeth Schlesinger Library, Radcliffe College, Cambridge, MA.

2. Charlotte Perkins Gilman, *Mer-songs and Others,* Schlesinger Library, folder 190.

3. Carol Farley Kessler, *Charlotte Perkins Gilman, Her Progress Toward Utopia.* (Syracuse: Syracuse University Press, 1995).

4. Jacqueline Rose, *The Case of Peter Pan or the Impossibility of Children's Fiction* (London: Macmillan, 1984), 1.

5. Gillian Avery and Julia Briggs, eds., *Children and Their Books: A Celebration of the Work of Iona and Peter Opie* (Oxford: Clarendon, 1990), 223.

6. Kessler, *Her Progress,* 17. See also 82–88, 94–95.

7. It is, of course, possible to challenge this blanket assumption. Not all children's texts prefer childhood to adult life; some include the move into adulthood and present

it as not only inevitable, but also desirable. *Peter Pan* would be an example here, where the Lost Boys long for a mother and family, and Wendy and her brothers always want to return home and get on with growing up. These are protagonists we are supposed to emulate. Peter is all very well as an idea, not a reality. Indeed, Barrie firmly contains Peter within the sphere of childhood and, more particularly, the recollection of childhood by the adult by having Peter mistake Wendy's daughter for Wendy at the end of the text. This leads to Wendy herself remembering her own childhood experience, which, as an adult and mother, she has clearly relegated to the realms of imagination. Wendy's access to her memory is possible only through the presence and reactions of her daughter, which reflects the relation between text and adult reader that I draw upon here.

8. Larry Ceplair, ed. *Charlotte Perkins Gilman: A Nonfiction Reader* (New York: Columbia University Press, 1991), 44.

9. Mary A. Hill, ed., *A Journey from Within: The Love letters of Charlotte Perkins Gilman* (Lewisburg: Bucknell University Press), 309.

10. Gilman, "A Fairy Story," in "The Literary and Artistic and Creative Vurks of the Princess Charlotte," op.cit.

11. Ann J. Lane, introduction to *Herland* (London: The Women's Press), xxii.

"Dreaming Always of Lovely Things Beyond": Living Toward *Herland,* Experiential Foregrounding

CAROL F. KESSLER

IN HER 1996 STUDY OF RELATIONSHIPS BETWEEN TALES AND TELLERS, *From the Beast to the Blonde,* Marina Warner observes that "utopian ambitions beat strongly in the heart of the fairy tale." Regarding self-projection into heroines of tales told, she finds that the "voiceless . . . voice their 'sovereignty' against the odds" and become the "protagonist"; that fairy tales can "flow with the irrepressible energy of inter-dicted narrative and opinion among groups of people who have been muffled in the dominant, learned milieux." Such a tale teller can express "forbidden, forgotten, buried, even secret matters." Comparably Ethel S. Person in her 1997 *By Force of Fantasy* claims, "Fantasies are among the most powerful of the catalysts that infuse and organize our lives, dictating romantic, familial, and professional goals; fueling behavior; engendering plans for the future. In turn, our experiences, and the myths and stories of the culture in which we live, shape our fantasies. Moreover, fantasy, as embodied in the works of the great artists of our time, is one of the crucibles in which those myths and stories are forged, and is thus a key element in cultural evolution and change." Person also comments, "At the heart of every fantasy are a germ of frustration and, consequently, a desire for change."[1]

Though folklorist Warner specifies the genre of fairy tale while psychiatrist Person writes of fantasy in general, their ideas seem applicable to several childhood stories of Charlotte Perkins Gilman (1860–1935), whose case demonstrates how "utopian ambitions," couched in imagery of upward vaulting, culminate in *Herland* as one current of imagery in her writing. First emerging about 1870 when she was ten, this imagery flows like an underground stream through Gilman's life, bubbling up during the 1880s and 1890s, until it fully surfaces in the 1915 *Herland.* The biographical foreground of *Herland* extends over at least four decades: at ten she was "dreaming always of lovely things beyond," and

89

during her teens, she loved the physicality of gymnastics. The twelfth
birthday in March 1897 of her daughter Kate (Katharine Beecher Stetson [Chamberlin], 1885–1979) recalled her own twelfth year and childhood frolicking with her recently rediscovered Beecher cousin, "Ho"
(George Houghton Gilman, 1867–1934, seven years her junior, who
would become her second husband in June 1900). The landscape described in her March 1897 letter to Kate—which inspired this essay and
provided the title quotation—was mutually experienced by Charlotte
and Ho as children. In her letter from this 1897 moment, Gilman seems
to recall childhood experience, echo her own childhood fantasies extant
in "The Literary and Artistic Vurks [sic] of the Princess Charlotte,"
express her personal "delight" in rediscovering Ho, and prefigure both
imagery that marks the meeting between visitors and Herlanders in the
1915 *Herland,* as well as this utopia's overall themes. In current scholarly parlance, "eutopia" designates a "good place," as "dystopia" does
a "bad"; "utopia," according to Sir Thomas More's eponymous pun,
once ambiguously suggested "no place" or "good place," but now includes all categories of alternative imaginary place.[2]

Tillie Olsen first alerted us in 1962 that to surmount silences such as
the long foreground awaiting the achievement of *Herland* can require
"immobilization of long illness," "lifting of responsibility," or particular "circumstances and encouragement." In their introduction to *Listening to "Silences",* Elaine Hedges and Shelley Fisher Fishkin review
Olsen's definition of "unnatural silences"—in their words, "those that
result from 'circumstances' of being born into the wrong class, race, or
sex, being denied education, becoming numbed by economic struggle,
muffled by censorship, or distracted or impeded by the demands of nurturing." Fishkin, in her essay in this collection, in addition to the foregoing, emphasizes Olsen's "draw[ing] our attention to a range of
silences, including 'work aborted, deferred, denied'" as well as those
"imposed by . . . corroded self-confidence, by 'the cost of "discontinu-
ity" (that pattern still imposed on women).'" These last are especially
pertinent to Gilman's case. Surely, in Olsen's words, "one on whom
nothing [was] lost," Gilman recalls her early fantasy life in her posthumously published autobiography, *The Living of Charlotte Perkins Gilman* (1935):

> I could make a world to suit me. All that inner thirst for glorious loveliness
> could be gratified now, at will, unboundedly. . . .
>   . . . no one had a richer, more glorious life than I had, inside. It grew into
> fairy-tales, one I have yet; it spread to limitless ambitions. With "my
> wishes" I modestly chose to be the most beautiful, the wisest, the best per-
> son in the world; the most talented in music, painting, literature, sculp-
> ture—why not, when one was wishing?

But no personal wealth or glory satisfied me. Soon there developed a Prince and Princess of magic powers, who went about the world collecting unhappy children and taking them to a guarded Paradise in the South Seas. I had a boundless sympathy for children, feeling them to be suppressed, misunderstood.[3]

The next paragraph from Gilman's autobiography expands her meaning for children's being "suppressed, misunderstood" (*Living* 23)—the placement of the two words indicating malaise close beneath the surface of "utopian" writing. She refers to her brother Thomas's incessant teasing and her mother's withheld caresses, both recurrent biographical topics, and contrasts her family life with the "pleasure[,] . . . courtesy and kindness" experienced in the home of her uncle Edward Everett Hale (1822–1909) in Roxbury, a suburb of Boston— "quite a revelation" to her. Among the "whole flock of cousins" she met there was the child Ho (*Living* 31).

Not "one" as stated in *Living,* but a full notebook of the ten-year-old Gilman's tales survives today, but no one tale exactly fits that which Gilman recollects in the 1897 birthday letter to her daughter Kate. Of comparable interest for readers of *Herland* is Gilman's acknowledgment of the compensatory and self-fulfilling function for her of fictional heroines, with whom—exemplifying Warner's observation—she often strongly identified. They show as well a legacy of ancestral Beecher do-goodism: Gilman felt called upon to create heroines as performers of good works, even when she was pleasurably engaged in fantasy-writing, an illustration of Person's claim that fantasy can organize life. This is one of several discrepancies existing between the autobiography and other extant documents. One of Gilman's purposes in writing *Living* was to inspire young women by presenting herself as an exemplary model. Therefore, she downplayed factors detracting from her personal heroism in overcoming difficulties. Her seemingly insatiable need for approval was, in fact, bred of insecurity, which over time—especially in her later life within a supportive second marriage—she was able to bring under a degree of control.

Also among Gilman's earliest extant writing is a substantially illegible and undated twenty-page fantasy called "A Dream." The first paragraph of the early "Dream" fantasy uncannily prefigures *Herland* imagery. It reads:

I had a dream, and I thought that I was wandering alone in a forest, the extent of which I did not know. . . . Strange noises and rustlings were heard on every side, and presently the clouds overhead having united in one black canopy it began to rain; not fiercely, nor gently, but heavily with a dull whispering sound *as if the elfish inhabitants of these trees and swamps were talking of me in muffled voices.* [my italics][4]

So, too, would the Herlanders speak of intruding male visitors from the United States.

At ten, she titled her notebook "Literary and Artistic Vurks [sic] of the Princess Charlotte." This title suggests that Gilman early gained a rudimentary sense of the parodic in her awareness of German language sounds and perhaps even of a nineteenth-century Germanic world view in her romantic self-inflation as "the Princess Charlotte," creator of art works. The royal title may also, of course, have bolstered her self-esteem as a female child, having an older, teasing brother, in a society valuing males more than females. She shows, in the beginnings of parodic wit and the capacity to bolster self-esteem, her early progress toward *Herland.*

In the fifteen-page "A Fairy Story" the child, Charlotte, imagined girls and women exhibiting effective public agency. Setting this tale on another planet before the creation of the earth, Charlotte suggests an interest in otherworldly science fiction not born in her adult writing. By the time she wrote *Herland,* she had gained sufficient optimism regarding the possibility of human self-actualization to locate her utopian society here on earth.

"A Fairy Story" presents a childish author's description of her version of the "Big Rock Candy Mountain" of American folklore, a veritable latter day "Land of Cockaygne." The girls explore a sensuously appealing Edenic garden: fragrant air, singing birds, fruit and ice cream brought to them in a "temple made entirely from flowers," where they stop to rest. Though Gilman freely borrows from "Cinderella," the culmination of her tale is not in the arrival of her prince, but in a rescue by the heroine's father, who has come "searching for her"—the young author's actual desire for her absent father (Frederick Beecher Perkins, 1826–99) gratified in fantasy. Since, as Freud has pointed out, young girls often fantasize their fathers as romantic strangers, Gilman's characterization of a father and daughter here is now a commonplace. Also typical is a daughter's absolving her father of responsibility while requiring it unremittingly of a mother. Warner, who hypothesizes that the fairy tale genre can release speechlessness, finds "Cinderella" the expression of a daughter's mourning for a lost or absent mother—or in Gilman's case, one emotionally absent, hence irresponsible (Mary A. Fitch Wescott, 1828–93). "A Fairy Story" concludes abruptly once father and daughter are reunited, continuation unnecessary.

When Gilman was fourteen or fifteen, she began a second version of "A Fairy Story." This time brother and sister protagonists named Gabriel and Araphenia replace the 1870 "only child," and an unnamed fairy princess functions as the fairy-savior "Elmondine" of the 1870 version. This gender change from two female protagonists in 1870 to male/female siblings saved by a female fairy reflects an adolescent writer's increased interest in heterosocial relations, as her nearest concurrent *Diaries* indicate.[5]

Readers might well place *Herland* against this deepest desire for a childhood in which a daughter receives her father's approval, here couched as rescue. *Herland*'s conclusion in reconstituting a two-sexed family and *With Her in Ourland*'s in the birth of a son thus begin the possibility of a future in which growing daughters can enjoy the presence of empathic fathers. While these outcomes may appear reactionary in terms of roles for adult women, we know from Gilman's fiction in the nine volumes of the *Forerunner* she imagined women functioning in equitably structured families. And in her *Concerning Children* (1900), while questioning many nineteenth-century truisms of childrearing, she explores strategies designed for rearing freely responsible children. For instance, she doubts the value of exacting absolute obedience from children in chapter 2, "The Effect of Minding on the Mind." Instead of benefits, Gilman argues that this practice develops docility, subservience, and quick surrender of purpose. She also stresses the importance of all adults' nurturance of all of a society's children, not just their own—what she calls "social," as opposed to individual, parenting. To this end in chapter 11, "Six Mothers," Gilman recommends a plan for creating a playgroup for the children of these "six mothers" so that each mother might be freed for her own pursuits for five days when her children are cared for by one of the other five mothers and so that on the sixth day she might observe the effectiveness of her own parenting practices as she takes her one-day turn to care for the group.[6]

Her adult concern for equitable families had not yet developed as a child; Gilman then portrayed young boys—brother surrogates—as "bad." The partial exception, Prince Cherry (see Jill Rudd's informative discussion), manages well for a while, guided by his "best friend" Fairy Candide, who, of course, is female, before he finally turns "bad." "The Story of a Bad Boy" and "The story of a good girl and a bad boy" (one-paragraph fragment) relentlessly imagine various naughty behaviors perpetrated by boys. Only one "bad" young female exists, the rabbit Bunch, from "The Story of Mr. and Mrs. Rabbit," who disobeys her parents, then gets caught in a snare—set by "bad boys." Behind the young Gilman's consistent refusal to see good in boys or very much bad in girls likely lay a persistently teasing older brother Thomas, who seemed to her younger eyes vastly more privileged than she in his freedom to hunt and set snares for animals. In a pre-1900 attempt at composing her autobiography, Gilman noted both the ceaseless teasing of her brother and the mischief that brother and sister together perpetrated, mischief not acknowledged in her published autobiography. By denigrating boys and elevating girls—a reversal of the priorities she experienced in real life as a child—Gilman wrote gender-biased fantasies to compensate herself for feeling less important than boys. By 1900 when she had concluded her therapeutic courtship correspondence with Ho, she had transformed life's deficits originating in relationships with father, brother, and first husband: throughout this period, Ho had demonstrated the actuality of male support in his understanding letters to her and in his desire not to intrude upon her work. A striking example of the life-transforming possibility of therapeutic speech is *The Words to Say It* (1975), an autobiographical novel in which the author Marie Cardinal records the verbal process whereby she regained her "appetite for life and for building as big as the earth itself." Similarly, Charlotte recovered her joy in life during the course of her correspondence with Houghton in which she likewise pushed herself on through dark anxiety and doubt to this bright outcome of a new life with him: she became aware that accommodating to another's life need not curtail her own goals, as she had experienced with Walter Stetson and feared might occur again; rather, Ho might offer her joyful compensation, even as she bound her life to his. As Carolyn Heilbrun notes of submitting to life's demands in *The Last Gift of Time* (1997), "Of course there is always a price. But the fear of paying it . . . is the highest price of all."[7]

Given the power to heal that childhood fantasy-writing provided, Gilman's distress when her "mother called on [her] to give it up" was boundless. In recollection, she bemoaned in *Living,* "Just thirteen. This had been my chief happiness for five years. It was by far the largest, most active part of my mind. I was called upon to close off the main building as it were and live in the 'L.'" To be sure, the notebook in question does carry the notation "1870–71," making Gilman about ten—up to five years before she was actually forbidden this pleasure. But for a Beecher, the mere experience of pleasure was questionable. Consider her comment in her published autobiography: "this was so delightful that it must be wrong"; this idea appears as well in an early autobiographical fragment. In a letter to George Houghton Gilman dated 18 May 1897, Charlotte writes, "I am well used to giving up what I like—thoroughly well trained in it." Fishkin's quotation from Olsen's *Silences* underscores Gilman's sentiment here: "I am of those who very strongly believe that this capacity to create is inherent in the human being. . . . I believe there is the strongest relationship between circumstances and actual creative production." Gilman's training in self-abnegation can be understood as a type of silence.[8]

There are additional steps in Gilman's development of the imagery of *Herland*'s instigating scene from childhood to its 1915 publication. During the 1880s, while living in Providence, she had enjoyed gymnastics. In *Living,* she recorded her

> special efforts . . . to the buildup of a sound physique. . . . [T]wice a week . . . I ran a mile. . . . I could vault and jump, go up a knotted rope, walk on my hands under a ladder, kick as high as my head, and revel in the flying rings. Best of all were the traveling rings. . . . To mount a table with one of those in one hand, well drawn back, launch forth in a long swing and catch the next with the other, pull strongly on the first to get a long swing back, carefully letting go when it hung vertically so that it should be ready for the return, and go swinging on to the next, down the whole five and back—that is as near flying as one gets. . . .

Behind Gilman's description of the three Herlanders' lithe scampering upward through tree branches, ahead of their pursuers, lies her experience of such joy in motion—noted both in the foregoing *Living* passage and in her 1897 letter to Kate.[9]

Between August and October 1895, Gilman resided at Hull House, the Chicago settlement founded in 1889 by Jane Addams (1860–1935).[10] During this residence, Gilman wrote three letters to Kate, prefiguring central utopian themes later expanded in *Herland.* The experience of living within a supportively communal environment and of enjoying supportive mothering both as daughter and as mother had not been part of her childhood life. Thus, following the pattern established in her childhood imaginative writing, Gilman's utopia provides what her life had lacked. Psychologist Jane Flax, in her essay on mother-daughter relationships, comments, "There seems to be an endless chain of women tied ambivalently to their mothers, who replicate this relation with their daughters." Though Gilman sought to rectify this ambivalence for herself in *Herland,* her daughter Kate would view her mother with great ambivalence and misunderstanding even as an adult, as Flax notes.[11]

Herland delineates a mother-centered society where the highest position is that of the mother, where the greatest social honor is to be deemed an Over Mother, permitted to bear more than one child, where mothers and daughters need not be at odds with each other. But Gilman's motherhood experience had held both bitterness and delight. She agonized over ceding her daughter to her first husband, Charles Walter Stetson (1858–1911), so that father and daughter might know each other and so that Kate might not "suffer the losses of my youth."[12] During the years that Gilman supported herself by lecture tours, 1894 to 1900, her lifelong friend Grace Ellery Channing (1832–1937, Stetson's second wife) acted as mother to Kate, who traveled East with Gilman's father in May 1894 to reside with Stetson and Channing one month before they married. Given Stetson's personality and views on a wife's duty, primary care for his child fell upon his second wife. Gilman was later delighted to restore Kate to her own household, when she married for a second time.[13]

Upon the occasion of Kate's twelfth birthday, on 14 March 1897, Gilman then in New York wrote to Kate with the Stetsons in Pasadena, California, where Channing's family resided. Gilman referred to one of her childhood tales. It sounds suspiciously reminiscent of those in "The Vurks of the Princess Charlotte" and also recalls her comments in *Living* about her fantasy writing. She wrote to Kate:

> Twelve years old! When I was twelve I was living in a wonderland of my own mostly. Shall I send you the fairy story I wrote at that time—"The Story of Elmondine and Ferolio"? It is a very philanthropic fairy story. I used to spend lots of time in the [Rehoboth, Massachusetts] woods, picking flowers, climbing the tall soft-boughed pine trees and swinging in their tops, wading in brooks, swimming in the little river, *dreaming always of lovely things beyond.* The outside world was fair, but I enjoyed the inside the best [my italics].[14]

Through a similar woodland scene, the paragraph joins Gilman's childhood experience, her memory and sharing of this experience with her daughter (both as lived and as written), and the *Herland* meeting between three intruding men and three Herland women that initiates narrative action. This scene evokes Gilman's childhood desire to create a "world in which to find a place to discover a self." It reveals Gilman returning, as one "among persons of genius, to this landscape of childhood in order to renew the power and impulse to create at its very source."[15] *Herland*'s emotional roots exist for Gilman first, in her own childhood fantasies; next, in her desires both to be with her daughter and for her daughter to enjoy the best possible from life; and also, in her relationships with her mother and father, and as well, with her two husbands and many women friends.

In her 1897 letter, just following the discussion of her fairy story written when she was twelve, and after her reference to "dreaming always of lovely things beyond," Gilman gloats, as if this phrase also sparked her mind concerning the next topic she shared with Kate:

> Last week I made a delightful discovery! Found a cousin! Cousins are real nice. They are better than brothers. You have one boy cousin on my side, and quite a lot on your father's side—five I believe—no, four. I hope you'll

enjoy them as much as I have mine. This cousin is Houghton Gilman—
George H. Gilman. He is now a grown man—nearly thirty; when I remember him [1879] he was just your age.[16]

Herself at twelve, Kate at twelve, Ho at twelve—the letter foreshadows
Herland's beginning, wherein past, present, future, living, and writing
are all prefigured, bound up closely together in these three paragraphs!
Context of memory remains unarticulated, in pregnant silences beneath
lines and words—text as deeply heteroglossic or polyvocalic as is *Herland*'s, where the voice of a child continues to sing through the words
of the woman, the images constant.[17]

In a 1 July 1898 letter to Houghton, speaking of her daughter Kate
and again anticipating *Herland*, she wrote, "And her little boy is lovely
beyond words—such as you read about—or see in pictures of *slim
wood fairies with long wings*" [my italics]. As a maternal adult, she
healed the bodily denial of her childhood through delight in her daughter's body: "I wish you could see us rioting together when I forcibly
undress her and kiss her all over in spots—she struggling and gurgling
in mingled anguish and delight." A listening Ho, the letter's recipient,
is the evidence here of the previously mentioned "circumstances and
encouragement" that Tillie Olsen claims necessary to break silence to
permit achievement in writing.[18]

From 1897 to 1900, Gilman explored in her correspondence with her
cousin Houghton Gilman the goals she expected marriage to meet. Her
subsequent productivity, especially in her magazine the *Forerunner*
(1909–16)—which annually included a novel, a nonfiction book, a
short story, as well as shorter articles, reviews, and editorials—suggests
that for her, their marriage was empowering. Theirs was one of several
such productive Victorian marital and writing relationships—one not
typically cited in research literature. Gilman was aware of models from
both the United States and Great Britain, both exemplary and cautionary. Among British examples are the five from *Parallel Lives: Five Victorian Marriages* (1984) by Phyllis Rose: Jane Welsh (1801–66) and
Thomas Carlyle (1795–1881); Effie Gray (1828–97) and John Ruskin
(1819–1900), their marriage annulled because of his impotence; widow
Harriet Taylor (1807–58) and John Stuart Mill (1806–73); ever-preg-
nant Catherine Hogarth (1815–79) and Charles Dickens (1812–70);
George Eliot (1819–80) and already married George Henry Lewes
(1817–78)—one female and four male luminaries in the group. Additionally, Gilman would have known of Elizabeth Barrett (1806–61) and
Robert Browning (1812–89) and was acquainted with Beatrice (1858–
1943) and Sidney Webb (1859–1947). Closer to Gilman in time and
place, though she could not have known of it, was the marriage of

Emily Dickinson's parents, their courtship correspondence foreshadowing a marriage of male dominance (Edward Dickinson, 1803–74) and female passive-aggression (Emily Norcross, 1804–82), expressed as dependent invalidism, the nervous exhaustion central to Jennifer Tuttle's essay in this collection—a model Gilman had approximated with Walter Stetson and greatly feared repeating. Eugenia Kaledin in *Mrs. Henry Adams* (1994) reveals Marian "Clover" Hooper (1843–85) as finally suicidally depressed, her creativity as an early photographer repressed in marriage to a highly critical, philandering, and eminent husband Henry (1838–1918). Susan K. Harris in *The Courtship of Olivia Langdon and Mark Twain* (1996) shows this literary couple to have aimed for a companionate marriage, a new possibility that blended traditional and innovative features: "Livy" (1845–1904) enjoyed considerable agency in her relation to Sam Clemens (1835–1910), though he alone attained public status. More autonomous as a woman was the author Elizabeth Stuart Phelps [Ward] (1844–1911), several of whose novels Gilman recorded reading and whom she cites as "Mrs. Ward" in a 10 December 1899 letter to Houghton Gilman as another instance of a couple more separated in age than they were, Phelps being seventeen years older than her young husband Herbert Dickinson Ward (1861–1932): this brief, disappointing marriage represented a gender role reversal. The Gilmans, however, apparently achieved a marriage happy for both in which she exemplified an independent "new woman." Houghton Gilman's presence in her "living" was one important condition for the appearance of *Herland* in the 1915 *Forerunner,* a fictional realization of principles enunciated in her 1898 *Women and Economics,* as was her marriage experiential actualization.[19]

Passages from Gilman's autobiography and correspondence prefigure imagery in the *Herland* meeting between three arriving adventurers and the three Herlanders who had observed them from their perches in trees:

> [The intruders] rushed in and looked up. There among the boughs overhead was something—more than one something—that clung motionless, close to the great trunk at first, and then, as one and all we started up the tree, separated into three swift-moving figures and fled upward. . . . [W]e could catch glimpses of them scattering above us. . . . [T]hey had left the main trunk and moved outward, each one balanced on a long branch that dipped and swayed beneath their weight. . . . [W]ith no more terror than a set of frolicsome children in a game of tag, [they] sat as lightly as so many big bright birds on their precarious perches and frankly, curiously, stared at us. . . . Then there was a torrent of talk tossed back and forth . . . clear musical fluent speech. (*Herland* 14–15)

As a young author, Gilman had imagined herself as an adventurer, an early demonstration of the agency that later, in *Herland,* she would stress for women. Having found her voice in self-healing letters to Ho, she gives voice in "clear musical fluent speech" to the Herlanders. Unlike Edith Wharton's (see Frederick Wegener's interesting comparison), Gilman's creativity expressed itself less in form or diction than in innovative reshaping of social content: her utopian writing, in particular *Herland,* smashes the established gender system.[20] Gilman alone cannot be credited with the totality of innovation expressed; however, she placed her life on the cutting edge of social reform and absorbed intellectual ferment occurring along the boundaries of human experience. She demonstrated M. M. Bakhtin's belief that *"the most intense and productive life of culture takes place on the boundaries of its individual areas"* [italics M. M. B.]—not necessarily nationally or internationally, but rather individually, within a human be/ing, the focus of this essay.[21] The imagery both of the correspondence and *Herland* suggest Gilman's stretching female gender boundaries both consciously and unconsciously. Her analyses of gender from *Women and Economics* until her death remain brilliant. This concern permeated all of her living.

The utopian dimensions of Gilman's juvenilia, correspondence, and *Herland* can thus be understood as but fragile surfaces covering painfully-lived experience, especially regarding her familial and marital relationships. Dystopian reality may well coexist with utopian vision: rather than obverses of each other, dystopia and utopia can be conceptualized as existing diagrammatically within a continuous spiral or circle, each implicit in the other. In Gilman's works are tracings of delight, imagined to compensate deficit, a potential transformation effected through moving silence into voice, through first imagining or fantasizing a reality later to be realized. In concluding her study of fairy tales, Warner cited a "maxim of Czech dissidents" to "live as if the freedoms you desire were yours already. Only by refusing the constraints that are imposed can they be broken" (415). Such "constraints" could be construed as dystopian pain lurking about utopian delight, not the least of which in Gilman's case was her experiencing the androcentric conditions of 1892 that compelled her to write "The Yellow Wall-Paper" (see Catherine Golden's illuminating essay). But gradually, by 1915, she had transformed her living into an affirmation of women's agency in *Herland.* This convergence of the literary, linguistic, and psychological in tracking metaphor through the corpus of an author's work emerges as a resulting epiphany for readers: in perceiving writers' transformations, readers, too, may transform themselves by moving beyond their silences.

NOTES

1. This essay expands facets of chapter 4 in Kessler, *Charlotte Perkins Gilman: Her Progress Toward Utopia, with Selected Writings.* Utopianism and Communitarianism series (Syracuse, NY: Syracuse University Press, 1990); Marina Warner, *From the Beast to the Blonde: On Fairy Tales and Their Tellers* (New York: Noonday / Farrar, Straus & Giroux, 1996), 411, 11; Ethel S. Person, *By Force of Fantasy: How We Make Our Lives* (New York: Penguin Books, 1996), 1, 6.

2. Charlotte Perkins Gilman Collection, Arthur and Elizabeth Schlesinger Library, Radcliffe [SLR], folder 89, correspondence with Kate, 14 March 1897: 6, and vol. 12, "Vurks" (1870). Subsequent references to this collection will appear in the text, abbreviated as SLR. Quotations from this collection appear with permission. A recent discussion of the definition of utopia is Ruth Levitas, *The Concept of Utopia,* Utopianism and Communitarianism series (Syracuse, NY: Syracuse University Press, 1990).

3. Tillie Olsen, *Silences* (New York: Delta / Seymour Lawrence, 1979), 6, 8, 10, 39; Elaine Hedges and Shelley Fisher Fishkin, introduction to *Listening to "Silences": New Essays in Feminist Criticism* (New York: Oxford University Press, 1994), 3; Fishkin, "Reading, Writing, and Arithmetic: The Lessons *Silences* Has Taught Us," in *Listening to "Silences",* 26; Charlotte Perkins Gilman, *The Living of Charlotte Perkins Gilman: An Autobiography,* introduced by Ann J. Lane (1935; reprint, Madison: University of Wisconsin Press, 1990), 20, 23.

4. SLR, folder 159, "Early Writing": "A Dream," 2.

5. SLR, vol. 12, "Vurks": "A Fairy Story" [1st version], 12, 14; for "Cinderella," see Warner, *From the Beast,* xxv, 206, 207; SLR, vol. 14, "A Fairy Story" [2d version], 32–36. *The Diaries of Charlotte Perkins Gilman,* ed. Denise D. Knight (Charlottesville: University Press of Virginia, 1994), vol. 1, 1879–87: 3–6. Here Knight provides a summary of entries from Gilman's first extant diary for 1876, when she was sixteen, through 1878; see also SLR, vol. 12, 13, 14 for juvenilia, the earliest extant writing.

6. *Forerunner* stories concerning mothers and daughters include "Martha's Mother," 1, no. 6 (1910): 1–6; "What Occupation?" 2, no. 8 (1911): 199–204; "My Poor Aunt" 4, no. 12 (1913): 309–13; "With a Difference (Not Literature)," 5, no. 2 (1914): 29–32; "Joan's Defender," 7, no. 6 (1916): 141–45; and "The Unnatural Mother," 7, no. 11 (1916): 281–85. Gilman also depicts mothers- and daughters-in-law as in "Old Mrs. Crosley," 2, no. 11 (1911): 283–87; "Making a Change," 2, no. 12 (1911): 311–15; and "A Strange Influence," 3, no. 5, (1912): 113–16. As an adult she was less concerned about fathering. On childrearing, see her *Concerning Children* (1900; reprint, Boston: Small, Maynard, 1900), esp. chap. 2, "The Effect of Minding on the Mind," 25–45, and chap. 11, "Six Mothers," 200–11.

7. "Prince Cherry" (3 pp.), "The Story of a Bad Boy" (2 pp.), and "The story of a good girl and a bad boy" (one-paragraph fragment) all appear in SLR, vol. 12, "Vurks." For Gilman's unpublished autobiography, see SLR, folder 234, chap. 2; Marie Cardinal, *The Words to Say It* (*Les mots pour le dire,* Paris: Editions Grasset & Fasquelle, 1975; reprint, Cambridge, MA: Van Vactor & Goodheart, 1984), 295; Carolyn G. Heilman, *The Last Gift of Time: Life Beyond Sixty* (New York: Dial, 1997), 35.

8. Gilman, *Living,* 20, 23; SLR, folder 234, "Autobiography," chap. 2; SLR, folder 41, letter to Ho, 18 May 1897; Fishkin, "Reading, Writing, and Arithmetic," 39, n. 16, quoted from Olsen, 28.

9. Jane Lancaster, in her article "I could easily have been an acrobat": Charlotte Perkins Gilman and the Providence Ladies' Sanitary Gymnasium 1881–1884" in *A[merican] T[ranscendental] Q[uarterly]* 8, no. 1 (1994): 33–52, explores Gilman's experience at the Providence Ladies' Sanitary Gymnasium between 1881 and 1884.

10. Among the reform and communal, or utopian, influences upon *Herland* in addition to Hull House must be noted Gilman's involvement in Edward Bellamy's Nationalist movement, predominantly during the 1890s (discussed in Hill 1980, Scharnhorst 1985, Lane 1990, and Kessler 1995); visiting, among others, Prestonia Mann's Summer Brook Farm community of Fabian socialists in New York's Adirondack Mountains, early August 1897; Sarah Farmer's Greenacres, a communal camp in Eliot, Maine, late August 1897; and the Ruskin Association's cooperative colony in Tennessee, January–February 1899, all of the foregoing reported by Gilman in letters to Ho, *A Journey from Within: The Love Letters of Charlotte Perkins Gilman, 1897–1900,* ed. Mary A. Hill (Lewisburg, PA: Bucknell University Press, 1995), chaps. 2, 10, and noted as well in her *Diaries* (ed. Knight), vol. 2, 1890–1935: 686–89, 761–62. Also see Charlotte Goodman's essay in this collection. The foregoing contexts offer directions for future investigation; see Janet Beer, who charts this path in *Kate Chopin, Edith Wharton, and Charlotte Perkins Gilman: Studies in Short Fiction* (London: Macmillan, 1997).

11. Jane Flax, "Mother-Daughter Relationships: Psychodynamics, Politics, and Philosophy," in *The Future of Difference,* ed. Hester Eisenstein and Alice Jardine (Brunswick, NJ: Rutgers University Press, 1985), 37. See also SLR, folder 156; Ann J. Lane, *To 'Herland' and Beyond: The Life and Works of Charlotte Perkins Gilman* (New York: Pantheon, 1990), chap. 12.

12. Gilman, *Herland: A Lost Feminist Utopian Novel,* introduced by Ann J. Lane (1915, reprint, New York: Pantheon Books, 1979), 69; *Living,* 163.

13. For Walter Stetson's views on wifehood, see Mary A[rmfield] Hill, *Endure: The Diaries of Charles Walter Stetson* (Philadelphia: Temple University Press, 1985).

14. This tale may not be extant. I have been unable to locate any story featuring Elmondine and Ferolio, though Elmondine functions as the savior-fairy in "A Fairy Story." For a discussion of these tales, see Kessler (1995), 84–89, Lane (1990), 47–49, and Hill (1980), 33–35, who call "A Fairy Story" "A Fairy Tale" (33). For letter, see SLR, folder 89, pp. 5–6.

15. Judith Fryer, in "From White City to *Herland,*" chap. 1 of *Felicitous Space: The Imaginative Structures of Edith Wharton and Willa Cather* (Chapel Hill: University of North Carolina Press, 1986), 46, quotes Edith Cobb's understanding of the childhood bases of adult creativity: see Cobb, "The Ecology of Imagination in Childhood," *Daedalus* 88, no. 3 (1959): 540.

16. SLR, folder 89, 14 March 1897: 6.

17. The concept of heteroglossia (multi-voiced textuality) was introduced by M. M. Bakhtin in the mid-1930s "Discourse in the Novel," in *The Dialogic Imagination: Four Essays,* translated by Caryl Emerson and Michael Holquist (Austin: University of Texas Press, 1981), 259–421. Recent feminist discussions extend his concept to include women writers, a category that he ignored; see esp. Dale M. Bauer, *Feminist Dialogics: A Theory of Failed Community* (Albany: State University of New York Press, 1988), and *Feminism, Bakhtin, and the Dialogic,* ed. Dale M. Bauer and Susan Jaret McKinstry (Albany: State University of New York Press, 1991).

18. SLR, folder 53, letter to Ho, 1 July 1899; for Olsen, see n. 3 above.

19. Texts cited include Phyllis Rose, *Parallel Lives: Five Victorian Marriages* (New York: Knopf, 1984); Vivian R. Pollak, *A Poet's Parents: The Courtship Letters of Emily Norcross and Edward Dickinson* (Chapel Hill: University North Carolina Press, 1988); Eugenia Kaledin, *Mrs. Henry Adams,* 2d ed. (Amherst: University of Massachusetts Press, 1994); Susan K. Harris, *The Courtship of Olivia Langdon and Mark Twain* (New York: University of Cambridge Press, 1996); Carol Farley Kessler, *Elizabeth Stuart Phelps,* Twayne's United States Authors Series, no. 434 (Boston: G. K. Hall, 1982); SLR, folder 78, letter to Ho, 10 December 1899; Gilman, *Diaries,* 1994, 1: 54, 301, 339; 2:

685; and 329–30. For a discussion of the "new woman" construct, see part 2 of *1915, The Cultural Moment: The New Politics, the New Woman, the New Psychology, the New Art & the New Theatre in America,* ed. Adele Heller and Lois Rudnick (New Brunswick, NJ: Rutgers University Press, 1991). For the Gilmans' courtship, see *Journey from Within: Love Letters* (1995).

20. For the general cultural climate of 1915, see *1915, The Cultural Moment: The New Politics, the New Woman, the New Psychology, the New Art & the New Theatre in America* (1991). For Gilman's utopian writings, see "A Cabinet Meeting" ([imitation of Edward Bellamy], Studies in Style series, *Impress* [5 January 1895]: 4–5); "A Woman's Utopia," chap. 1–4, *The Times Magazine* 1 (January–March 1907): 215–20, 369–76, 498–504; chap. 5 [page proofs], SLR box 21, folder 260, reprinted in *Daring to Dream: Utopian Fiction by United States Women before 1950* [an anthology that contextualizes Gilman's utopian writing], compiled and edited by Carol Farley Kessler, Utopianism and Communitarianism series (Syracuse, NY: Syracuse University Press, 1995), 131–74; and the reprints in Kessler, *Charlotte Perkins Gilman,* (1995).

21. M. M. Bakhtin, "Response to a Question from *Novy Mir,*" in *Speech Genres and Other Late Essays,* trans. Vern W. McGee; ed. Caryl Emerson and Michael Holquist (1970; reprint, Austin: University of Texas Press, 1986), 2.

Rewriting the West Cure:
Charlotte Perkins Gilman, Owen Wister,
and the Sexual Politics of Neurasthenia

JENNIFER S. TUTTLE

SINCE ITS REISSUE BY THE FEMINIST PRESS IN 1973, CHARLOTTE PERKINS Gilman's story "The Yellow Wall-Paper" has sparked an abundance of investigations into Gilman's struggle against the patriarchal medical establishment of the late nineteenth century. Over the past twenty-five years, feminist scholars have honored Gilman's attempts to speak authoritatively about the nervous breakdown she had at the age of twenty-four and have analyzed extensively the ways she negotiated her identity as a professional woman while contending with the constraining roles of wife and mother as well as the aftermath of her physician S. Weir Mitchell's infamous "Rest Cure."[1] Consisting of extended bed rest, seclusion, massage, electrical treatments, and overfeeding, this cure was prescribed largely, though not exclusively, for women, especially in its more extreme forms, which often prohibited intellectual pursuits and creative expression. Though Mitchell was quite popular among many of his women patients, contemporary scholars generally view the Rest Cure as a means of subduing women who had strayed from their domestic role. While much of their research has focused on "The Yellow Wall-Paper," Gilman's critique of Mitchell's treatment and the domestic ideology behind it also comprises some of the most commonly cited passages in her autobiography, *The Living of Charlotte Perkins Gilman*. In the chapter called "The Breakdown," she details Mitchell's prescription for healthy femininity: "Live as domestic a life as possible. Have your child with you all the time," and "never touch pen, brush, or pencil" again. She then explains the result, now hauntingly familiar: "I went home, followed those directions rigidly for months, and came perilously near to losing my mind."[2]

The explicit engagements with the Rest Cure in Gilman's story and her autobiography are central to her critique of the gender ideologies shaping medical discourse, providing as well an alternative case history

103

that enhances understanding of Mitchell's treatment. I seek here, however, to expand the possibilities for analyzing Gilman's attack on medicalized patriarchy, as well as for assessing Mitchell's treatments for nervous prostration, by focusing on those parts of Gilman's autobiography that are not commonly consulted, but are, nevertheless, central to these inquiries. After her initial breakdown, but before seeking Mitchell's cure, Gilman resolved to "go away, for a change," in an effort to regain her health and peace of mind (*Living* 92). She writes in her diary: "I contemplate wintering in California. Hope dawns. To come back *well!*"[3] Invited by the Channing family (who had fled West in an effort to restore the health of Gilman's childhood friend Grace Channing) to spend the winter with them in Pasadena, Gilman set off on her journey, leaving her husband and daughter behind and visiting her brother in Utah en route. In chronicling these events, Gilman compares a party she attended in Ogden, Utah, to one portrayed in Owen Wister's 1902 Western novel *The Virginian.* Though it may seem to be merely a passing reference to one of Gilman's favorite books,[4] this invocation of Wister, with its surrounding discussion of Gilman's sojourns in the American West, deserves greater analysis, for it is an integral part of her critique of Mitchell's medical practices and the repressive ideologies of gender they both relied upon and helped to perpetuate. Further, this reference illuminates Gilman's choice of the far West as the curative region in which she would remake herself as a public writer, speaker, and social activist.

Gilman's reference to Wister's novel is significant because in *The Virginian,* considered the prototype of the modern Western, Wister fictionalized his own treatment by Mitchell.[5] A member of the Philadelphia aristocracy, Wister had long desired to be a composer, having enrolled at the Conservatoire in Paris and played for an appreciative Franz Liszt. Persuaded by his father, however, that "American respectability accepted lawyers" while it "rejected composers," Wister returned home reluctantly to work as a bank clerk while awaiting his entry into Harvard Law School.[6] In 1885, just two years before Gilman sought Mitchell's medical help, Wister's health "very opportunely broke down," and he approached Mitchell with painful neurasthenic symptoms.[7] Instead of putting Wister to bed, however, Mitchell sent him to a cattle ranch in Wyoming to recover. Unlike Gilman's Rest Cure, this "West Cure" was enormously effective. Before his trip West, Wister complained of exhaustion, vertigo, oversensitiveness, and other ailments. But after having settled into his cattle roundup routine in Wyoming, he became "a picture of health," leading hunting expeditions and mounting horses to join the cowboys in " 'cutting out' the black cattle from the herd" (White 89).

Though the Rest Cure is by far the treatment better known today, it reveals only half of the picture: as Wister's case suggests, the Rest Cure and the West Cure were complementary parts of one process through which normative gender identities were constructed and reinforced, and the two cures were arguably equally familiar to Mitchell's contemporaries.[8] While their therapeutics were clearly antithetical, the cures were inherently linked precisely in that they were mutually defining: they were each other's opposites. Having common origins in Mitchell's service as a contract surgeon during the Civil War, these treatments were also developed to target a common disease, neurasthenia.[9] Understood to be a depletion of the body's limited supply of "nerve force," neurasthenia was viewed simultaneously as a disease distressingly common among elite, white northeasterners and as a by-product of modern life and advanced civilization;[10] indeed, the prevalence of this protean disease in the United States in the second half of the nineteenth century was viewed as proof of America's cultural superiority.[11] As a growing body of scholarship has shown, discourses of neurasthenia were central to articulations of American national and cultural identities, as well as to justifications of American imperialism and economic expansion.[12] Like the theories of the disease, then, its treatments held great cultural and national significance, as both Gilman and Wister were certainly aware.

Mitchell considered Gilman and Wister's ailments—symptoms of the same disease—to have gendered causes and, therefore, to necessitate gendered cures. He believed, in accordance with the medical orthodoxy of the day, that women's inherently weak and excitable nervous systems would suffer from the slightest physical, emotional, and especially mental strain. Conversely, since men were not considered pathological by nature, they suffered temporary nervous debility as a result of overtaxing their brains in the very professional endeavors that marked them as a superior class. While the Rest Cure enforced passivity, submission, and domesticity in order to discipline wayward women like Gilman into what was considered proper femininity, the West Cure urged supposedly feminized men to embrace the more "masculine" traits and pursuits embodied in a western model of manliness. The West Cure's therapeutic value lay in the male patient's immersion in (and symbolic appropriation of) a wild, natural space clearly outside of what was imagined to be feminized, debilitating urban civilization; here his manliness and vigor would be regained through contact with "uncivilized" men and participation in some form of outdoor sport, the ultimate goal being a return to productive involvement in the very civilization he had fled.

This practice was widespread in the second half of the nineteenth century, though it did not actually begin with Mitchell. Earlier in the century, for example, scores of young men fled the Mississippi Valley to take a "prairie cure" on the Santa Fe trail.[13] Francis Parkman, who later sought Mitchell's medical advice from time to time, helped to develop the ideal of the West as a cure for ailing masculinity through his own health-seeking trips as well as his histories. Later in the century, there was an explosion of interest in such pursuits. Many northeastern men, among them Theodore Dreiser, Thomas Eakins, Henry and William James, and Frederic Remington, sought the treatment in various forms. Tom Lutz calls this phenomenon the "exercise cure," illustrating the growing appeal of rough riding and dude ranches, mountain hikes, resort spas, even (temporary) manual labor among the urban upper classes during this period (Lutz 32). Gail Bederman, Michael Kimmel, and E. Anthony Rotundo cite the importance of the increasing popularity of male muscularity and sports like boxing and baseball as well as men's recreational associations encouraging hunting and excursions into the wilderness. This was, after all, the era in which numerous national parks were established, concurrent with the founding of such groups as the Boy Scouts of America, the Boy Pioneers, the Boone and Crockett Club, the Appalachian Mountain Club, the Sierra Club, and the Improved Order of Red Men.[14] Central to these cultural phenomena was a construction of what Rotundo calls "primitive masculinity": an ethos through which middle- and upper-class white men appropriated what they saw as the "savagery" and "barbarism" of racial others and working-class men in order to claim ultimately superior manliness and racial supremacy (Rotundo 227). The most well-known benefactor and advocate of the West Cure was Teddy Roosevelt, a feeble asthmatic who inspired epithets like "Jane Dandy" and "Punkin-Lily" until he undertook a vigorous hunting and ranching life in the Dakotas, masculinizing his frail political image and marketing himself as an embodiment of the "strenuous life."[15] Indeed, it seems entirely fitting that Wister dedicated *The Virginian* to Roosevelt, an exemplar of the West Cure.

Like many men of his day, Mitchell himself took frequent West Cures, camping, hiking, fishing, and occasionally hunting in Maine, upstate New York, the Great Lakes, and Yellowstone Park. Pronouncing that "the surest remedy for the ills of civilized life is to be found in some form of return to barbarism," Mitchell immersed himself in the "barbarous" life of what he called "the simple-minded, manly folk who live on the outposts of civilization—'the lords of the axe and the rifle.'" Through escaping all female society—the "tourists and parasols"— and immersing himself in the usually all-male "social life of the camp," Mitchell temporarily and calculatedly communed with "primitives" like trappers, packers, and Native American guides in the wilderness, seeking the revitalizing masculinity supposedly embodied by such "manly folk."[16] Though Mitchell variously called his version of the remedy the "open-air treatment," the "out in the air life," and the "camp cure," it is appropriately labeled the West Cure because, regardless of its actual geographical location, it partakes of the symbolic West conjured by the cure's defining elements.[17] Less a specific locale than an idealized space, the West was a shifting signifier with strong cultural and national significance. As a place where "men could be men," the West represented an escape not only from civilization and urban life, but also from domesticity and all of the roles, expectations, and constraints it imposed upon individuals. As Mitchell's best known patient, Wister mythologized the West's curative powers in *The Virginian,* thus helping to popularize the already legendary status of the West as a cure for declining virility. The novel's narrator is very much like Wister: he is a sickly, northeastern, upper-class white man who travels to Wyoming for his health, which he eventually regains by learning the presumably masculine skills of rough riding and hunting. He achieves these skills largely through emulating the novel's title hero: the manly, laconic, and mysterious cowboy known as "The Virginian."[18]

Gilman's description of her curative journeys to the West, especially with her reference to *The Virginian,* can be understood, then, as a fairly explicit and certainly quite radical engagement with this widespread practice. Though Gilman does not, of course, literally herd cattle or shoot wild game, she does claim for herself her own successful West Cure, which she juxtaposes against a miserable, and quite threatening, Rest Cure. Ultimately, she appropriates the West Cure for her own purposes. In her autobiography, she claims to have devised her own healthful way of life in the West, which provided her with the freedom to launch the career as a speaker, writer, and reformer for which she is now so famous. Gilman begins her description of this long process with the very first moments of her journey to Pasadena: "Feeble and hopeless I set forth," she explains, "armed with tonics and sedatives, to cross the continent. From the moment the wheels began to turn, the train to move, I felt better" (*Living* 92). Though "armed with tonics and sedatives," Gilman indicates that her health was aided by the very movement westward—and, perhaps equally, by the movement away from home, marriage, and domestic codes and responsibilities. This section of the chapter "The Breakdown" illustrates the healthful effects for a woman of both an escape from the home and an immersion in the culture and landscape of the West—the very components that Mitchell's West Cure attempted to claim were healthy practices for men only.[19]

It is in her direct reference to Wister's novel, however, that Gilman signals the full implications of her experiences in the West. Describing her brother's town in Utah, she writes: "Society in Ogden at that time was not exacting," revealing in her sarcasm an awareness that the ideal of liberation in the "uncivilized" West was dependent upon its being contrasted with the "exacting," class-bound social codes of the East Coast—codes to which Gilman herself appeals at times, even as she flees their constraints. "[T]he leading lady," she explains, "was the wife of a railroad conductor." At the beginning of her description of "a species of ball" she attended with her brother and his family, she initiates a series of references and allusions to Wister's novel: "The bedrooms were all occupied by sleeping babies," she says, "as described in *The Virginian.*" The scene to which Gilman refers is one in which the community of Bear Creek, Wyoming, equally as unexacting as Ogden, has gathered for a dance and barbeque. Since many of the settlers have babies, they have laid them all down in a quiet room, away from the noise and commotion of the party. The Virginian and his friend Lin McLean, both of whom had rejected vociferously the domesticating tendencies of the settlers, avoid the heterosexual rituals of the dance and come upon this quiet room in their wanderings.[20] Counting twelve "sleeping strangers" altogether, the Virginian decides to switch the babies and dress them in each other's clothes, so that when the parents gather up their children at the end of the night, they all bring home the wrong ones and only discover later, amid much confusion and panic, what has been done (*Virginian* 75). This offense against social order, domesticity, and procreation, an offense met with "mirth" by the fathers but with "crie[s] for vengeance" by the mothers, represents precisely the curative world in which Wister's narrator immerses himself (*Virginian* 79). The world of the West Cure was one of homosocial male bonding, of escape from the domestic ties which the babies (and their angry mothers) represent. In likening her experience at the "ball" to this scene in Wister's novel (like the Virginian, Gilman tells us that she "did not dance" [*Living* 93]), Gilman draws an explicit comparison between her own West Cure—with its escape from feminine domesticity and the obligations of motherhood—and Wister's.

The remaining sentences of this paragraph in Gilman's chapter "The Breakdown" enhance the parallels between Wister's (and his narrator's) experience and her own, for they describe events which similarly correspond to aspects of *The Virginian.* "Among the dancers," she reveals, "there was pointed out to me a man who had killed somebody—no one seemed to hold it against him; and another who had been scalped three times—the white patches were visible among the hair. I had thought scalping a more exhaustive process." Following the dance, she reports, "we had a game of whist, and I was somewhat less than pleased to see each of the gentlemen playing bring a large cuspidor and set it by his side. They needed them" (*Living* 93). As a place in which the rules of propriety and the conventions of eastern "society" are irrelevant, the West of Gilman's sojourn is identical to the West of Wister's novel and cure. The man who had "killed somebody" but was not shunned in the least recalls the Virginian himself. He admits naively to the mother of his fiancée Molly Wood in a letter that "I have seen plenty rough things but can say I have never killed for pleasure or profit" (*Virginian* 234), a revelation which scandalizes both Molly and her family—all representatives of eastern social propriety. Yet in Bear Creek, where a different set of laws condones killing for frontier justice, the Virginian is revered for his willingness, as ranch foreman, to mete out the punishment of death to those men who violate Wyoming's code of ethics. Bringing her eastern codes of respectability with her, Gilman resembles Wister's fictional neurasthenic narrator, in that both of them view many aspects of life in the West through the lens of their East Coast cultural biases. In her discussion of scalping, which (with characteristic dry humor) Gilman admits she had previously misunderstood, she draws another parallel between herself and Wister. Just as Wister (and then his narrator) was a "tenderfoot" who had to learn to separate the realities of life in the West from eastern fallacies about it, Gilman gives up her mistaken notions about the region. In the same moment, of course, she reminds her readers that she, too, has seen firsthand the wildness of life among violent white men and "Indians." The rough life Gilman describes, in which a different kind of law rules behavior and ethics, echoes strikingly the world painted by Wister in his novel. Furthermore, Gilman's description of herself taking part in a card game at which spittoons are ubiquitous and these images of violence linger calls to mind the fateful card game described by Wister's narrator in which, among "[v]oices and cards, the click of chips, the puff of tobacco, glasses lifted to drink" (*Virginian* 19), the Virginian and the novel's villain Trampas have their first ominous encounter that will end eventually in a shootout near the novel's end. The card game in *The Virginian* is a vehicle through which Wister represents the essence of the West's curative powers, for it shows "the cow-boys at their play. . . . Here were lusty horsemen ridden from the heat of the sun, and the wet of the storm, to divert themselves awhile. Youth untamed sat here for an idle moment, spending easily its hard-earned wages" (*Virginian* 20). This card game illustrates again the masculine, homosocial world of Wister's cure, in which young men "untamed" by civilization and domesticity bond together, "spending easily" those economic resources and energies which the neurasthenic East would seek to regulate.[21] In the context of her reference to *The Virginian,* Gilman's card game suggests an implicit parallel to Wister's, though she plays the admittedly tamer game of whist among "gentlemen."

The similarities between Gilman and Wister's experiences extend, however, beyond their social activities, because the West as both an idea and a vast, idyllic space was equally curative for both of them. Like Gilman, Wister describes his own train journey as immediately health-inducing. He writes in the journal of his West Cure, on which his novel is clearly based, "Sorry to leave the train. Had begun to feel as if I grew there. A sort of Eastern air-feeding orchid."[22] Describing himself as a rare, delicate, eastern flower that has finally begun to grow, Wister indicates both his initially feminized state as well as the healthful effects of simply moving toward the West, away from the pressures of the East and "civilization." Upon reaching Wyoming, Wister continues: "This existence is heavenly in its monotony and sweetness. Wish I were going to do it every summer. I'm beginning to be able to feel I'm something of an animal and not a stinking brain alone" (*Owen Wister,* 8 July 1885, 32). In *The Virginian,* his narrator echoes this idealized description of the West, calling it "a world of crystal light, a land without end, a space across which Noah and Adam might have come straight from Genesis" (*Virginian* 8). In this Edenic place, Wister, like the sickly eastern narrator of his autobiographical fiction, is renewed, noting the physical effects of the vast and beautiful expanse of wilderness and the freedom it represents. Wister and his narrator's references to growth and Genesis highlight, in fact, the way that the West Cure nurtured a kind of rebirth, allowing practitioners to return East and undertake their professions with renewed vigor. It was even more of a transformative process for Wister, of course, since it provided him with not only the enthusiasm but the material for his career as chronicler of a supposedly dying way of life in the West; as Jane Tompkins notes, "Wister created himself and his vocation out of the experiences he had" there (137).

Gilman's West Cure was likewise transformative, providing a healing landscape in which to remake herself and develop her vocation. While in Utah, her brother took her for a ride "in that vast, shining, mile-high valley, and pointing to some sharply defined little hills," asked her "how far I thought they were." She replied, " 'Three hundred miles.' They were forty, but that didn't sound like much" (*Living* 92–3). This seems to echo Wister's "land without end," and the land has the same effect upon Gilman, particularly when she reaches Pasadena.[23] "So down the great inland plain of California," she describes her journey, "over the Mojave Desert, and to heaven" (*Living* 93). Shortly after her arrival in Pasadena, Gilman's health was, in fact, restored. She explains, "This place did not seem like earth, it was paradise. Kind and congenial friends, pleasant society, amusement, out-door sports, the blessed mountains, the long, unbroken sweep of the valley, with snow-peaks at the far eastern end—with such surroundings I recovered so fast, to outward appearance at least, that I was taken for a vigorous young girl" (*Living* 94). Like Wister, Gilman found the land and the lifestyle it provided to be curative: regaining her "vigor," renewed in a place she described as "heaven" and "paradise," Gilman was restored to health, showing that immersion in a West Cure, with its escape from the literal and figurative walls of the home and society, was just as refreshing for her as it was for Wister.

Of course, Gilman's autobiography was written with the benefit of hindsight, and she hints in the above passage that while the West Cure alleviated her symptoms, it did not address what she discovered was the cause of her illness: her domestic role. When she returned to the East—indeed, during the very train ride away from California—her illness returned. "This was a worse horror than before," Gilman admits in the same chapter, "for now I saw the stark fact—that I was well while away and sick while at home" (*Living* 95). Significantly, Wister had a parallel experience. In a revelation remarkably similar to Gilman's "stark fact," Wister, who had given up a less acceptable career as a composer to assume the respectable, presumably more "manly," profession of law, wrote in his journal that his journeys West had been "holidays from the law and my perfunctory days at the office—the forgetting for a moment a detested occupation," while "the homecoming and prospect of the office and driveling legalities was a gloomy thing" (*Owen Wister,* 29 April 1894, 201). This suggests that Gilman and Wister suffered from what was at root a similar cause: both of them became ill (at least in part) as a result of inordinate pressures to fulfill appropriate social and gender roles; though Wister's West Cure was designed to buttress his efforts to perform his role, Gilman's allowed her to reject that role altogether. The success of Gilman's West Cure, as well as its inability to alleviate the ultimate cause of her distress (a situation she would later attempt to rectify by separating from her husband), was noted by Grace Channing's father, William F. Channing, in a letter sent to S. Weir Mitchell in 1887. "You have among your patients," he writes, "a lady, Mrs. Charlotte Perkins Stetson, who spent the winter of 1885–6 with us. . . . [A]nd in our large, quiet sphere, free from the home frictions, [she] regained apparently perfect health. We regretted to hear that the nervous symptoms recurred sometime after her return to Providence."[24] Despite her relapse, however, Gilman's discussion of the West Cure in her autobiography is extremely important for our understanding of her complex relationship to Mitchell and Wister, because in it Gilman indicates a comprehension of the gender dynamics of Mitchell's treatments and of what was at stake in this construction of "healthy" spaces and identities for men and women. By healthfully performing those acts and characteristics associated with masculinity, Gilman called into question both Mitchell's medical discourses and the supposedly natural "truths" about gender on which these discourses were based.

The implications of Gilman's West Cure, however, exceed a critique of gendered definitions of health and illness. The Rest Cure was designed to keep women like Gilman from writing and undertaking other "unfeminine" practices, while the West Cure enabled weakened men to resume their professional work. In her invocations of the West, Gilman ultimately moves beyond the comparison of herself with Owen Wister and his West Cure, transforming its principles and using them to launch her own professional career. Like other easterners in the nineteenth century, Wister used the West as an escape valve which temporarily restored him to vigor and productivity; Gilman did the same. However, in events described at the end of "The Breakdown," Gilman makes an abrupt change. After her ineffective Rest Cure and the mutual decision with her husband to separate, she resolves to return to California with her daughter, this time to live. This move carries great significance for her: it represents an embracing of the principles of the West Cure not as a temporary salve, but as a way of life. Her husband Walter, whom she suggests doubts her ability to be self-sufficient, questions her decision. She describes his challenge when she proposes to employ carpenters to help her move:

"How can you engage them when you have no money?" asked Walter.
"I shall get the money by selling my property."
"How do you know you can?"
"I shall have to, to pay the carpenters."
And I did. (*Living* 105)

On the following page, Gilman concludes the chapter with her friends' reactions to her decision to move to Pasadena, lines which echo Walter's stereotypically masculine distrust of her capabilities:

"What will you do when you get there?" asked anxious friends.
"I shall earn my own living."
"How do you know you can?"
"I shall have to when I get there." (*Living* 106)

And she did. Though admittedly Gilman does not choose to live in a space so "wild" as that described in *The Virginian,* with its saloon gambling and gun fights, she, nevertheless, imagines this move in related terms. In the face of societal expectations to the contrary, she will learn to be self-reliant, facing unknown obstacles with stoicism and clarity of purpose brought by the necessity of survival.

Despite the anxieties these independent acts caused in others, Gilman presents herself as determined to strike out on her own. In fact, in an event described later in the autobiography, she implicitly contrasts herself with what has become a stereotype of feminine helplessness in the West, a stereotype classically rendered in *The Virginian.* Near the beginning of his novel, Wister introduces the aforementioned Molly Wood, soon to become the fiancée of the Virginian, a blue-blooded (and blue-stockinged) spinster schoolmarm. She goes West from Vermont in what Wister portrays as a ridiculous quest for "the unknown," and finds herself "helpless" inside a "lurching" stagecoach with a driver drunk on whiskey (*Virginian* 62). When the stage careens into a river, Molly sees the Virginian for the first time, "a tall rider" who lifts her "out of the stage on his horse so suddenly that she screamed." Despite his encouraging words, "her wits were stock-still, so she did not speak and thank him" (*Virginian* 63). The Virginian then berates the driver, helps to right the stage, and rides off, leaving Molly embarrassed for her speechlessness and hoping in a "maidenly" fashion to see her rescuer again (*Virginian* 64). Likewise, Gilman describes a journey in which she sits on the front seat of a "rocking stage" in a trip through the mountains, "talking to the driver now and then." As they "began a swift descent" on a "narrow road" with "hairpin turns," the driver "did not slacken speed," and they nearly collided with another stage. She reports: "It was a close shave, but they managed to wriggle out of it in safety, and when we were on our way again I took up the conversation where it had broken off. The driver looked at me as if I were uncanny, probably thought I was not intelligent enough to be afraid; maybe I wasn't" (*Living* 177). Unlike Wister's Molly, Gilman is not afraid, and needs—indeed, desires—no cowboy rescuer, an assertion which complements her earlier pronouncement that she "has never known fear," though "if the streets were not safe for women" who wanted the "freedom to go alone," "let them carry a pistol" rather than suffer protection by a man (*Living* 72). Hers is an adventure purposely lacking a romance plot, an adventure in which an articulate Gilman (not the speechless Molly cowering inside the stage) converses, unscathed, with her male driver. More like Wister's male narrator than his female character, Gilman inverts conventional images of eastern women in the West, establishing her fearlessness, her independence, and her unwavering voice.

It is significant, then, that Gilman found her professional voice in the West. In the early years of her life in California, she launched her ca-

reer, "formulat[ing]," as Gary Scharnhorst writes, quoting Gilman's
own words and enhancing her medical metaphors, "the social critique
with which she diagnosed 'what ailed society' and the reform program
'to improve it.' "25 Struggling as a single mother but determined to live
independently of marriage, Gilman "began to reconstruct her life"26:
not only did she write some of her best-known poetry and short fiction
and co-write plays with Grace Channing, but she also became active
in the fight for woman suffrage and joined the Nationalist movement,
inspired by Edward Bellamy's socialist utopianism ("California, always
fertile," she explains, "blossomed with" Nationalist clubs [*Living* 122]),
delivering public lectures and sermons, serving in the Pacific Coast
Women's Press Association, and editing its newspaper the *Impress*—all
of which Gilman calls "a surprising output of work, some of it my best"
(*Living* 98). With this move to the West, then, Gilman both demonstrated that she was capable of "earn[ing her] own living" and initiated
a career in which she would argue, among other things, that other
women were entitled to do so as well, freed from such obligations as
child-rearing, cooking, and unequal roles within marriage. Her claim to
a public, professional identity for women was, of course, directly opposite to Mitchell and others' medical advice that such an inclination was
"unnatural" in women; professional and public identities were still considered inherently masculine. Gilman reinforces this assertion of both
her desire and her implicit right to have a career outside the bounds of
marriage and eastern gender codes by constructing it in the terms of
a West Cure, indicating that she will be aided in this endeavor by her
immersion in the healing western landscape. She makes this clear from
the very beginning of the chapter immediately following "The Breakdown," called "Pasadena": "With Pasadena begins my professional
'living.' Before that, there was no assurance of serious work. To California, in its natural features, I owe much. Its calm sublimity of contour,
richness of color, profusion of flowers, fruit, and foliage, and the steady
peace of its climate were meat and drink to me" (*Living* 107). The "natural features" of California prove instrumental in Gilman's personal
transition from a "feeble and hopeless" wife and mother to a professional with growing "assurance of serious work." Yet contrary to Wister
and Mitchell's masculinist association of health with the West's spittoons and shootouts, Gilman's long-term West Cure focuses ultimately
on "calm sublimity" and "steady peace." "Everywhere there was
beauty," she opines later, "and the nerve-rest of steady windless
weather" (*Living* 107). She redefines the West Cure so that it is livable
for her, noting repeatedly the freedom and health enabled by her western lifestyle. "It was free expression of a growing philosophy," she says

of what she accomplished there, "and a power of delivery which increased with use" (*Living* 131).

A great deal of this "growing philosophy" was delivered, in fact, in Gilman's fiction. As Scharnhorst argues, "In her art no less than in her life, . . . Gilman revised the traditional pattern of male flight to the geographical frontier."[27] She arguably began this work as a child in the stories which prefigured her later utopian writings, as Carol Farley Kessler suggests in her essay included in this collection. In these early tales she described Edenic gardens where young girls enjoyed gymnastics and exercise, and the youthful Gilman pictured herself as an adventurer, anticipating the powerful self-determination for women that she would later espouse in *Herland.* In much of her fiction, such liberatory adventures are associated explicitly with the West, a region which often proves to be a panacea. As Catherine Golden points out in her essay in this volume, Gilman's works "The Widow's Might" (1911) and *Unpunished* (ca. 1929) both end with women characters who find freedom by traveling West. Similarly, *What Diantha Did* (1909–10) as well as "My Poor Aunt" (1913) portray heroines who escape conventional feminine roles to go West, where they undertake meaningful professions. According to Deborah Evans, "Gilman's repeated use of the western setting and western conventions . . . speaks to her urge to reject some of those same constricting values of the female sphere," the same "constraining limits of eastern society," critiqued by her "male counterparts" writing Westerns. Unlike these male writers, however, Gilman "sees the west as a site for female heroism."[28] It could be argued, in fact, that Gilman claims a successful, and transformed, West Cure for women in this fiction. For example, her novella *The Crux* (1911), which Evans asserts is an appropriation of the Western genre exemplified by Wister's novel, presents a woman physician, significantly named Doctor Bellair, who urges her female patients to "rough it" in the West, where they forge a new and enlightened form of community. This "calm" and "steady" civilizing community is, of course, a predictable and powerful twist on the "barbarous," homosocial community undergirding the West Cure. Similarly, "Dr. Clair's Place" (1915) pictures a woman physician prescribing a kind of West Cure; in what seems a direct response to Mitchell, Gilman describes "how a female physician might treat neurasthenia."[29] Complaining that "The trouble with Sanatoriums . . . is that the sick folks have nothing to do but sit about and think of themselves and their 'cases' " (Mitchell commonly berated women invalids for precisely this behavior, which he inculcated through the Rest Cure), she sets up a sanatorium in Southern California where patients are encouraged to "keep . . . busy" with artistic, physical, and intellectual pursuits, and generally to amuse themselves.[30]

Like these stories, Gilman's "The Giant Wistaria" (1891) portrays a
woman who attempts to flee Old World oppression by traveling to an
Edenic West; unlike many of Gilman's western heroines, however, this
young unwed mother "fails to realize the freedom and independence
promised in the west" and meets her death in a horrific version of the
idyllic western garden.[31] As this story suggests, Gilman found that the
West, though curative, was not entirely free of the social constraints she
had rejected in the East. Certainly she struggled economically during
her years in California, supporting herself, her daughter, and later her
mother, and still battling the effects of her nervous breakdown. Though
she praises the transformative properties of the West, she admits that
this period there "was the hardest of my life" (*Living* 98). She also had
to contend with public censure for her divorce, her decision to let her
ex-husband and his new wife rear her daughter Katharine, and, by
some, for her participation in public discourse as a published writer.
The scandal caused by her personal life forced the *Impress,* under her
editorship, to fold; as for her professional work, she incurred constant
public ridicule by some in the male-dominated California literary establishment—especially Ambrose Bierce, with whom she feuded and
who condemned what he saw as her masculine pretensions to author-
ship.[32] Despite the attempts of other literary notaries to claim her as a
"California Literary Genius"—among them "Colonel Irish, a prominent newspaper man" (*Living* 132, 131) and Charles Lummis, the editor of *Land of Sunshine*[33]—Gilman, discouraged by "creeping slanders"
(*Living* 171) and disgusted with the "immoral[ity]" of "the San Francisco mind" (*Living* 173), ultimately clung to a "New England innocence" (*Living* 151). "[A]ll my early impressions," she explains, "had
been of life in New England, among people of clean and dignified traditions. Now I was to live and teach among an entirely different sort"
(*Living* 133). Though Gilman does experience and portray the West as
a curative, free space for female independence as well as community,
and though she transforms the West Cure into a healthful way of life,
in the end she cannot free herself of her cultural identification with a
supposedly more "innocent" and "tradition[al]" East, populated by a
presumably "cleaner" (and perhaps more racially and ethnically homo-
geneous) "sort" of people.[34] Like male West Cure patients, Gilman
pulls back from complete identification with those whose way of life
she appropriates; the very essence of the West Cure, after all, was its
revitalization—not its renunciation—of eastern society and cultural superiority.

Ultimately, it is unclear to what degree Gilman recognized the com-
plicity of this idealized New England culture in the very oppression she
had fled originally, but such identification with the East does reinforce

her resemblance to other partakers of the West Cure such as Owen
Wister. Indeed, Gilman portrays her life in the West as a protracted
West Cure from which she must inevitably return once she is healed. At
the end of this phase of her life, in a passage that tellingly echoes the
description of her first journey to Pasadena, she explains her departure
from California in 1895: "The sense of hope and power rose up afresh
as the train rolled eastward. . . . I was alive and I had my work to do,
. . . I had a wholly reliable religion and social philosophy" (*Living* 180).
Moving eastward, however, Gilman does not close this chapter of her
life with a simple resumption of her former manner of living; rather,
free of marriage and motherhood and sporting a "religion and social
philosophy" developed in the West, she leaves California newly em-
powered to begin her profession as a nomadic citizen of the world.
Asked when leaving Los Angeles to give a forwarding address, Gilman
"cheerfully inscribed, 'Charlotte Perkins Stetson. At large.' For the next
five years," she writes triumphantly, "that was a legitimate address.
Back and forth and up and down, from California to Maine, from
Michigan to Texas, from Georgia to Oregon, twice to England, I wan-
dered" (*Living* 181). Unlike the narrator of "The Yellow Wall-Paper,"
whose quest for mobility is hampered by a medically justified gender
ideology and which results in circular "creeping" in an ancient, interior
pattern, the autobiographical Gilman, having appropriated the West
Cure, is free to "wander" the globe in pursuit of a meaningful profession. "As I had planned the programs for those Congresses of Women"
in California, she writes, "I planned programs for the world" (*Living*
183). Reconsidered in this light, "The Yellow Wall-Paper," written during Gilman's first year living in California and long viewed as a fictionalization of her Rest Cure, may also be considered a central aspect of
her West Cure, which, unlike the former treatment, encouraged writing
as therapy. Gilman's diverse portrayals of the West Cure, then, deserve
consideration alongside her more familiar critiques of the Rest Cure,
particularly "The Yellow Wall-Paper." Her best-known story is thus
part of a body of lesser-known autobiographical and fictional work, including *The Living of Charlotte Perkins Gilman,* in which she turns a
critique of the gendering of Rest and West into a personal and professional transformation.

NOTES

I am grateful to David Kuchta, Catherine Golden, and Joanna Zangrando for their
comments on drafts of this essay, as well as to the participants of the Second International Charlotte Perkins Gilman Conference, the Western Literature Association 32nd

Annual Meeting, and the College of Physicians of Philadelphia History of Medicine Seminar for their responses to earlier versions of my research on the West Cure and Charlotte Perkins Gilman. I would also like to thank the Library of the College of Physicians of Philadelphia for permission to quote from the papers of the S. Weir Mitchell Collection.

1. There are dozens of articles analyzing Gilman's critique of the treatment in "The Yellow Wall-Paper." For excellent reviews of this scholarship, see Catherine Golden, "One Hundred Years of Reading 'The Yellow Wallpaper,' " in *The Captive Imagination: A Casebook on* The Yellow Wallpaper, ed. Catherine Golden (New York: The Feminist Press, 1992), 1–23, and Elaine R. Hedges, " 'Out at Last'? 'The Yellow Wallpaper' after Two Decades of Feminist Criticism," in *The Captive Imagination,* 319–33.

2. Charlotte Perkins Gilman, *The Living of Charlotte Perkins Gilman: An Autobiography* (1935; reprint, New York: Harper & Row, 1975), 96. All subsequent quotations are from this edition and are cited parenthetically in the text as *Living,* followed by the page number.

3. 8 October 1885. *The Diaries of Charlotte Perkins Gilman,* ed. Denise D. Knight, 2 vols., (Charlottesville: University Press of Virginia, 1994), 1: 338. Italics in original.

4. Gary Scharnhorst, *Charlotte Perkins Gilman* (Boston: Twayne Publishers, 1985), 98. See also Scharnhorst and Denise D. Knight, "Charlotte Perkins Gilman's Library: A Reconstruction," *Resources for American Literary Study* 23, no. 2 (1997): 181–219.

5. Despite this mythical status among literary historians, *The Virginian* represents more accurately one stage in the long development of the genre, which began much earlier. See Sanford E. Marovitz, "Testament of a Patriot: The Virginian, the Tenderfoot, and Owen Wister," *Texas Studies in Literature and Language* 15, no. 3 (1973): 551–52; Gary Topping, "The Rise of the Western," *Journal of the West* 19, no. 1 (1980): 29–35; and Barbara Will, "The Nervous Origins of the American Western," *American Literature* 70, no. 2 (June 1998): 311 n.5.

6. Quoted in G. Edward White, *The Eastern Establishment and the Western Experience: The West of Frederic Remington, Theodore Roosevelt, and Owen Wister* (New Haven: Yale University Press, 1968), 70.

7. Owen Wister, *Roosevelt: The Story of a Friendship* (New York: MacMillan, 1930), 28.

8. The contrasts between the two treatments, as well as Wister's fictionalization of Mitchell's West Cure, have been nicely discussed by Barbara Will in "The Nervous Origins of the American Western," where she furthers significantly the scholarship on neurasthenia by illustrating how Mitchell's treatment for men enlisted the patient's writing in an effort to "revalue" the feminized struggle with nervousness as manly, strenuous "self-conquest" (300). See also her essay "Nervous Systems," in *American Bodies: Cultural Histories of the Physique,* ed. Tim Armstrong (New York: New York University Press, 1996), 86–100.

9. It has long been understood that, though the Rest Cure developed over many years, it was inspired in part by various aspects of Mitchell's treatment of Civil War soldiers. See Ernest Earnest, *S. Weir Mitchell: Novelist and Physician* (Philadelphia: University of Pennsylvania Press, 1950), 81; S. Weir Mitchell, "The Evolution of the Rest Treatment," *Journal of Nervous and Mental Diseases* 31 (1904): 368–73; Suzanne Poirier, "The Weir Mitchell Rest Cure: Doctors and Patients," *Women's Studies* 10 (1983): 15–40; and Richard D. Walter, M.D., *S. Weir Mitchell, M.D.—Neurologist: A Medical Biography* (Springfield, IL: Charles C Thomas, 1970), 47. Likewise, the West Cure was inspired in part by Mitchell's realization that ill and wounded soldiers, particularly those suffering from gangrene, healed much more quickly in "tent-hospitals." Mitchell, *Nurse and Patient; and, Camp Cure* (Philadelphia: J. B. Lippincott, 1877), 49–50; see also Earnest, 53–54, and Walter, 101.

10. Though neurasthenia was seen as an elite disease, this did not mean that non-whites and the poor and working classes did not suffer from the same symptoms—but their symptoms were diagnosed, understood, and treated differently. See Barbara Ehrenreich and Deirde English, *For Her Own Good: 150 Years of the Experts' Advice to Women* (New York: Anchor Books, 1978), 115; E. Anthony Rotundo, *American Manhood: Transformations in Masculinity from the Revolution to the Modern Era* (New York: Basic Books, 1993), 340 n.51; and Carroll Smith-Rosenberg, *Disorderly Conduct: Visions of Gender in Victorian America* (New York: Alfred A. Knopf, 1985), 200.

11. Neurologist George M. Beard, who coined the term "neurasthenia" in 1869, argued that the "stupendous" prevalence of the disease in America proved this country's development was greater than any other at any time in history, including Greece and Rome in the highest "days of their glory" (Beard, *American Nervousness: Its Causes and Consequences,* ed. Charles E. Rosenberg [1881; reprint, New York: Arno Press, 1972], viii). See also Mitchell's *Wear and Tear, or Hints for the Overworked,* ed. Gerald N. Grob, 5th ed. (1887; reprint, New York: Arno Press, 1973).

12. See especially Joan Burbick, *Healing the Republic: The Language of Health and the Culture of Nationalism in Nineteenth-Century America,* Cambridge Studies in American Literature and Culture (New York: Cambridge University Press, 1994); Diane Price Herndl, *Invalid Women: Figuring Feminine Illness in American Fiction and Culture, 1840–1940* (Chapel Hill: University of North Carolina Press, 1993); Tom Lutz, *American Nervousness, 1903: An Anecdotal History* (Ithaca: Cornell University Press, 1991); Barbara Sicherman, "The Uses of a Diagnosis: Doctors, Patients, and Neurasthenia," in *Sickness and Health in America: Readings in the History of Medicine and Public Health,* ed. Judith Waltzer Leavitt and Ronald L. Numbers (Madison: University of Wisconsin Press, 1978), 25–38; and Will, "The Nervous Origins of the American Western" and "Nervous Systems."

13. See Barton H. Barbour, ed. *Reluctant Frontiersman: James Ross Larkin on the Santa Fe Trail 1856–67* (Albuquerque: University of New Mexico Press, 1990), and his "Westward to Health: Gentlemen Health-Seekers on the Santa Fe Trail," *Journal of the West* 28, no. 2 (1989): 39–43.

14. See Gail Bederman, *Manliness and Civilization: A Cultural History of Gender and Race in the United States, 1880–1917,* Women in Culture and Society (Chicago: University of Chicago Press, 1995); Michael Kimmel, *Manhood in America: A Cultural History* (New York: The Free Press, 1996); and Roderick Nash, *Wilderness and the American Mind* (New Haven: Yale University Press, 1967), 147–54.

15. For a discussion of Roosevelt's uses and views of the West, particularly regarding its supposedly transformative properties, see, for example, Bederman; Lutz; and Kim Townsend, *Manhood at Harvard: William James and Others* (New York: W. W. Norton, 1996).

16. Mitchell, *Camp Cure,* 45, 56–75, and 61. I concur with Barbara Will, who points out that Mitchell's West Cure represents "less a return to barbarism than a leisured connoisseurship of it" ("The Nervous Origins of the American Western" 301). In fact, despite its vociferous calls to leave behind the comforts and technologies of "civilization," the cure is enabled by implements like the barometer, opera glass, and sketchbook, as well as by the race and class hierarchies it claims to suspend. Tellingly, the erasure of those classes of laborers who make treatment possible is common to both the West and Rest Cures. Though evident in Mitchell's travel journals, the work of guides, cooks, and packers is not generally mentioned in his published accounts of his cures. Similarly, Gilman presumably is able to take her Rest Cure (as well as her earlier trip to Pasadena) because she could leave her daughter with her mother and "an excellent maid" (*Living* 92), a situation echoed by her narrator in "The Yellow Wall-Paper,"

whose cure is enabled by her sister-in-law's housekeeping and by Mary, presumably a servant, who is "so good with the baby" ("The Yellow Wall-Paper" [1892; reprint, New York: The Feminist Press, 1996], 14).

17. S. Weir Mitchell, unpublished autobiography, ca. 1900, box 16, folder 4, p. 183, S. Weir Mitchell Papers, Library of the College of Physicians of Philadelphia; Mitchell to Sarah Butler Wister, 1889, Ristigouche Salmon Club, Matapedia, Quebec, box 9–10, folder 18, Mitchell Papers; *Camp Cure.*

18. Wister's fictionalization of his curative experience in the West in *The Virginian* has been widely noted, as has the therapeutic nature of this writing. See, for example, Marovitz, 554–55; Jane Tompkins, *West of Everything: The Inner Life of Westerns* (New York: Oxford University Press, 1992), 136–37; Topping, 29; Ben Merchant Vorpahl, "Roosevelt, Wister, Turner, and Remington," in *A Literary History of the American West,* ed. J. Golden Taylor, et al. (Fort Worth: Texas Christian University Press, 1987), 276–302; Leslie T. Whipp, "Owen Wister: Wyoming's Influential Realist and Craftsman," *Great Plains Quarterly* 10 (1990): 246–47; White, 52; and Will, "The Nervous Origins of the American Western."

19. In less extreme cases, Mitchell did recommend exercise for many of his patients, both women and men, admitting later in his career that "camp-life" was "in a measure attainable by many women." Though it might seem to do so, however, this does not entirely undermine his earlier gendering of the Rest and West Cures, for Mitchell continues to conceive of camp-life as "a man's life" and, in contrast to Gilman's view of her own invigorating West Cure, celebrates a woman patient's successful Camp Cure because it allows her to fulfill her biological destiny as a "vigorous wife and mother." See Mitchell, *Doctor and Patient* (Philadelphia: J. B. Lippincott, 1888), 155–58.

20. Tellingly, the first depiction of the Virginian has him insisting, "What's the use o' being married?" (Owen Wister, *The Virginian: A Horseman of the Plains* [1911; reprint, New York: New American Library, 1979], 4). Though the novel was originally published in 1902, Wister changed its subtitle for his 1911 edition. All subsequent quotations are from the above reprint of the 1911 edition and are cited parenthetically in the text as *Virginian,* followed by the page number.

21. The economic metaphors used to construct nervous exhaustion have been discussed widely. See especially Burbick; Lutz; and Will, "The Nervous Origins of the American Western" and "Nervous Systems."

22. Owen Wister, journal entry (3 July 1885), *Owen Wister Out West: His Journals and Letters,* ed. Fanny Kemble Wister (Chicago: University of Chicago Press, 1958), 30. All subsequent quotations are from this edition and are cited parenthetically in the text as *Owen Wister,* followed by the date and page number.

23. In her essay in this collection, Charlotte Margolis Goodman argues convincingly for the influence of "The Yellow Wall-Paper" on Edith Summers Kelley's novel *Weeds.* Conversely, though to my knowledge there is no direct evidence that Gilman was familiar with Kelley's work, Gilman's portrayal of her West Cure strikes a suggestive parallel with this novel, written in California, with its yearning to escape the demands of domesticity for the "endless" landscape outdoors.

24. William F. Channing to Mitchell, 16 June, box 10, folder 3, Mitchell Papers. This letter corroborates, of course, Gilman's own account of her West Cure, as well as her understanding that the cause of her illness was in reality "home frictions," facts she presumably revealed to Mitchell in a letter she sent him before beginning his Rest Cure. Tellingly, however, Mitchell reportedly dismissed Gilman's "history of [her] case" as "self-conceit" (*Living* 95).

25. Gary Scharnhorst, "Making Her Fame: Charlotte Perkins Gilman in California," *California History* (Summer 1985): 192.

26. Ann J. Lane, *To* Herland *and Beyond: The Life and Work of Charlotte Perkins Gilman* (New York: Pantheon Books, 1990), 142.

27. Gary Scharnhorst, "Charlotte Perkins Gilman's 'The Giant Wistaria': A Hieroglyph of the Female Frontier Gothic," in *Frontier Gothic: Terror and Wonder at the Frontier in American Literature,* ed. David Mogen, Scott P. Sanders, and Joanne B. Karpinski (Rutherford, NJ: Farleigh Dickinson University Press, 1993), 159.

28. Deborah Evans, " 'Come out to Colorado with me—and Grow': *The Crux* and Gilman's New Western Hero(ines)" (Paper delivered at "Many Wests, Many Traditions," the Western Literature Association 32nd Annual Meeting, Albuquerque, NM, 16 October 1997; and the Second International Charlotte Perkins Gilman Conference, Skidmore College, Saratoga Springs, NY, 28 June 1997), 5.

29. Scharnhorst, *Charlotte Perkins Gilman,* 97.

30. Gilman, "Dr. Clair's Place," *Forerunner* 6, no. 6 (1915): 142. In his biography of Gilman, Gary Scharnhorst has argued that this story was inspired by Dr. Mary Putnam Jacobi's treatment of Gilman (97).

31. Scharnhorst, "Charlotte Perkins Gilman's 'The Giant Wistaria,' " 159.

32. For an extended study of the Bierce-Gilman relationship, see Lawrence J. Oliver and Gary Scharnhorst, "Charlotte Perkins Gilman v. Ambrose Bierce: The Literary Politics of Gender in Fin-de-Siècle California," *Journal of the West* 32, no. 3 (1993): 52–60.

33. See Lummis, "In Western Letters," *Land of Sunshine* 12, no. 5 (April 1900): 302.

34. As the present volume testifies, scholars have become increasingly attuned to Gilman's problematic views on race. For an extended and insightful study of this issue, see also Susan S. Lanser, "Feminist Criticism, 'The Yellow Wallpaper,' and the Politics of Color in America," *Feminist Studies* 15, no. 3 (Fall 1989): 415–41.

Caging the Beast: The Radical Treatment for "Excessive Maleness" in Gilman's Fiction

Catherine J. Golden

COMMENTING ON THE VIOLENCE IN CHARLOTTE PERKINS GILMAN'S feminist detective novel *Unpunished* (ca. 1929), Ann J. Lane remarks that Gilman "gave in to the frustration she felt at having devoted a life to struggling for changes that did not occur. If she could not destroy patriarchy in reality, she could do it in literary fantasy."[1] In *Unpunished* and much of Gilman's oeuvre, the patriarch emerges as a figure to be reckoned with and "destroyed." Gilman's decision to eliminate a leading man in her fiction places her in the company of turn-of-the-century American women writers who envisioned utopias, such as Caroline Mason and Alice Ingelfritz Jones. Such writers subverted the conventions of romance, got rid of their fictional patriarchs (who often died of natural causes), and thus allowed their heroines to escape a constrained marriage and perhaps engage in meaningful work outside the home.[2] Whereas many women writing utopian fiction between 1890–1920, some of whom were not professional writers, leave but one novel behind them, as Carol A. Kolmerten notes in her examination of American women envisioning utopia, Gilman stands apart. A prolific writer, Gilman had an international reputation as a lecturer at the turn of the century, and she wrote numerous works in which she imagined a better world without men and created a new breed of man. Her rich legacy reveals, moreover, that Gilman consistently and increasingly implemented strategies that her contemporary reformers also used in their works criticizing male-dominated culture, as Kolmerten indicates: "If the women writers do not physically eliminate men, they criticize what they perceive to be destructive societal values most often linked with men."[3]

Gilman repeatedly argues that "All the hate and rivalry between nations is not woman's, but man's," that "The whole pouring stream of tradition behind us is man-made."[4] The failings Gilman considers man-made include "a despotic government, a savage soldiery, a false and corrupt church, crippled industry, and deficient education."[5] The

122

world urgently needed a "New Motherhood" to bring forth a nonsexist
generation in which democracy and cooperation would reign supreme.
Both in her poetry (e.g., "Women of Today," "Girls of Today") and
countless nonfiction essays published in *Forerunner* and other journals,
Gilman's solution was to rally "the New Mothers of the New World"
to rebuild their nations and teach their children gender equality, community service, and true cooperation ("New Mothers" 148). In her
treatise *The Man-Made World or, Our Androcentric Culture* (1911), Gilman explains that in order to achieve what she calls a "human world":
"It is not a question of interfering with or punishing men . . . but purely
a matter of changed education and opportunity for every child."[6] But
in her fiction Gilman suggests that the patriarch must be "punished"
or at least removed if a woman's "natural atmosphere of peaceful industry, of tender watchful care, of far-seeing affection, now jealously
secluded by each man in the home, for his own satisfaction, is to be
unloosed, expanded, spread far and wide throughout the world" ("New
Mothers" 149).

   In her fiction, over time, Gilman created increasingly more corrupt
and idiosyncratic patriarchal figures whom she dispensed with in ever
more violent ways in an effort to rid her world of the "unprecedented
dominance of the male" (*Man-Made World* preface). Three texts spanning Gilman's career well demonstrate this progression: her early, now
best-known short story, "The Yellow Wall-Paper" (1892); "The Widow's Might" (1911), published in the *Forerunner,* the feminist periodi-
cal she launched at the height of her career; and *Unpunished* (ca. 1929),
her lone feminist detective novel written when her own reputation was
dwindling and the mass women's movement was declining. While John,
the husband/doctor of "The Yellow Wall-Paper," swoons at the end of
the story, Mr. McPherson of "The Widow's Might" dies of natural
causes, and Wade Vaughn of *Unpunished* ends up as a fatality of premeditated murder. The fate of Terry Nicholson of Gilman's utopian
novel *Herland* (1915) presents an interesting and less violent alternative
to punishment by death—banishment. And the work of other women
writing between the 1870s and 1920s, such as Kate Chopin, Margaret
Oliphant, Edith Summers Kelley, and Olive Schreiner, further illuminates Gilman's treatment for "excessive maleness" and her argument
for women's emancipation from patriarchy.

   Gilman wrote extensively on the subject of "excessive maleness"
(155) in *The Man-Made World,* where, from her opening animal analogy,[7] she explores "the effect on our human life of the unbridled dominance of one sex" (19). The work is indebted to Lester Ward's
Gynaecocentric Theory of Life, which Gilman acknowledges in her
preface. Much like Ward, she believed that woman originated first in

the process of evolution: "The female is the race-type" (238). But the family unit quickly became patriarchal, and the prehistoric period of female superiority was never reclaimed. The enslavement of woman gave rise to "Androcentric Culture," a still ongoing "unchecked [male] supremacy" (235) that has "warped" and "disfigured" (255) human development. Gilman concedes that men and women have inherently opposite natures, though in her view exclusively masculine and feminine traits have been overstated. She advocates that adequate attention be given to "the human qualities shared by both, owned by neither" (154). Still, in *The Man-Made World,* she claims that if women could influence our world, we would achieve "world-progress. An economic democracy must rest on a free womanhood; and a free womanhood inevitably leads to an economic democracy" (260).

Regrettably, in Gilman's view, man—a hunter and fighter in primitive times—remained saddled with his primal predatory sex characteristics. As he took charge of industry and corrupted it, he made it exclusively a public, productive, male sphere. In man-made culture, we find "the unnatural mastery of the patriarch, owning and governing his wives, children, slaves and cattle, and making such rules and regulations as pleased him" (181). Women, as a result, were limited to the private, domestic sphere, "stunted, crippled" (181).

A humanist who repudiated the term feminist, Gilman realized that the world could not progress unless women and men cooperated.[8] Still, in *The Man-Made World,* she privileges women's innate abilities: "the distinctly feminine or maternal impulses are far more nearly in line with human progress than are those of the male; which makes her exclusion from human functions the more mischievous" (235).[9] Moreover, in *Herland,* Gilman achieves "human progress" in her utopian world of "highly civilized women" who reproduce parthenogenically.[10] The culture of the Herlanders is scientifically advanced and informed by the traits she deemed feminine: love, nurture, and nonviolence. The misogynist Terry Nicholson, who enters Herland, provides a prototype for the evil Wade Vaughn of *Unpunished,* and also harkens back to John in "The Yellow Wall-Paper." Thus Gilman's treatment of Terry offers an interesting point of comparison to her other fiction about patriarchy.

At the opening of *Herland,* three men—rich playboy Terry Nicholson, sociologist Vandyck Jennings, and poet/botanist Jeff Margrave—stumble upon this utopian world populated by strong, calm, capable, athletic, short-haired, comfortably clothed women (in typical Gilman fashion, their clothes have pockets, too). Impressed by this civilization, the men declare: "There must be men . . . let's find 'em" (11). Instead, the Herlanders "find" the three male intruders and attempt to civilize " 'em." While Jeff totally embraces Herland and Van comes to recognize its merits, sexist Terry Nicholson sneers at the idea of woman-centered culture.

To the peace-loving Herlanders, who embrace Gilman's ideal of the "New Motherhood," Terry embodies "Androcentric Culture" and its inherent evils. Following "his pet conviction that a woman loves to be mastered" (132), Terry uses "brute force" (132) to conquer his Herland wife Alima and is convicted of marital rape. Moreover, at the end of the novel, Terry himself is "mastered." He receives the supreme sentence in this pacifist community—expulsion from utopia.

Banishment of patriarchy becomes a solution for Gilman only in a fictional utopian world. Over time, Gilman expunges the sins of male domination from her non-utopian fictional worlds and sentences her patriarchs more harshly. Admittedly, in her early 1892 "The Yellow Wall-Paper," John receives a light sentence: a fainting spell. In the extensive scholarship about the story, Doctor John is often criticized for his patronizing ways.[11] The nameless narrator continually refers and defers to "dear John," who infantilizes his wife; under John's direction, she undergoes a Rest Cure for a postpartum depression. As Elaine R. Hedges and others have noted, "The Yellow Wall-Paper" can easily be read as an indictment of the patriarchal institution of marriage in American Victorian society.[12] Clearly an embodiment of patriarchy, John "scoffs" and "laughs" at the narrator who sadly "expects that" in marriage.[13] Underdeveloped as a character, John is handicapped by his practical nature and his sexist ways. Still, Doctor John is not cruel like Gilman's later patriarchs and might well be compared to other sympathetically drawn contemporary male characters including Judith Pippinger's husband Jerry Blackford in Kelley's *Weeds* (1923) and Edna Pontellier's husband Léonce in Chopin's *The Awakening* (1899).

Although *Weeds* has been situated in the tradition of working-class women's writing—it recounts the story of a spirited young woman growing up in the rural tenant farms of Kentucky—Judith Pippinger shares the creative aspirations of the narrator of "The Yellow Wall-Paper." As Charlotte Goodman notes, the young Judith draws comic and satiric chalk and crayon pictures on walls, desks, window casings, tree trunks, and flat stones; likewise, the nameless narrator continually writes in her journal to express her thoughts and feelings, even though John forbids her. Whereas Gilman's nameless narrator writes only in a secret journal while Judith leaves her artist's mark on public property and the natural world, neither is encouraged to develop her talent and ambitions are "laid away."[14] Judith's husband Jerry seems kinder than the narrator's John, but her hardworking farmer husband does not share in the overwhelming demands of housework even when Judith falls ill and finally retreats to her bed to rest, much as the more privi-

leged nameless narrator is ordered to do. Despite their crucial class differences, both Gilman and Kelley's heroines fail to achieve autonomy
in a patriarchal world, which is far harsher to the tenant farmer Judith
than to the privileged narrator.

Doctor John more closely resembles another sympathetic but underdeveloped male character from a privileged class in a novel written in
the same era—Léonce Pontellier. A traditional Creole husband, Léonce
watches over his wife as if she were "a valuable piece of personal property."[15] Edna Pontellier does "admit" that Léonce, on the surface, "was
the best husband in the world. Mrs. Pontellier was forced to admit that
she knew none better" (9). Léonce provides generously for his wife and
spoils his sons with sweets, but he fails as a husband simply because
he cannot understand Edna's soul and the source of her discontent.
Like Léonce, John truly misunderstands his wife's nature because he,
too, is "practical in the extreme" ("Yellow Wall-Paper" 39). The nameless narrator, like Edna, becomes a "solitary soul" until she finds her
soulmate trapped behind the bar-like patterns of the wallpaper.[16]
Rather than elect suicide as Edna does, the narrator frees her double
and succumbs to madness as she challenges the authority of patriarchy
to which she initially defers: "There comes John, and I must put this
away—he hates to have me write a word" ("Yellow Wall-Paper" 41).[17]

In its dramatic denouement, the narrator chooses literal madness
over John's prescribed cure to make her a docile, obedient wife. Theat-
rical conclusions were a specialty of Gilman's, and this conclusion dramatically reverses the dynamics of gender.[18] The narrator "creeps" over
her husband, who—in a stereotypically feminine gesture—has swooned
before her on the floor. The woman is undeniably, if only temporarily,
on top; the illustration that accompanied the story's original publication in *New England Magazine* graphically illustrates this point. Face
down, John appears senseless; his hands are limp, and his body curls
slightly in a near fetal position. However, the narrator, whose hands
squash the top of John's head and back, crawls right over him.

In "The Yellow Wall-Paper," patriarchy is momentarily "skirted" but
not destroyed. Gilman leaves her ending open: the reader cannot help
but wonder what action Doctor John will take when he awakes from
his dead faint. The narrator who exclaims " 'you can't put me back!' "
("Yellow Wall-Paper" 53) may, in fact, be "put back" in her place. Even
worse, she may discretely be "put" away for life, sharing the fate of
Lady Audley of Mary Elizabeth Braddon's *Lady Audley's Secret* (1862),
who is locked away in a Belgian asylum when her inherited insanity and
related crimes are revealed.

In other late-nineteenth-century works by women writers, patriarchy
is also circumvented temporarily. In Chopin's "The Story of an Hour"

(1899), Louise Mallard experiences temporary freedom when she learns that her husband, Brently Mallard, has been killed in a train accident. Though Brently, like John, is underdeveloped in Chopin's very brief short story, we learn of his oppressive effect on his wife through the description of Louise's face: "She was young, with a fair, calm face, whose lines bespoke repression and even a certain strength."[19] Not overcome by sadness at Brently's death as her relatives anticipate, she utters: " '[F]ree, free, free,' " "under her breath" (12) so that no one can detect her joy. As Virginia Woolf so aptly recognized, one brief hour upstairs in a "room of one's own" leads to a revelation. Keenly aware of the repression she experienced in her married life, Louise relishes the prospect of freedom for all of her days: "a long procession of years to come that would belong to her absolutely. And she opened and spread her arms out to them in welcome" (12). But when she learns that her husband was not a victim of a fatal accident, she realizes the impossibility of resuming her former restricted life. In this story, the patriarch lives, and the protagonist—who momentarily becomes "like a goddess of Victory"—dies, as Chopin tells us satirically, "of joy that kills" (13).

In Margaret Oliphant's 1870s "A Story of a Wedding Tour," the protagonist Janey, likewise, exclaims " 'Safe!' " when the train, pausing for a brief stop, accidentally leaves behind Mr. Rosendal, her husband of just one week.[20] Rosendal is "a thick-set little man" (405), insensitive to his wife's interests and needs. Taking a second train, later, to leave her husband truly behind her, Janey discovers "Janey herself, the real woman, whom nobody had ever seen before" (412). Ten years later, living independently in the small French town of St. Honorat with her son, she remeets her husband through another accident of the railway and loses her autonomy. Mr. Rosendal, traveling on a rapide passing through the St. Honorat railway station, by chance looks out the train window and spies his wife Janey who left him many years before. Taken by surprise, Mr. Rosendal dies of a heart attack. Although Janey had never blamed herself for escaping her miserable marriage, she suddenly "seemed to herself no less than the murderer of her husband" (424). Although the patriarch is dead, Janey experiences a dread that, Oliphant tells us, "she never quite got over all her life" (424).

These examples confirm that for the repressed woman of the late-nineteenth and early-twentieth century, death of the patriarch must result solely from natural causes if the woman is to gain true autonomy. Gilman does not secure the freedom of the narrator in "The Yellow Wall-Paper," given its richly ambiguous ending. However, she liberates the protagonist of her 1911 "The Widow's Might" through the demise of the patriarch, who dies from natural causes.

This story more boldly indicts patriarchy than Chopin's "The Story of an Hour," Oliphant's "A Story of a Wedding Tour," and her own "The Yellow Wall-Paper." Mr. McPherson dies after a " 'long illness' " so that Mrs. McPherson, different from Janey of "A Story of a Wedding Tour," emerges truly "free" and blameless.[21] Brently Mallard and Doctor John pale next to Mr. McPherson, whose death liberates his dutiful wife from " 'an awful life' " (101). Had Janey stayed with Mr. Rosendal, she might have experienced this same kind of coldness and repression that Mrs. McPherson bore as her " 'duty' " (104).

Through comments other characters make, we can reconstruct the character of Mr. McPherson, whom we never actually meet. At his funeral, daughter Ellen tells us that " 'He was a man who always did his duty . . . But we none of us—loved him—very much' "; she adds, " 'Nobody could be affectionate with Father . . . and Mother—poor Mother! She's had an awful life' " (101). Understatement is key in this story, but "poor Mother" admits that the last thirty years of marital servitude to Mr. McPherson have been " 'hard' " (106). Rejecting her children's offers to move in with them, the middle-aged Mrs. McPherson exclaims " 'I'm tired of duty' " (104) and vows: " 'I'm going to do what I never did before. I'm going to *live!*' " (105) At the close of the story, she throws off her mourning clothes and appears "in a well-made traveling suit of dull mixed colors" (105), exclaiming much as Louise Mallard does in "The Story of an Hour," " 'Now, I'm free' " (106).

Mrs. McPherson's success cannot all be attributed to the death of a repressive patriarch. Described by her lawyer Mr. Frankland as a "woman of remarkable intelligence" (104), Mrs. McPherson convinces her husband to deed his property to her so that he would escape pressure from creditors.[22] Later, to afford a nurse and doctor during his illness, she ingeniously turns her home into a " 'rancho-sanitarium' " (105). A real entrepreneur, Mrs. McPherson, in just three years, makes a six thousand dollar profit, enough to finance her travel plans. Although she devoted her life to serving the patriarch, she gains freedom as a mature woman, and she embraces it. Thus, as Lane concludes, Mrs. McPherson is "Not a helpless, broken, distraught woman after her husband's death[;] she discovers resources within herself never before explored."[23]

The death of Mr. McPherson, then, becomes an occasion for rejoicing and thus anticipates the death of Wade Vaughn of *Unpunished.* Gilman's lone feminist detective novel, written ca. 1929 and first published in 1997, depicts the most perverted patriarch of the Gilman canon. Wade Vaughn, like Terry Nicholson of *Herland,* is a marital rapist, but Nicholson pales in comparison. Vaughn is an unscrupulous blackmailer, a sadist, a misogynist, and a corrupt villain. In Gilman's fiction, the punishment fits the patriarch's crime, and Vaughn, ironically a criminal lawyer, dies a criminal's death. While John is momentarily paralyzed, and Mr. McPherson dies from a lingering illness, Wade Vaughn is poisoned, shot, bludgeoned, knifed, choked, and frightened to death.

As in "The Widow's Might," we begin with the death of the patriarch. We never meet Wade Vaughn just as we never encounter Mr. Mc-Pherson, but Vaughn's wicked and loathsome character reverberates throughout this novel. *Unpunished* offers a groundbreaking argument against what we refer to today as battered women's syndrome and also demonstrates Gilman's vision for gender equality, but it contains racist and ethnic references to blacks and Italians—a mixed legacy indeed. While Gilman's prejudices in this later work are blatantly visible, so is her vehemence against a corrupt patriarchy as Denise D. Knight and I have noted in our afterword to The Feminist Press edition of this hitherto unpublished work. More than the other patriarchs, Wade Vaughn emerges as an extreme case. Initially thwarted in his attempt to marry Iris Smith, Vaughn succeeds when a terrible car accident kills Iris's first husband and her sister's husband. Iris, left mentally unstable, succumbs to Vaughn, who agrees to care for Iris's daughter (also named Iris), Iris's sister Jacqueline ("Jack") Warner (disfigured in the accident), and Jack's son Hal. Vaughn attempts to control Iris, and, when she recoils from his sexual advances, he torments her with the prospect of institutionalization. He comments: " 'If you make any noise or disturbance of any sort I am sure that an examining physician would quite agree with me that—restraint was necessary, and seclusion. . . . Come back to bed.' "[24] In his mandate for quiet, his threat of "seclusion," Vaughn recalls the character of Doctor John of "The Yellow Wall-Paper," who declares that he will send his wife to Dr. S. Weir Mitchell in the fall if her condition does not "pick up faster" (44).[25] Rather than undertake a Rest Cure, which Gilman had endured, or surrender to madness, as the narrator does in "The Yellow Wall-Paper," Iris hangs herself with her favorite scarf.

Responsible for more than the death of his wife, Vaughn—for his own profit—arranges for young Iris, against her will, to marry a crooked sleuth named Gus Crasher. Jack succeeds in avenging her sister's death and saving her niece Iris. She is but one of many who kill Wade Vaughn.[26] But Jack, undeniably Gilman's heroine, suffers no guilt. While Vaughn was alive, Jack makes clear, "We were in slavery, pure and simple!" (81); her son Hal confirms, " 'we couldn't call our souls our own' " (164). Following Vaughn's death, Jack exclaims, " 'We are *free*' " (143). And at the end, Jack is truly "free," much as her Victorian sisters Louise Mallard of Chopin's "The Story of an Hour" and Janey of Oliphant's "A Story of a Wedding Tour" longed to be. Slave master is but one more atrocity that Gilman piles on a dead patriarch deemed " 'worse than Jack the Ripper' " (135). Gilman exonerates the murderer of a villain: "If ever a man needed killing it was that one' " (161–62). Moreover, after hearing Jack's confession, detectives Bess and Jim Hunt and Dr. Ross Akers concur that the official verdict of Vaughn's death will remain heart disease even though, we later learn, Jack actually frightened him to death. Vaughn's death emerges as a justifiable homicide, not unlike the case of Minnie Wright, who murders her abusive husband in Susan Glaspell's "A Jury of Her Peers" (1917).[27] In Glaspell's work, Minnie's culpability is not questioned, but her women neighbors withhold the key evidence necessary to convict her. Gilman exonerates Jack much as Glaspell absolves Minnie: the years suffered under the abusive patriarchal rule of Wade Vaughn—who does not go unpunished—more than stand as her sentence.

In "The Widow's Might" and *Unpunished*, the death of the patriarch allows the true natures of the female protagonists "to be unloosed, expanded" to benefit their worlds. Interestingly, both women move westward, decisively reversing the progress of evil Wade Vaughn who came to the East (153). Mrs. McPherson tells her children of her plans to visit New Zealand, Australia, Tasmania, and Madagascar, and the concluding words of the story where she parts from her children for some time—"three going east, one west" ("Widow's Might" 106)—invoke the importance of going to the West. Likewise, Jack Warner "took herself off" (*Unpunished* 196) to California to repair the damages from the car accident that the wicked Vaughn refused to pay for: "he said I was sufficiently useful to him as I was, and more likely to stay! Like the Chinese women" (71). She travels "At first to a quiet southern beach accompanied by a competent and agreeable woman Dr. Akers found for her, half maid, half nurse, and there she basked in sunshine and rest, good food and pure air. Then, refreshed and strengthened, to a sanitarium, and a long period of treatment under the artistic skill of modern surgery" (196). Healing in the California sunshine with nutritious food, rest, and reconstructive surgery, Jack seemingly takes what Jennifer Tuttle refers to as the "West Cure." The West emerges as a panacea in this and other fiction (e.g., *The Crux* [1911]) as it also served in Gilman's own life. When feeling overwhelmed after the birth of her daughter Katharine, Gilman visited California and moved there following her separation from Walter Stetson. Freed from the tyrannical Vaughn, Jack emerges at the end of the novel as Gilman herself did from her own "West Cure"—with strength and purpose, almost a new woman.

Despite the vehemence with which Gilman eradicates patriarchy, she also reformulates the Victorian ideology of the male patriarch in her creation of a New Man figure to help build a more "human world." In New Woman fiction of the 1880s and 1890s by authors such as Olive Schreiner and Mona Caird, there emerges what Joseph Bristow calls "A new breed of man, desiring to transgress his allotted sexual place."[28] Bristow's description of the New Man illuminates the character of Gregory Nazianzen Rose of Schreiner's *The Story of an African Farm* (1883), the initially repugnant English farmer who bravely cross-dresses to nurse the dying Lyndall (even though she scorns him). But Bristow's description of this new, sensitive "breed" of man also applies to male characters who populate Gilman's early-twentieth-century fiction.

Perhaps Gilman's most liberated New Man is Ford Mathews of "The Cottagette" (1910), a writer and a cook whose father also was a professional cook. At the opening of the story, the artist Malda, rents a kitchenless cottagette for the summer and takes her meals in a common eating area so that she can devote her energy to her embroidery and drawing. To attract Ford Mathews, Malda reluctantly abandons her artistic calling to "play house," following the advice of her divorced friend Lois who insists " 'what they [men] want to marry is a homemaker.' "[29] The installment of the kitchen in the cottagette leads to endless chores that encroach on Malda's time to pursue her " 'beautiful and distinctive art' " (55), as Ford Mathews deems it. Fortunately, Ford rescues Malda from her ill-hatched plan " 'that the way to a man's heart is through his stomach' " (56). After proposing, he asks Malda to give up her stint at cooking and resume her artwork. Praising her New Man, Gilman concludes her story with a rhetorical question: "Was there ever a man like this?" (56).

Another man "like this," Vandyck Jennings of *Herland* is not quite as liberated as Ford Mathews. Whereas rebellious Terry vehemently renounces the principles of Herland, and the romanticized Jeff wholeheartedly adopts the views of that society, Van, a sociologist, observes the society carefully and undergoes a slow, believable conversion. He is not "perfectly satisfied" (145) with the ways of Herland, as Jeff is at the end of the novel (Van critically observes, "I never saw an alien become naturalized more quickly than that man in Herland" [145]). When Ellador "trembled" as he kisses her "hungrily" (138), he admits: "I begin to see—a little—how Terry was so driven to crime" (139). But Van sympathizes with Terry only "a little." Van possesses patience, an important quality that John of "The Yellow Wall-Paper" sorely lacks. He rejects the sexist ways of Ourland, magnified in Terry's animalism, and welcomes the companionship that Ellador graciously offers him. At the end of the novel, as he embarks on his journey to Ourland with Ellador, he has achieved a bond based on mutual respect.

Yet another man "like this," Ross Akers of *Unpunished* falls in love with Jack Warner despite her physical disabilities. Jack's sole friend during the years of Vaughn's tyranny, Ross Akers emerges as a man of principles who is also under the control of Vaughn. He pleads with Vaughn without success to allow Jack to have surgery. In one development, we learn that Wade Vaughn has solid evidence against Akers for "killing a patient, a very dear friend of his, who was slowly and hopelessly dying in constant agony" (99).[30] Vaughn threatens to expose Akers for his actions unless he remains useful to Vaughn. Thus, the death of the blackmailing patriarch of *Unpunished* also frees Gilman's New Man, who appreciates Jack for her "good head" (32), much as Vandyck Jennings of *Herland* comes to esteem Ellador. The death of patriarchy, symbolized in Vaughn's multiple murder, liberates not only women but also men.

Despite her theoretical insistence in *The Man-Made World,* Gilman demonstrates in her fiction that it takes more than "a matter of changed education and opportunity for every child" (*Man-Made World* 247) to make a "human world." Increasingly over time, she shows in her fiction that there is a need for "punishing [corrupt] men" (*Man-Made World* 247) handicapped by what she viewed as excessive male predatory traits. Caging the beast, Gilman makes room for a New Man, who will contribute to the creation of " 'a mother-world as well as a father-world, a world in which we shall not be ashamed or afraid to plant our children' " ("New Mothers" 149).

NOTES

1. Ann J. Lane, *To Herland and Beyond: The Life and Work of Charlotte Perkins Gilman* (New York: Pantheon, 1980), 344.

2. For example, in *Woman of Yesterday* (1900), author Caroline Mason kills off her heroine's husband Keith so that Anna Mallison can go to India as she had always hoped. Moreover, she rejects a marriage offer from her soulmate, who is also the head of the utopian community Fraternia, in order to pursue meaningful work. In Alice Ingelfritz Jones's second novel entitled *Beatrice* (1895), her heroine Beatrice does not marry because her beloved dies; rather, she finds a calling helping natives on a remote island. For more information on these novelists and Gilman's utopian fiction, see Carol A. Kolmerten's essay "Texts and Contexts: American Women Envision Utopia, 1890–1920" in *Utopians and Science Fiction by Women,* eds. Jane A. Donawerth and Carol A. Kolmerten (Syracuse: Syracuse University Press, 1994), 121.

3. Kolmerten, *Utopians,* 110.

4. Gilman, "The New Mothers of a New World," *Forerunner* 4 (June 1913): 149. All further references are cited parenthetically in the text.

5. Gilman, "The World's Mother," *Woman's Journal* (2 January 1904): 2.

6. Gilman, *The Man-Made World or, Our Androcentric Culture* (New York: Charlton, 1911), 246–47. All further references are cited parenthetically in the text.

7. This was a favorite trope of Gilman's. She makes extensive use of animal analogy to explore gender relations in *Women and Economics* (1898) and in countless poems (e.g., "Females" and "Wedded Bliss" from *In This Our World*) and parables (e.g., "Two Storks" and "The Lady Oyster").

8. Although she repudiated the term, today we recognize her as a feminist.

9. For more discussion of *Man-Made World,* see Gary Scharnhorst, *Charlotte Perkins Gilman* (Boston: Twayne, 1985), 75–80; Lane, *To Herland and Beyond,* 278–81.

10. Charlotte Perkins Gilman, *Herland,* introduction by Ann J. Lane (New York: Pantheon, 1979), 25. All further references are cited parenthetically in the text.

11. There are over two dozen articles about the story since its 1973 republication by The Feminist Press, with an afterword by Elaine R. Hedges.

12. See Elaine R. Hedges, "Afterword to 'The Yellow Wallpaper,' " in *The Captive Imagination: A Casebook on "The Yellow Wallpaper,"* ed. Catherine Golden (New York: The Feminist Press, 1992), 124, 131–34.

13. Charlotte Perkins Gilman, "The Yellow Wall-Paper," in *"The Yellow Wall-Paper" and Selected Stories of Charlotte Perkins Gilman,* ed. Denise D. Knight (Newark: University of Delaware Press, 1994), 39. All further references are cited parenthetically in the text.

14. Edith Summers Kelley, *Weeds,* afterword by Charlotte Margolis Goodman (New York: The Feminist Press, 1996), 329.

15. Kate Chopin, *The Awakening,* ed. Margo Culley (New York: W. W. Norton, 1994), 4. All further references are cited parenthetically in the text.

16. Chopin intended to name her novel "A Solitary Soul," and the term well describes Edna Pontellier.

17. For a detailed discussion of the narrator's language as an indication of her change in self-presentation when her actions compromise her sanity, see my essay entitled "The Writing of 'The Yellow Wall-Paper': A Double Palimpsest," *Studies in American Fiction* 17 (1989): 193–201. Reprint, *The Captive Imagination,* 296–306. Reprint, *Charlotte Perkins Gilman: A Study of the Short Fiction,* ed. Denise D. Knight (New York: Twayne Publishers, 1997), 155–65.

18. See, for example, "Turned," in which Mrs. Marroner and her husband's mistress, holding Mr. Marroner's illegitimate child, unite to confront the adulterous husband.

19. Kate Chopin, "The Story of an Hour," in *Fictions,* 3rd ed., ed. Joseph F. Trimmer and C. Wade Jennings (New York: Harcourt Brace, 1994), 12. All further references are cited parenthetically in the text.

20. Margaret Oliphant, "A Story of a Wedding Tour," in *Nineteenth-Century Stories by Women,* ed. Glennis Stephenson (Peterborough, Ontario: Broadview Press, 1993), 408. All further references are cited parenthetically in the text.

21. Charlotte Perkins Gilman, "The Widow's Might," *The Charlotte Perkins Gilman Reader,* introduction by Ann J. Lane (New York: Pantheon Books, 1980), 101. All further references are cited parenthetically in the text.

22. Her lawyer is aptly named Mr. Frankland. Giving characters clever names was a specialty of Gilman's; this becomes particularly apparent in *Unpunished.* See the afterword to *Unpunished,* by Catherine J. Golden and Denise D. Knight (New York: The Feminist Press, 1997).

23. Lane, introduction, *Charlotte Perkins Gilman Reader,* xxii.

24. Charlotte Perkins Gilman, *Unpunished,* ed. with an afterword by Catherine J. Golden and Denise D. Knight (New York: The Feminist Press, 1997), 88. All further references are cited parenthetically in the text.

25. In her introduction to *The Charlotte Perkins Gilman Reader* (xxxii), Lane makes

an allusion that *Unpunished* harkens back to "The Yellow Wall-Paper" but does not develop it. For more discussion, see my afterword to *Unpunished,* with Denise Knight, 230.

26. The murderers include several household servants and Doctor Ross Akers—but Jack is the first to kill him. She dons a death mask, made from Iris's face, and puts on a black-and white scarf identical to the one Iris used to hang herself. Jack discloses: "when he saw me standing there he put up his hands before his face at first—then gave a choked cry, clutched at his heart" (207).

27. The one-act play version, produced in 1916 and published in 1920, is called *Trifles.* For more discussion of this connection, see my afterword to *Unpunished,* with Denise Knight, 222, 231.

28. Olive Schreiner, *The Story of an African Farm,* ed. with an introduction by Joseph Bristow (Oxford: Oxford University Press, 1992), xxi.

29. Charlotte Perkins Gilman, "The Cottagette," *Charlotte Perkins Gilman Reader,* 51.

30. Although in real life Gilman favored a woman doctor, Akers is exactly the type of physician she hoped to find when, in 1935, she was preparing for her own death by suicide. As the plot unfolds, we learn that Akers inflicted one of the postmortem wounds.

Charlotte Perkins Gilman, Edith Wharton, and the Divided Heritage of American Literary Feminism

FREDERICK WEGENER

ASSEMBLING ITS MONTHLY COMPENDIUM OF HIGHLIGHTS FROM OTHER journals and magazines, Charlotte Perkins Gilman informed readers of the *Impress,* early in 1894, "There is a story in the December *Scribner's* [*Magazine*] called 'The Fullness of Life,' by Edith Wharton, of a most surprising nature."[1] Only her second work of fiction, Wharton's tale probably seemed worth noting to Gilman as a parable of a joyless marriage in which an unnamed woman experiences on her deathbed "a vague satisfaction in the thought that she had swallowed her noxious last draught of medicine . . . and that she should never again hear the creaking of her husband's boots—those horrible boots—and that no one would come to bother her about the next day's dinner . . . or the butcher's book."[2] Greeted in the hereafter by the Spirit of Life, who asks her if she ever experienced "the fullness of life" with her husband, Wharton's heroine admits, "Oh, I was fond of him, and we were counted a very happy couple," before evoking an image to which Gilman must have keenly responded: "But I have sometimes thought that a woman's nature is like a great house full of rooms: there is the hall, through which everyone passes in going in and out; the drawing room, where one receives formal visits; the sitting room, where the members of the family come and go as they list; but beyond that, far beyond, are other rooms, the handles of whose doors perhaps are never turned; no one knows the way to them, no one knows whither they lead." To the Spirit's next question ("And your husband . . . never got beyond the family sitting room?"), the woman replies that "the worst of it was that he was quite content to remain there. . . . He was different. His boots creaked, and he always slammed the door when he went out, and he never read anything but railway novels and the sporting advertisements in the papers—and—and, in short, we never understood each other in the least" (*CS* 1 : 14).

Wharton's story takes an unexpected turn, however, when the protagonist—offered a life in eternity with a male figure identified as her
"kindred soul"—also learns that her husband does not have such a
companion similarly awaiting his own arrival beyond the grave. Overwhelmed with misgivings, and knowing that "[h]e will never be happy
without me," the woman abruptly dismisses her kindred soul and decides to wait for her husband, explaining to the Spirit of Life,

> don't you understand that I shouldn't feel at home without him? It is all
> very well for a week or two—but for eternity! After all, I never minded the
> creaking of his boots, except when my head ached, and I don't suppose it
> will ache *here*; and he was always so sorry when he had slammed the door,
> only he never *could* remember not to. Besides, no one else would know how
> to look after him, he is so helpless. His inkstand would never be filled, and
> he would always be out of stamps and visiting cards. He would never re-
> member to have his umbrella re-covered, or to ask the price of anything
> before he bought it. Why, he wouldn't even know what novels to read. (*CS*,
> 1 : 19–20)

As one might have guessed, Gilman makes short work of such backped-
alling rationalizations, and of the tale itself: "To begin a story with the
death of the heroine is novel treatment surely, but to represent the new-
freed soul as instantly seeking a mate—searching for a complementary
angel out of all the joys of heaven—seems still somewhat of the earth
earthy. She is left waiting patiently at the gates for the husband left
behind, in order that they may set up housekeeping again" (*Impress* 2).

An admittedly slight and unskillful affair, Wharton's tale was not included in her first collection, omitted along with other "old stories" that
she "regard[ed] . . . as the excesses of youth. They were all written 'at
the top of my voice,' & The Fulness of Life is one long shriek."[3] What
disqualifies the tale in her eyes, however, is its tone and lack of control,
as opposed to the concluding embarrassments on which Gilman focuses. Most striking of all, perhaps, about Gilman's comment on the
story is the fact that it would remain her only significant reference,
apart from a brief and perfunctory nod in one of her last essays, to the
work of a writer soon to become one of the luminaries among American
literary women of their era.[4] And the fact that she discusses only one of
Wharton's earliest works of fiction, and does so in a single dismissive
paragraph written at a comparably early stage of her own career,
should illustrate the perils greeting any attempt to place these two figures alongside each other in a mutually illuminating way. It is presumably for reasons like these that Gilman and Wharton are seldom jointly
discussed even in the increasingly voluminous body of scholarship on
both careers. Yet this persistent interpretive separation of the two seems

in other respects peculiar, for in the process of resurrecting both figures, literary historians and critics have lately come to assign Gilman and Wharton a commanding position among American women prose writers between the 1890s and the Great Depression. In light of this shared predominance, and of their numerous and considerable incompatibilities, one can now observe that Gilman and Wharton—the very writers who might be said almost to divide between them the legacy of American literary feminism in their time—have been on a collision course ever since their importance in literary studies began to be restored nearly a generation ago. Any pairing of figures so unalike and yet equally central poses a uniquely provocative challenge to the continuing task of reconfiguring the period in which they both flourished and of delineating a usable, authoritative lineage of writing by American women.

At first glance, Gilman and Wharton represent a very promising, almost inevitable encounter between two literary women whose careers mirror each other in various, often unexpected ways. Enormously prolific writers who were born, and who also died, only two years apart, Gilman and Wharton were, of course, exact contemporaries whose work reflects a number of overlapping themes and concerns. Both authored reticent, carefully guarded memoirs published in successive years by the same firm, Appleton-Century, and offered remarkably similar accounts of childhood and adolescence. In a largely self-taught youth, each read widely and miscellaneously, Wharton in what she would later call "the kingdom of my father's library," Gilman under the guidance, at least in part, of her father, literally a librarian, who "was always effective in book advice," she later recalled, "none better."[5] Like Gilman, who remarks, "My passion for beauty dates far back," and who "keenly recall[s] my delight in specially beautiful things" (*L* 17, 18), Wharton elsewhere observes, "I had been fed on beauty since my babyhood," resulting in what she called "my love of pretty things— pretty clothes, pretty pictures, pretty sights."[6] Such inclinations, as one might expect, had on each of them an effect described in language closely echoed by the other. Much as Wharton enjoyed "a secret ecstasy of communion" with her father's books, Gilman declared that "no one had a richer, more glorious life than I had, inside," fondly evoking a bookish girlhood marked by "all that inner thirst for glorious loveliness" (*BG* 69–70; *L* 23, 20). Since "none of my companions had any imagination, or any taste for books or pictures," Wharton recalled, "I lived one side of life with them, gaily & thoroughly," while "of the other wonderful side they never had so much as a guess!" (*N* 1082). According to Gilman, "My dream world was no secret" in the sense that "I was but too ready to share it, but there were no sympathetic listeners" in her environment any more than in Wharton's: "It was my life, but lived entirely alone" (*L* 23).

In Gilman's memory, "this inner life"—reminiscent of what Wharton called "my long inner solitude"—stemmed from circumstances described as more or less identically estranging. "Young people are commonly unhappy at being 'misunderstood,' and alone," she notes, "but this usual condition was added to in my case," not unlike that of Wharton, who recalls that "from the first I kept my adventures with books to myself," in the course of acknowledging, "perhaps it was not only the 'misunderstood' element, so common in meditative infancy, that kept me from talking of my discoveries" (*L* 76; *BG* 70). The disjunction that Gilman laments in remembering "the wide range of my studies, hopes and purposes, and the complete lack of understanding or sympathy in those about me" (*L,* 76), corresponds poignantly to the contrast with what Wharton calls "my complete mental isolation" as a young woman: "All the people I have known who have cared for 'les choses de l'esprit' have found some degree of sympathy & companionship either in their families or among their youthful friends" (*N* 1077, 1082).

Later in life, both survived disastrous marriages that ended in divorce at a time when that similarity would have been far more notable, while Wharton is thought to have undergone in 1898 a version of the "Rest Cure" administered to Gilman with such catastrophic results a decade earlier.[7] Each voluntarily embarked upon a period of exile about as distant from where she started, if in opposite directions (Gilman in California, Wharton in France), as the other. Although inclined to the sort of pacifism that Wharton bitterly detested, Gilman surprised many of her admirers by speaking against German aggression soon after the outbreak of the first world war, a crisis that drew Wharton for the first time into various forms of social relief work, the effects of which on those around her would have been easily recognizable to Gilman: "Many women with whom I was in contact during the war had obviously found their vocation in . . . philanthropic activities. The call on their co-operation had developed unexpected aptitudes which, in some cases, turned them forever from a life of discontented idling, and made them into happy people" (*BG* 356). A serious acquaintance with Darwin's writing and with evolutionary thought in general performed an equally decisive role in forming their imaginations, while both became ardent Whitmanites not long after a time that saw "*Leaves of Grass* . . . kept under lock and key," as Wharton remembered it, "and brought out, like tobacco, only in the absence of 'the ladies,' to whom the name of Walt Whitman was unmentionable."[8] Both were vehemently anti-Freudian and became increasingly puritanical in their remarks on the flapper generation in postwar America, while Gilman, radical as she was, had nothing much better to say than Wharton about what she called "the Jewish-Russian nightmare, Bolshevism" (*L* 320)—a reminder also of the racial and ethnic antipathies compromising Gilman's social prognoses, and all too familiar to Wharton's readers as well.

Perhaps most significant, however, is the way in which their trajectories as writers so closely intersected, from the somewhat delayed emergence of both to the fluctuating posthumous fortunes of their work. Like so many others of their generation, both Gilman and Wharton benefited from the sponsorship of William Dean Howells, who helped to launch Wharton's career by publishing one of her poems in the *Atlantic Monthly,* where he later tried without success to place "The Yellow Wall-Paper" thirty years before reprinting it, along with one of Wharton's tales, in *The Great Modern American Stories* (1920)—the only volume in which their work appeared together during their lifetimes. Fervent readers of verse from an early age, both first appeared in print (but for one trifling exception in Gilman's case) as poets, while their first freestanding publications—Wharton's privately printed *Verses* (1878) and Gilman's *In This Our World* (1893)—were collections of poetry rather than exercises in any of the modes of writing by which either became principally known. More important, both became nationally prominent figures at the same time, each steadily gathering an audience throughout the mid-1890s before publishing several full-length works between 1898 and 1904. On the other hand, each lived to witness a severe decline in her reputation, an eclipse that lasted almost as long in Wharton's case as in Gilman's. Finally, it would be difficult to think of another American literary woman among their contemporaries whose career has been revived so assiduously, or her works reissued as extensively, over the past thirty years as those of Gilman and Wharton.

And yet, upon closer examination, the dissimilarities—often dramatically conflicting—start to become far more salient and to outweigh in value even the most intriguing resemblances or parallels between these two figures. A descendant of the Beecher family, and friend of the Channings, Gilman celebrates in *The Living* precisely the crusading, reformist New England heritage to which Wharton eagerly and gratefully contrasts her own New York ancestry in *A Backward Glance,* with predictably differentiating consequences.[9] Unlike Gilman, who stresses "that desire to help humanity which underlay all my studies" and who declares that, as a young woman, "I looked ahead to a steady lifetime of social study and service" (*L* 70, 74), Wharton confessed more than once to what she called "my innate distaste for anything like 'social service,' " admitting even as she recalled her own heroic role in the war-relief effort, "I am conscious of lukewarmness in regard to organized beneficence" (*BG* 348, 356). According to Gilman, with such "benefi-cence" at least partly in mind, "The main distinction of human virtue is what we roughly describe as altruism," involving the duty "[t]o love and serve one another, to care for one another, to feel for and with one another."[10] Wharton, on the other hand, once sardonically attributed what she called "the other-regarding virtues" to the characters in an anachronistic historical drama, while commending the work of another playwright who "has had the audacity to draw his characters as Italians of the Middle Ages, and not as scrupulous and sentimental modern altruists" (*UCW* 83, 92).

Such contrarieties may be traced, in part, to the obviously vast differ-ences in their social background and formative experiences. Between the mid-1860s and 1872, as the young Charlotte Perkins moved with her mother and brother from boarding house to boarding house or from one relation's home to another, Edith Jones's equally peripatetic family traveled in Rome, England, Spain, Paris, and Germany. Gilman struggled through adolescence and early married life in Providence from 1872–73 through the late 1880s even as Wharton summered com-fortably nearby, yet a world apart, in Newport. Particularly revealing in this respect is the use to which each writer, early in her memoirs, puts a quotation from the same Longfellow poem, "Maidenhood." Depicting herself at "[s]ixteen, with a life to build" as well as "a passion . . . for scientific knowledge, for real laws of life," along with "an insatiable de-mand for perfection in everything," Gilman proudly claims that "in-stead of 'Standing with reluctant feet where the brook and river meet,' I plunged in and swam" (*L* 44). At the start of a chapter entitled "Unre-luctant Feet," remarking that "[i]n one of the most famous poems of [Longfellow] the Maiden is supposed to arrive with reluctant feet 'where the brook and river meet,' " Wharton likewise declares, "I can-not say that my own feet were thus hampered" (*BG* 77). Alongside the earnestness with which Gilman remembers "the desperately serious 'living' which was going on" at that time of her life, as well as "the cumulative effort toward a stronger, nobler character" (*L* 44, 45), the point of Wharton's allusion, however, is bound to seem comparatively mundane: "I longed to travel and see new places, and . . . was by no means averse to seeing new people, and especially to being regarded as 'grown up' " (*BG* 77). Fortunately for her, Wharton recalls, "I had not long to wait, for when I was seventeen my parents decided that I spent too much time in reading, and that I was to come out a year before the accepted age" (*BG* 77), a recollection clashing rather hilariously with Gilman's: "In my seventeenth year I wrote to my father, saying that I wished to help humanity, that I realized I must understand history, and where should I begin" (*L* 36).

It is no surprise, therefore, to discover that the most grievous drawback of their youth, as each remembered it—the absence of sympathetic understanding and encouragement on the part of family and peers—should have had a decidedly different impact, and generated wholly separate aspirations, in the lives of both writers. Whereas Wharton knew at first-hand what it was like "for the creative artist to grow up in an atmosphere where the arts are simply non-existent," and where "I had to fight my way to expression through a thick fog of indifference, if not of tacit disapproval" (*BG* 121, 122), Gilman describes an altogether divergent source of strife and tension: "No one that I knew had any interest in 'the human race,' their interests were all for individuals, and as for plans for improving social conditions—such ideas seemed utterly absurd" (*L* 76). An interest in "the arts," on the one hand, and an "interest in 'the human race' " on the other—such a distinction becomes fundamentally defining, and may be said to have determined the significantly different outlets that an otherwise shared expressive impulse quickly found in each case. As Wharton recalled, "The imagining of tales . . . had gone on in me since my first conscious moments; I cannot remember the time when I did not want to 'make up' stories" (*BG* 33); according to Gilman's memoirs, by contrast, "I did not compose, make stories like Frances Hodgson in her childhood, but was already scheming to improve the world" (*L* 21). A sensibility for which the composition of narrative and "world-work" appear to have remained mutually exclusive tended to favor a correspondingly different medium, as Gilman more than once denied any aptitude for the genre most closely associated with Wharton, who never felt comfortable writing in the critical, discursive, and polemical forms in which Gilman excelled.

Such a preference reflects Gilman's allegiance, moreover, to a creed that would have been essentially meaningless to Wharton, as articulated, for example, in her remarks on "The Yellow Wall-Paper," about which she famously "assured" Howells "that it was no more 'literature' than my other stuff, being definitely written 'with a purpose.' In my judgment it is a pretty poor thing to write, to talk, without a purpose" (*L* 121). In a late essay, Wharton included Gilman's great-aunt, Harriet Beecher Stowe, among "the pleaders of special causes" who "produced . . . that unhappy hybrid, the novel with a purpose," while she once counseled the avowedly purposeful Upton Sinclair, "I have never known a novel that was good enough to be good in spite of its being adapted to the author's political views" (*UCW* 175; *LEW* 500).[11] Like other similarly driven writers, Gilman often favored in her narratives the sort of utopian mode from which Wharton consistently abstained throughout her career. To be sure, both attached an inherent social value, each in her own way, to the nurturing and exercise of an artistic capacity. "Where you find great beauty," according to Gilman, "you find a great civic sense,"[12] a postulate with which Wharton would not have disagreed: "If art is really a factor in civilization, it seems obvious that the feeling for beauty needs as careful cultivation as the other civic virtues."[13] A writer with a purpose like Gilman, who frankly belittled "such small sense of art as I have" and who once unabashedly maintained that her work "is not, in the artistic sense, 'literature' " (*L* 6, 284), would have had little patience, however, with the insularity of Wharton's axiom that "the only rules to be considered in art evolve from the inside, and are not to be applied ready-made from without" (*UCW* 161). By the same token, a writer of Gilman's bent would have seemed intolerably tendentious or topical to one as proficient and sophisticated as Wharton, who would have been nonplused, at the very least, to hear a fellow practitioner admit as casually as Gilman did, "I was never a careful writer" and "I have never made any pretense of being literary," or ascribe to her own prose "the natural expression of thought, except in the stories, which called for composition and were more difficult—especially the novels, which are poor" and "by which I definitely proved that I am not a novelist!" (*L* 241, 284, 100, 306).

It will seem ironic in this light, to take the most obvious of the disparities between them, that her fiction should have earned Wharton an extraordinary amount of money, while Gilman, whose "method . . . was to express the idea," in her words, "with clearness and vivacity, so that it might be apprehended with ease and pleasure" (*L* 284–85), nonetheless found writing a stubbornly unremunerative activity. Yet the gap between Wharton's punctiliously aesthetic emphasis and what might be called the "functionalism" of a writer like Gilman also underlies many of the more significant, not-unrelated differences that quickly start multiplying the further one pursues any juxtaposition of their careers. Whereas Gilman achieved renown as a ubiquitous and tirelessly itinerant lecturer on a wide variety of topics, Wharton frequently satirized lecturing women in her fiction and once began an address to American soldiers in France by confessing, "I have never expected to speak in public. I consider it a man's job and not a woman's."[14] Examining in a late essay "the true importance of the motion picture," Gilman underscored "its value in social advancement" along with "the inescapable supremacy of this art in social progress" and announced, "The motion picture is the greatest instrument for stimulating the imagination yet offered"[15]; Wharton, however lucrative she found the early screen adaptations of her novels, made a point of placing "the cinema" among the "world-wide enemies of the imagination" (*UCW* 271). Even their few mutual enthusiasms only end up widening the distance between them. As "one point in the introduction of the automobile which is not generally noted," for example, Gilman considers "the effect of the vehicle upon the human character" and proposes "[t]he automobile as a moral agent"; Wharton, famously among the first American writers to own one, emphasizes assets that Gilman might have found insufficiently elevated: "The motor-car has restored the romance of travel" and "given us back the wonder, the adventure and the novelty which enlivened the way of our posting grand-parents."[16] With reference to "garden-craft," "garden-composition," and "garden-art," Wharton adopts a characteristically sculptural perspective in remarking that "the garden must be studied in relation to the house, and both in relation to the landscape," and that "[t]he inherent beauty of the garden lies in the grouping of its parts."[17] In Gilman's eyes gardening involved, above all, "plenty of honest-to-goodness physical labor, in which I exult," with results at once more practical and more productive than those of Wharton's architecturally oriented approach: "about thirty kinds of vegetables," as Gilman recalls proudly (*L* 327).

On weightier matters of importance to both of them, their views are even more difficult to harmonize with each other. Whereas Gilman presents the eponymous utopian community of "Bee Wise" (1913) as a place where "[t]he great art of child-culture grew apace . . . with the best methods now known," and where "Montessorian ideas and systems were honored and well used," Wharton once scornfully defined "the fundamental principle of the Montessori system" as "the development of the child's individuality, unrestricted by the traditional nursery discipline," arguing that "a Montessori school is a baby world where, shut up together in the most improved hygienic surroundings, a number of infants noisily develop their individuality."[18] Nor is this the only issue on which she targeted a peculiarly American progressivist advocacy and rhetoric of the sort exemplified throughout Gilman's work. As demonstrated in her characterization of ludicrously misguided reformers like Pauline Manford in *Twilight Sleep* (1927) or the Princess Buondelmonte in *The Children* (1928), the satirical fiction of Wharton's later period amounts to a derisive pastiche of the very ensemble of ideas, values, and convictions (on styles of child-rearing, household hygiene, birth control, and "physical culture") with which Gilman had become so closely associated.[19] Both of them were doubtless more alive than Howells could have been to the irony of uniting "The Yellow Wall-Paper," as he did in his 1920 anthology, with a tale like "The Mission of Jane" (1904), in which Wharton's portrayal of a middle-aged couple's adopted daughter, who "seemed extraordinarily intelligent" and "a prodigy of wisdom" (with "no difficulty in fixing her attention"), soon evolves into almost a caricature of a Gilmanian model child:

> Before she was fifteen she had set about reforming the household. . . . She instructed Mrs. Lethbury in an improved way of making beef stock, and called attention to the unhygienic qualities of carpets. She poured out distracting facts about bacilli and vegetable mold, and demonstrated that curtains and picture frames are a hotbed of animal organisms. She learned by heart the nutritive ingredients of the principal articles of diet, and revolutionized the cuisine by an attempt to establish a scientific average between starch and phosphates. (*CS* 1 : 372–73)

As a result, "Four cooks left during this experiment, and Lethbury fell into the habit of dining at the club," thereafter "enduring with what grace he might the blighting edification of Jane's discourse" (*CS* 1 : 373).

That Wharton's animus, here as in a novel like *Twilight Sleep*, should have focused on therapeutic improvements in domestic management becomes particularly suggestive when one revisits her first book, *The Decoration of Houses* (1897), in tandem with its counterpart among Gilman's writings, *The Home* (1903), published only a few years later and conceived with works like Wharton's influential treatise at least partly in mind.[20] At one point in her study, Gilman concerns herself no less urgently than Wharton with the question, "may we not furnish and decorate our homes beautifully? . . . What do we know, what do we care, for the elementary laws which make this thing beautiful, that thing ugly, and the same things vary as they are combined with others!" (*H* 148). According to Wharton, "Each room in a house has its individual uses" that "are seriously interfered with if it be not preserved as a small world by itself," without which "all [rooms] will be equally unfitted to serve their special purpose" (*DH* 22); similarly, Gilman observes, "In the furnishing and decoration of a home . . . each room may be treated separately according to its especial purpose," thanks to which "the domestic architect is under the necessity of separating as far as possible these discordant purposes [of the various rooms], while obliged still to confine them to the same walls and roof" (*H* 148, 146). Much as Wharton stipulates that, "In deciding upon a scheme of decoration, it is necessary to keep in mind the relation of . . . the room as a whole to other rooms in the house," while "this plan must be carried out with such due sense of the relation of the rooms to each other that there shall be no violent break in the continuity of treatment," so Gilman recommends a plan whereby "we can accustom ourselves to the aesthetic jar of stepping from one [room] to another, or even bring them all under

some main scheme" (*DH* 24; *H* 148). At times, both adopt the organi-
cist vocabulary informing Wharton's emphasis on "fitness of proportion," or her argument that "much of the sense of restfulness and
comfort produced by certain rooms depends on the due adjustment of
their fundamental parts" and on "the expression of . . . the sense of
interrelation of parts, of unity of the whole"—a sense also animating
Gilman's approach to "[t]he laws of applied beauty," which involve
"no devious meandering, but the direct clear purpose and result: Unity,
Harmony, that unerring law of relation which keeps the pa[r]t true to
the whole—never too much here or there—all balanced and at rest"
(*DH* 19, 198; *H* 144–45).

Concerning the many departures from such precepts that one may
find in "the average American house," as Wharton calls it, Gilman's
remarks indicate an entirely different orientation, however, to the problems that both writers confront in their studies. Whereas Wharton
glibly blames the incoherence of fashionable interior decoration on
"the feminine tendency to want things because other people have them,
rather than to have things because they are wanted" (*DH* 17), Gilman
traces this circumstance to origins conspicuously ignored in *The Decoration of Houses,* placing at the core of her analysis a set of matters
that receive no attention in Wharton's treatment of domestic space. For
Gilman, any lack of "harmony" or "proportion" in household decor
ultimately constitutes not so much a lapse in taste as a symptom of
certain underlying social conditions that govern domestic life itself. In
a correlation that Wharton would not have had any interest in making,
"The bottled discord of the woman's daily occupations," according to
Gilman, "is quite sufficient to account for the explosions of discord on
her walls and floors"; because "she continually has to do utterly inharmonious things," such a woman "must develop a kind of mind that
does *not object to discord.* Unity, harmony, simplicity, truth, restraint—
these are not applicable in a patchwork life, however hallowed by high
devotion and tender love. This is why domestic art is so low—so indis-
tinguishable" (*H* 151–52). Gilman's argument here develops more fully
her remarks on "the question . . . of household decoration and furnishing" in *Women and Economics* (1898), where she contends, under the
running head "The Tyranny of Bric-a-brac," that "[t]he economically
dependent woman, spending the accumulating energies of the race in
her small cage, has thrown out a tangled mass of expression" and "has
crowded her limited habitat with unlimited things,—things useful and
unuseful, ornamental and unornamental, comfortable and uncomfortable" (*WE* 256–57). On the other hand, "The free woman, having room
for full individual expression in her economic activities and in her social
relation, . . . will learn to love simplicity at last," so that "the trend of

the new conditions, . . . developing the sense of beauty, will be toward a delicate loveliness in the interiors of our houses" (*WE* 257). By contrast, Wharton's chapter on "Bric-à-Brac," in which she reconsiders "the natural desire to 'make a room look pretty' . . . with the purpose of inquiring whether such an object is ever furthered by the indiscriminate amassing of 'ornaments' " (much as Gilman declares that "the mere accumulation of beautiful objects is not decoration; often quite the contrary" [*H* 149]), advances a more detached solution to the problem: "It is surprising to note how the removal of an accumulation of knick-knacks will free the architectural lines and restore the furniture to its rightful relation with the walls" (*DH* 185).

For an aesthetically motivated understanding like Wharton's, "The vulgarity of current decoration has its source in the indifference of the wealthy to architectural fitness," whereas Gilman is more inclined to perceive "no pathos, rather a repulsive horror, in the mass of freakish ornament on walls, floors, chairs, and tables, on specially contrived articles of furniture, on her own body and the helpless bodies of her little ones, which marks the unhealthy riot of expression of the overfed and underworked lady of the house" (*DH* iv; *H* 220). According to her diagnosis, "A larger womanhood, a civilised womanhood, specialised, broad-minded, working and caring for the public good *as well as the private,* will give us not only better homes, but homes more beautiful" (*H* 158). For many, such a vision will present a breadth and capaciousness missing from what might be considered the hermeticism of Wharton's approach, reflected even in the organization of both studies, as Gilman reserves only one part of the shortest chapter of *The Home,* "Domestic Art," for the subject of Wharton's entire volume, which dwells exclusively on the structural aspects of interior decoration. Whereas Gilman finds such questions inextricably entangled with phenomena like marriage, parenthood, the sexual division of labor, and many other facets of the home as "a human institution" (*H* 4). Wharton's carefully and scrupulously arranged interiors belong to "houses" that often seem to be designed without inhabitants in mind, while the word "home," astonishingly enough, hardly ever occurs in *The Decoration of Houses.*[21]

Wharton's inability or unwillingness to think critically about the home in more, or other, than purely compositional terms ultimately points to the matter on which her divergence from Gilman is sure to be of greatest concern to students of their work. For when she does evoke the domain explored in such iconoclastic detail by Gilman in *The Home,* her pronouncements are scarcely reassuring, as Wharton mourns the disappearance of "that ancient curriculum of house-keeping which, at least in Anglo-Saxon countries, was so soon to be swept aside by the 'monstrous regiment' of the emancipated: young women taught by their elders to despise the kitchen and the linen room, and to substitute the acquiring of University degrees for the more complex art of civilized living" (*BG* 60). One could not ask for a better example of the sort of affirmation that Gilman sought to undermine in exposing various hierarchical realities effectively camouflaged by this kind of sanctifying language about the traditional home. Indeed, Wharton's lofty re-mythologization of "civilized living" as a "complex art" associated with sites of conventional domestic work (deemed, in turn, of implicitly greater value than the advantages of emancipation and higher learning for women) should be more than enough to illustrate the most disquieting aspect of any comparison of Wharton and Gilman, their largely antithetical views on the "woman question" itself.

At first, numerous passages from *Women and Economics* and, for example, *French Ways and Their Meaning*—Wharton's fullest statement, outside her fiction, on the subject—seem to agree on the asphyxiating effects of the predicament in which women of their time invariably found themselves. "Her restricted impression, her confinement to the four walls of the home," Gilman observes, "have done great execution, of course, in limiting her ideas, her information, her thought-processes, and power of judgment[,] and in giving a disproportionate prominence and intensity to the few things she knows about," from which she concludes that "[t]his condition tends to magnify the personal and minimize the general in our minds," much as Wharton declares, "No matter how intelligent women are individually, they tend, collectively, to narrow down their interests, and take a feminine, or even a female, rather than a broadly human view of things" (*WE* 65–66, 83; *FWM* 119). Attacking "the reduction in voluntary activity to which the human female has been subjected," and arguing that "[a]ll . . . human progress has been accomplished by men," while "[w]omen have been left behind, outside, below, having no social relation whatever," Gilman draws a distinction between "[t]he absolutely stationary female and the wide-ranging male," which is not all that far from the one drawn by Wharton: "The woman whose mind is attuned to men's minds has a much larger view of the world, and attaches much less important to trifles, because men, being usually brought by circumstances into closer contact with reality, insensibly communicate their breadth of view to women" (*WE* 65, 74, 65; *FWM* 119).

If anything, Wharton may be said to have advocated a greater degree of parity along such lines no less strenuously than Gilman, who could have had little with which to quarrel in a passage that finds the novelist at her most expansive on the benefits of transcending a restrictive domesticity. "The more civilized a society is," according to Wharton, "the wider is the range of each woman's influence over men, and of each man's influence over women. Intelligent and cultivated people of either sex will never limit themselves to communing with their own households. Men and women equally, when they have the range of interests that real cultivation gives, need the stimulus of different points of view, the refreshment of new ideas as well as of new faces" (*FWM* 112). Her opposition to "[t]he long hypocrisy which Puritan England handed on to America concerning the danger of frank and free social relations between men and women" (*FWM* 112) places Wharton in close sympathy with what Gilman calls "[t]he demand for a wider and freer social intercourse between the sexes" and "[f]or women as individuals to meet men and other women as individuals, with no regard whatever to the family relation," even though "its right development is greatly impeded by the clinging folds of domestic and social customs" (*WE* 296, 295–96). Wharton herself found a model of this "freer" mingling in an institution like the French *salon,* "based on the belief that the most stimulating conversation in the world is that between intelligent men and women who see each other often enough to be on terms of frank and easy friendship" (*FWM* 117).

From other passages, however, it becomes clear that such exemplary gatherings in France owed their strength, in Wharton's eyes, to precisely the sort of imbalance that needed to be completely redressed as far as critics like Gilman were concerned. "In circles where interesting and entertaining men are habitually present," Wharton observes, without demur, "the women are not expected to talk much," and "above all they are not to air their views in the presence of men worth listening to," men whose talk is aided by "the rare quality of the Frenchwoman's listening," a trait on which she later notoriously elaborated: "This power of absorbed and intelligent attention is one of the Frenchwoman's greatest gifts, and makes a perfect background for the talk of the men" (*FWM* 24, 25; *BG* 274). Such remarks, along with the more general corollary that "[w]omen (if they only knew it!) are generally far more intelligent listeners than talkers," or that "intelligent women will never talk together when they can talk to men, or even listen to them" (*FWM* 25, 26), should dissolve any superficial concordance one might detect between her views on the "woman question" and Gilman's, which become even harder to reconcile with certain accompanying presuppositions warmly endorsed by the novelist. In another of their virtues, according to Wharton, "the French have always recognised that, as a social factor, a woman does not count until she is married" (*FWM* 116), implicitly ratifying what Gilman calls "the enforced attitude of the woman toward marriage" whereby, in a famous passage, "all that she may wish to have, all that she may wish to do, must come through a single channel and a single choice. Wealth, power, social distinction, fame,—not only these, but home and happiness, reputation, ease and pleasure, her bread and butter,—all, must come to her through a small gold ring" (*WE* 86, 71). It would not have occurred to Wharton to assert, as Gilman does, that "[w]oman has been checked, starved, aborted in human growth" (*WE* 75) through the institution of marriage and its confinement of one sex to the domestic sphere; on the contrary, as far as Wharton is concerned, "Marriage, union with a man, completes and transforms a woman's character, her point of view, her sense of the relative importance of things. . . . A girl is only a sketch; a married woman is the finished picture" (*FWM* 114–15).

In any event, the alternative envisioned by Gilman, who predicts that "as men and women move freely together in the exercise of common racial functions, . . . we shall live in a world of men and women humanly related, . . . working together, as they were meant to do, for the common good of all" (*WE* 313), would have been anathema to Wharton, whose preference in this regard may be discerned in her characterization of marriage in France, and in her claim that "the Frenchwoman of the middle class is her husband's business partner" (*FWM* 105). Although "[t]he French wife has less legal independence," as she acknowledges, "than the American or English wife, and is subject to a good many legal disqualifications from which women have freed themselves in other countries," such constraints turn out to be negligible, for "the Frenchwoman has gone straight through these theoretical restrictions to the heart of reality, and become her husband's associate, because, for her children's sake if not for her own, her heart is in his job" (*FWM* 105–6), which thus becomes hers as well, whatever it might be. "In small businesses," for example, "the woman is always her husband's bookkeeper or clerk, or both; above all, she is his business adviser" (*FWM* 103). Such an argument would have struck Gilman as disingenuous at best, a version of "the commonly received opinion," as she puts it, "that, although it must be admitted that men make and distribute the wealth of the world, yet women earn their share of it as wives" and that "assumes either that the husband is in the position of employer and the wife as employee, or that marriage is a 'partnership,' and the wife an equal factor with the husband in producing wealth" (*WE* 10). For Gilman, as for Wharton, "Man and wife are partners truly in their mutual obligation to their children" and in "their common love, duty, and service"; Gilman adds, however, that "a manufacturer who marries, or a doctor, or a lawyer, does not take a partner in his business, when he takes a partner in parenthood, unless his wife is also a manufacturer, a doctor, or a lawyer. . . . She is in no sense a business partner, unless she contributes capital or experience or labor, as a man would in like relation" (*WE* 12). Although the French businessman's wife, in Wharton's account, makes just such a contribution, she does so in what for Gilman would have amounted to merely an extension of the unremunerated household labor that "enables men to produce more wealth than they otherwise could" (*WE* 13).[22]

Indeed, Wharton herself concedes as much in observing that the middle-class Frenchwoman's husband "has long since learned that the best business partner a man can have is one who has the same interests at stake as himself. It is not only because she saves him a salesman's salary, or a book-keeper's salary, or both, that the French tradesman associates his wife with his business; it is because he has the sense to see that no hired assistant will have so keen a perception of his interests" (*FWM* 106). The supposition that "[t]here is no drudgery in this kind of partnership, because it is voluntary, and because each partner is stimulated by exactly the same aspirations" (*FWM* 106), would have made little difference to Gilman's hard-nosed, unromanticizing sense of this aspect of the relations between husband and wife. "If she likes the work, does it satisfactorily, and is willing to do it," Gilman once proposed, "let them settle it upon that basis, honestly, at market rates," while "if she would rather work for him without pay, than do some other work for pay, then they should face the condition honestly, and he should admit that she contributes to their common establishment five dollars a week in labor; that she is entitled to that much, even though she does not get it; that he owes to her. . . . Let him count up the weeks that they have been married, what she has earned in that time above what she has received, and feel a new sense of their business relation."[23] It would be hard to imagine such an adjustment on the part of Wharton's representative middle-class French couple, much less the option that Gilman dramatizes in the aptly named story "A Partnership" (1914). A housewife who "had always held the pleasant theory that marriage was a partnership" in which "she had done her part . . . as faithfully as Mr. Haven had paid the bills," Maggie Haven is left with nothing to do after their children's departure while "his business went right on" (*YW* 253, 254), and she proceeds to start a bread-baking enterprise so successful that her husband soon offers to serve as *her* business manager. In a complete inversion of the marital ideal underlying Wharton's claim that "it is this practical, personal and daily participation in her husband's job that makes the Frenchwoman more grown up than others" (*FWM* 106), such an arrangement leads the wife along a rather different path to maturity: "Best of all, if she concludes that she can earn more by some other work she likes better, she ceases to be her husband's employee, and becomes a business partner as well as a

parental one, earning her share, contributing her share, glorying in a
new sense of independence and equality" ("BSM" 9).

For Wharton, there is something chimerical and illusory about this
sort of exultation. "Compared with the women of France," she main-
tains, "the average American woman is still in the kindergarten," while
it would appear to be precisely the sort of activist reformer epitomized
by Gilman whom Wharton has in mind when defending her impulse
"to compare the American woman's independent and resonant activities—her 'boards' and clubs and sororities, her public investigation of
everything under the heavens from 'the social evil' to baking-powder,
and from 'physical culture' to the newest esoteric religion—to compare
such free and busy and seemingly influential lives with the artless exercises of an infant class" (*FWM* 101). Accordingly, whereas Gilman declared that "[t]he woman's club movement is one of the most
important sociological phenomena of the century" (*WE* 164), Wharton
memorably burlesqued women's clubs and their pursuits throughout
her fiction. Indeed, she seldom displayed an inclination to address the
"woman question" itself, or any of the issues that so agitated Gilman
regarding the situation of women in their time. When the editor of the
Yale Review solicited "an article on the problem of feminism which goes
beneath the surface," for example, her secretary replied that Wharton
"cannot write the article" in part because "she does not feel prepared
to deal with the question that you suggest."[24] Over a decade later, she
declined more caustically another magazine editor's invitation "to write
an essay on the question 'Women: Have They Got What They
Want?' "[25] An especially dispiriting sense of the gulf separating her
from someone like Gilman may be derived from another letter in which
Wharton unequivocally declared that she was "not much interested in
travelling scholarships for women . . .—they'd much better stay at
home and mind the baby."[26] Given such an antagonistic posture, along
with the male-oriented consciousness pervading so much of her work
(to say nothing of her well-documented preference for the company of
men), "We can be sure," as Mary Suzanne Schriber drily notes, "that
Edith Wharton would have been as unhappy to be relegated to Charlotte Perkins Gilman's *Herland* as would Twain to John Bunyan's
heaven."[27]

Thus, the lines dividing Gilman from Wharton could not be drawn
more graphically and starkly, and the figures who have re-emerged as
the two leading American literary women of their generation turn out
to be almost complementary opposites, aligning themselves on the
spectrum of opinion and attitude about as far from each other as possible. Their admirers, and American literary historians generally, will find
it sobering to contemplate the fact that these twin pillars of early-twen-

tieth-century writing by American women should have had so little to say about each other and taken virtually no notice, it seems, of each other's accomplishment. Is there no way to bridge the evidently insurmountable temperamental, ideological, and programmatic differences between them? Or are we to conclude that Gilman and Wharton generate two parallel or asymptotic lines of literary descent? Or, does this mutual avoidance or indifference encourage yet another of those traditional, convenient dichotomies (Tolstoy or Dostoyevski? Kafka or Thomas Mann? Camus or Sartre? aestheticism vs. "engagement"?) still not uncommon in the conceptualization of literary history, thus ironically duplicating what many would regard as a fundamentally male gesture of critical polarization?

Some initially attractive points of conjunction come to mind without offering much of a way, however, out of the impasse in which two such discordant figures apparently leave us. For example, Zona Gale, the novelist who contributed a preface to *The Living* and whose friendship with Gilman almost exactly coincided with the little-known correspondence that she and Wharton started conducting in 1922, somehow fails to mention either of them anywhere in her remarks to or about the other.[28] A more substantial possibility revolves around "Vernon Lee," the prolific art critic, novelist, and aesthetician who received a visit from Gilman in Tuscany in 1904, only a year and a half after escorting Wharton on the tour that resulted in the publication of *Italian Villas and Their Gardens.* Two years earlier, moreover, she had provided the Italian translation of *Women and Economics* with a lengthy and enthusiastic introduction that appeared in English in the same issue of the *North American Review,* as Katherine Joslin observes, as Wharton's first extensive piece of critical writing, an essay on three dramatic adaptations of the Paolo and Francesca episode from the fifth canto of Dante's *Inferno.*[29] Also in 1902, Lee published a review of *The Valley of Decision,* a historical novel that was not only Wharton's first longer work of fiction but also the one occasion on which, in William Vance's words, "she attempted to imagine an intellectual woman engaged in radical politics who might nevertheless by sympathetic."[30] Strangely, however, Lee's review never mentions that character, who is accidentally and abruptly murdered, even so, just after she succeeds in completing her doctoral oration. In any event, one finds no evidence elsewhere in Wharton's writing to corroborate the additional surmise that "her friendship with Vernon Lee . . . may well have led her to the work of Charlotte Perkins Gilman."[31]

As it turns out, the source of perhaps the most fruitful rapprochement is even more remote, originating in the person of one of Wharton's closest Parisian friends, Jean du Breuil de Saint-Germain, an essayist and social commentator who took an urgent interest in women's issues throughout the waning years of the *belle époque*. The presiding spirit of an organization constituted by an influential group of French male suffragists in 1910, du Breuil is now a forgotten, practically irretrievable figure, seldom if ever mentioned even by historians in France.[32] Eulogizing him in 1915, Wharton cites two of Breuil's relevant essays, "Suffrage and the Social Misery of Women" (1911) and "On the Interest of Men in Women's Suffrage" (1913), both published partly under the auspices of the Union of Frenchwomen for Women's Suffrage (UFSF), a moderate national suffragist league whose founder, the redoubtable activist Jeanne Schmahl, had written to Gilman in 1899 proposing to prepare a translation of *Women and Economics* and edited for over a decade one of the leading French feminist journals of the time, *Avant-Courrière* (literally, "The Forerunner"). Schmahl's interest in Gilman, whose authority she cites in her own writing on "l'émancipation économique" of women,[33] offers more than a hint of Gilman's French reception not long before Wharton moved to Paris in 1907. Her interest also makes it all the more difficult to believe that du Breuil—who was fluent and widely read in English and who once addressed the International Woman's Franchise Club in London—would not have been aware of Gilman's work by the time he composed the two essays cited by Wharton.

As evidence of what she calls a "constant disdain for popularity" on du Breuil's part, Wharton dwells at length on "the devotion with which he served the feminist cause" and on the "reasons . . . that Jean du Breuil asks that women be enfranchised in France: it is because there are, in this beautiful country 'where they always talk of women's grace and charm, and never of their rights,' several million women, widowed or single, who depend solely on themselves." Applauding him for having "understood that the only practical way to come to [their] aid was to obtain for [them] the right to vote," Wharton offers a remarkable concession in a passage likely to astonish even those readers extensively familiar with her work:

> It is Jean du Breuil who opened my eyes to a question of which—I admit it to my shame—I had not until then understood the immense social implications. In a few words, he made me see that the only thing that matters, in the feminist movement, is the fate of those women, . . . those poor hard-working women who accept their long misery with an animal fatalism because they do not know that they have a right to a more humane existence. In short, one would be tempted to say that women who argue for the right to vote could very well do without it, but it is necessary for those women, so much more numerous, who do not even know what it is, or why others are demanding it in their name! (*UCW* 200–201)

Apart from the peculiarity of considering enfranchisement dispensable in the lives of its advocates, nothing in such an argument would have seemed invalid to Gilman, who so frequently subordinated the question of suffrage to the sorts of issues raised in Wharton's essay on du Breuil, and who once recalled that "the suffragists thought me a doubtful if not dangerous ally on account of my theory of the need of economic independence of women" (*L* 198).

Here, if anywhere, lies a significant area of kinship with Wharton, whose heroines had already dramatized the economic uncertainties and terrors that du Breuil deplored and that Gilman made such a dominant theme of her own writing about women as well. And their underlying affinity in this regard places Gilman and Wharton in genuine conversation with each other on a basis that should considerably facilitate the ongoing effort to re-orient an American feminist critical tradition habitually inattentive to issues of class. Unlike Gilman's, to be sure, Wharton's financially straitened women achieve stasis at best or capitulate and decline, while apart from unfortunate exceptions like Gerty Farish, the stereotypically drab social worker in *The House of Mirth* (1905), Wharton seems to have been imaginatively incapable of portraying the sort of woman who, in Gilman, manages to find salvation in recuperative and rewarding work. Even more than Gilman, however, this far more tightly class-bound novelist was able to acknowledge the reality of economic dependence in the lives of impoverished and leisured women alike and to endow several protagonists (from Lily Bart to Bessy Westmore to Undine Spragg), as more than one scholar has noted, with the sort of "parasitism" that Gilman decried and that Vernon Lee emphasized in her consideration of *Women and Economics*.[34] Accused by Mr. Westmore of being "still imprisoned in the old formulas," even the conventional Mrs. Ansell, in *The Fruit of the Tree*, issues the sort of challenge that such a remark might have elicited from Gilman herself: "Isn't that precisely what Bessy is? Isn't she one of the most harrowing victims of the plan of bringing up our girls in the double bondage of expediency and unreality, corrupting their bodies with luxury and their brains with sentiment, and leaving them to reconcile the two as best they can, or lose their souls in the attempt?" (*FT* 281).

Perhaps nowhere, however, is their consensus on such a state of affairs more powerfully evident than in *The Custom of the Country* (1913), begun shortly after Wharton had moved to France, and laboriously written during a five-year period largely overlapping her friendship with du Breuil. As she follows its heroine's pathologically acquisitive and opportunistic career, her novel becomes virtually an extended meditation on what Gilman called "the training of women as non-productive consumers," capturing in Undine's antics and in her effect on those closest to her "a world torn and dissevered," in Gilman's words, "by the selfish production of one sex and the selfish consumption of the other" (*WE* 227, 313). With such a formulation in mind, one begins to hear a more than faintly Gilmanesque note in the words, say, of Charles Bowen, the wry, sardonic observer who considers the peculiarities of Undine's marriage with Ralph Marvell in attempting "a general view of the whole problem of American marriages."[35] Contemplating the American businessman's chronic neglect of his wife ("How much does he rely on her judgment and help in the conduct of serious affairs? . . . Why haven't we taught our women to take an interest in our work?"), Bowen at first seems merely to anticipate Wharton's own remarks on the dubious "partnership" at work in French marriages of the commercial class: "Why does the European woman interest herself so much more in what the men are doing? Because she's so important to them that they make it worth her while! She's not a parenthesis, as she is here—she's in the very middle of the picture" (*C* 206, 207). When he asks more generally about the American woman's husband, "How much does he let her share in the real business of life?" (*C* 206), Bowen's insight, however, becomes more probing, as he illuminates "the custom of the country" that governed the predicament even of economically secure American women at the time by offering an explanation almost worthy of Gilman's incisiveness and wit: "All my sympathy's with them, poor deluded dears, when I see their fallacious little attempts to trick out the leavings tossed them by the preoccupied male— the money and the motors and the clothes—and pretend to themselves and each other that *that's* what really constitutes life! Oh, I know what you're going to say—it's less and less of a pretense with them, I grant you; they're more and more succumbing to the force of suggestion; but here and there I fancy there's one who still sees through the humbug, and knows that money and motors and clothes are simply the big bribe she's paid for keeping out of some man's way!" (*C* 208).

NOTES

1. Charlotte Perkins Gilman, "Exchanges and Others," *Impress* 1 (January 1894): 2.

2. Edith Wharton, "The Fullness of Life," in *The Collected Short Stories of Edith Wharton,* 2 vols. (New York: Scribner's, 1968), 1 : 12. Hereafter referred to in the text as *CS.*

3. Edith Wharton, *The Letters of Edith Wharton,* ed. R. W. B. Lewis and Nancy Lewis (New York: Macmillan, 1988), 36. Hereafter referred to in the text as *LEW.*

4. "Edith Wharton still holds her high place in American letters," Gilman remarked over thirty years later, also acknowledging the work of at least a dozen other novelists,

however, including such quickly forgotten writers as Ann Parish, Martha Ostenso, and Anne Douglas Sedgwick ("Woman's Achievements Since the Franchise," *Current History* 27 [October 1927]: 12–13).

5. Edith Wharton, *A Backward Glance* (New York: Appleton, 1934), 43 (hereafter referred to in the text as *BG*); Charlotte Perkins Gilman, *The Living of Charlotte Perkins Gilman* (New York: Appleton, 1935), 36 (hereafter referred to in the text as *L*).

6. Edith Wharton, "Life and I," in *Novellas and Other Writings* (New York: Library of America, 1990), 1080, 1074. Hereafter referred to in the text as *N*.

7. Regarding its role in their experience, and in that of other women among their contemporaries, see, for example, Suzanne Poirier, "The Weir Mitchell Rest Cure: Doctors and Patients," *Women's Studies* 10 (1983): 15–40. For a discussion based on this biographical coincidence (arguing that "Gilman and Wharton found that writing could be curative, whether they had consciously undertaken it as therapy or not," and that, "By writing, Gilman and Wharton produced irrefutable evidence of their changed position from invalid women to writers"), see Diane Price Herndl, *Invalid Women: Figuring Feminine Illness in American Fiction and Culture, 1840–1940* (Chapel Hill: University of North Carolina Press, 1993), 123–49. The received wisdom regarding the exact nature of Wharton's treatment, however, has been vigorously disputed in Shari Benstock, *No Gifts From Chance: A Biography of Edith Wharton* (New York: Scribner's, 1994), 93–96.

8. Edith Wharton, "A Little Girl's New York," in *Edith Wharton: The Uncollected Critical Writings,* ed. Frederick Wegener (Princeton: Princeton University Press, 1996), 282. Hereafter referred to in the text as *UCW*.

9. As it turns out, however, the New York of Wharton's youth was not entirely unknown to Gilman, who spent several months as a young girl "[i]n a New York boarding-house, for description of which see Henry Alden's *Old New York*—he even mentions 'little Charlotte Perkins,' " and where she remembered repeatedly antagonizing "Mrs. Swift, the landlady," with her brother (*L* 15). "[A] most comfortable boarding-house, kept by that comfortable woman, Miss Anne Swift," according to New York journalist William Livingston Alden (who appears to be the source Gilman has in mind here), "the tall yellow brick house on the northeast corner of Tenth Street and Fourth Avenue might fairly have been called one of the literary centres of New York" at the time, home to Richard Henry Stoddard, Edmund Clarence Stedman, Bayard Taylor, and other avatars of the genteel belletristic culture of Wharton's old New York. Among its habitués, in Alden's account, "Fred Perkins, as every one called him, did not live at the Swift house, but his wife and two children boarded in the house," including "[h]is little daughter Charlotte." See W. L. Alden, "Some Phases of Literary New York in the Sixties," *Putnam's Monthly* 3 (February 1908): 554, 555–56.

10. Charlotte Perkins Gilman, *Women and Economics* (Boston: Small, Maynard, 1898), 323. Hereafter referred to in the text as *WE*.

11. Her own attempt at such a novel, *The Fruit of the Tree* (1907), adopts a distinctly Gilmanesque idiom, in fact, in its depiction of John Amherst, assistant manager at a wretched textile factory in a New England mill-town, and an impassioned reformist whose visions reflect "that yearning to help the world forward that, in some natures, sets the measure to which the personal adventure must keep step." Amherst's many unorthodox "scheme[s] of social readjustment" include "a night-school for the boys in the mills" and well as "the establishing of a library, a dispensary and emergency hospital, and various other centres of humanizing influence," which have precisely the sort of effects that Gilman might have foreseen: "Westmore prospered under the new rule. The seeds of life they had sown there were springing up in a promising growth of bodily health and mental activity, and above all in a dawning social consciousness. . . .

And outwardly, also, the new growth was showing itself in the humanized aspect of the place" (Edith Wharton, *The Fruit of the Tree* [New York: Scribner's, 1907], 94, 48, 110, 118–19, 621; hereafter referred to in the text as *FT*).

12. Charlotte Perkins Gilman, *The Home: Its Work and Influence* (Chicago: McClure, Phillips, 1903), 156. Hereafter referred to in the text as *H*.

13. Edith Wharton and Ogden Codman, Jr., *The Decoration of Houses* (New York: Scribner's, 1897), 174. Hereafter referred to in the text as *DH*.

14. Edith Wharton, "Talk to American Soldiers," Edith Wharton Collection, Beinecke Rare Book and Manuscript Library, Yale University, 1. (Quoted with the kind permission of the Estate of Edith Wharton and the Watkins/Loomis Agency.)

15. Charlotte Perkins Gilman, "Public Library Motion Pictures," *Annals of the American Academy* 128 (November 1926): 143, 144.

16. Charlotte Perkins Gilman, "The Automobile as a Reformer," *Saturday Evening Post,* 3 June 1899: 778; Edith Wharton, *A Motor-Flight Through France* (New York: Scribner's, 1908), 1.

17. Edith Wharton, *Italian Villas and Their Gardens* (New York: Century, 1904), 5, 7, 6, 8.

18. Charlotte Perkins Gilman, *The Yellow Wallpaper, and Other Stories,* ed. Robert Shulman (Oxford: Oxford University Press, 1995), 233 (hereafter referred to in the text as *YW*); Edith Wharton, *French Ways and Their Meaning* (New York: Appleton, 1919), 101 (hereafter referred to in the text as *FWM*).

19. Regarding eugenics, perhaps the one issue on which current readers are likely to find her views more agreeable, Wharton has been somewhat hyperbolically commended at Gilman's expense (and in defiance of her reactionary stance on most other social issues); see Dale M. Bauer, *Edith Wharton's Brave New Politics* (Madison: University of Wisconsin Press, 1994), 50, 116–18, 171.

20. "In varying fields of work," as she observes, "there is a strong current of improvement, in household construction, furnishing, and decoration. . . . Whole magazines are devoted to this end, articles unnumbered, books not a few, and courses of lectures" (*H* 143).

21. Its blindspots in this regard thus go well beyond the fact, as Judith Fryer notes, that Wharton's study contains "chapters on boudoirs, drawing-rooms and libraries but no mention of the kitchen," whereas "[t]he kitchen was . . . the focus of Charlotte Perkins Gilman's criticism of bourgeois domestic life" (*Felicitous Space: The Imaginative Structures of Edith Wharton and Willa Cather* [Chapel Hill: University of North Carolina Press, 1986], 35). Inasmuch as the "kitchenless" home constituted one of her chief domestic renovations, Gilman would have found such an oversight, ironically, among the least of Wharton's sins in *The Decoration of Houses.*

22. On such grounds, it seems implausible to argue that Wharton "approved the French expectation that a middle-class woman will be her husband's business partner" as sanctioning "a role which allowed her to be influential outside the merely domestic sphere" or as one of "many ways French women seemed to Wharton to be more emancipated than Anglo-Saxon women" (Margaret B. McDowell, "Viewing The Custom of Her Country: Edith Wharton's Feminism," *Contemporary Literature* 15 [1974]: 526). According to a more cogent analysis of her position, "the husband-wife partnership Wharton describes is one that is really dictated by the husband," in which "the wife begins to emerge not as equal (surely implied in the very term 'partner') but as unpaid employee." If anything, "in an era in which Engles [*sic*] in Europe and feminists like Charlotte Perkins Gilman in the United States had argued the nearness of marriage to prostitution, . . . Wharton's view of the unpaid labor of these wives seems either remarkably naive or consciously conservative. Indeed, Wharton goes to the opposite ex-

treme in the argument about women and economics, celebrating the fact that French wives go unpaid for their work." In the light of these nuances and incongruities, far from "constitut[ing] a feminist statement," according to this analysis, "Wharton's argument in *French Ways and Their Meaning* . . . suggests Wharton's unstated belief in the fundamental inferiority of women. Although the Frenchwoman may be, as she claims, the Frenchman's 'partner,' in no way do Wharton's examples of this partnership suggest that it is an equal one." (See Julie Olin-Ammentorp, "Wharton's View of Woman in *French Ways and Their Meaning*," *Edith Wharton Review* 9 [Fall 1992]: 16, 15.) Her recalcitrance along such lines obviously complicates the already difficult search for a critical consensus on Wharton's work, which will seem less assimilable than ever to any feminist paradigm when reconsidered in the light of Gilman's example.

23. Charlotte Perkins Gilman, "The Business Side of Matrimony," *Physical Culture* 31 (January 1914): 8, 9. Hereafter referred to in the text as "BSM."

24. Wilbur Cross to Edith Wharton, 28 October 1912, and Edith Wharton to Cross, 15 November 1912 (Beinecke Rare Book and Manuscript Library, Yale University). Quoted with the kind permission of the Yale Review and of the Estate of Edith Wharton and the Watkins/Loomis Agency.

25. Benstock, *No Gifts From Chance*, 265.

26. Quoted in Benstock, *No Gifts From Chance*, 387.

27. Mary Suzanne Schriber, *Gender and the Writer's Imagination: From Cooper to Wharton* (Lexington: University Press of Kentucky, 1987), 182.

28. Revealingly, despite this intersection, Gilman's name is not mentioned in Deborah William's otherwise informative "Threats of Correspondence: The Letters of Edith Wharton, Zona Gale, and Willa Cather," *Studies in American Fiction* 25 (Autumn 1997): 211–39.

29. Vernon Lee, "The Economic Dependence of Women," *North American Review* 175 (July 1902): 71–90. Joslin identifies the text as "Vernon Lee's review of Charlotte Perkins Gilman's *Women and Economics,* a book for which Lee had also written the introduction" (*Edith Wharton* [New York: St. Martin's, 1991], 55); that the two are one and the same, however, is clear from Lee's own reference to "this preface for a translation of Mrs. Stetson's 'Women and Economics' " in reprinting the *North American Review* essay, under the title "The Economic Parasitism of Women," in *The Gospels of Anarchy, and Other Contemporary Studies* (1908). As Joslin suggests, "We can reasonably assume Wharton read the review (she had even referred to Lee in her own article)," but it is "The Three Francescas," the essay accompanying Lee's text in the *North American Review,* that contains Wharton's aforementioned quip about "sentimental modern altruists," among other remarks on which Gilman would not have smiled.

30. William L. Vance, *"The Valley of Decision*: Edith Wharton's Italian Mask," in *The Cambridge Companion to Edith Wharton,* ed. Millicent Bell (Cambridge: Cambridge University Press, 1995), 187.

31. Joslin, *Edith Wharton,* 54.

32. For a rare, albeit brief, reference to du Breuil, see Steven C. Hause, with Anne R. Kenney, *Women's Suffrage and Social Politics in the French Third Republic* (Princeton: Princeton University Press, 1984), 156.

33. "Partout, à mesure que l'émancipation économique de la femme se confirme, la conviction s'impose qu'il est impossible de continuer dans le désordre domestique où nous sommes et que pour y remédier, il faut—comme le démontre si bien Mme Stetson—nous résoudre à perdre nos cuisines, comme nous avons perdu nos boulangeries et nos buanderies [Everywhere, to the extent that the economic emancipation of woman is confirmed, one cannot escape the conviction that it is impossible to maintain the domestic disorder in which we live and that in order to remedy it, we must—as

demonstrated so well by Mme. Stetson—resolve to discard our kitchens, as we have discarded our bakeries and laundries]"; Jeanne E. Schmahl, *Économique domestique* (Paris: Lamy, 1902), 20.

34. On *The House of Mirth,* for example, with reference to Gilman in this context, see Joslin, *Edith Wharton,* 49–50, 55, 57–58, 69. Some germane remarks on *The Fruit of the Tree* in connection with Gilman may be found in Janet Goodwyn, *Edith Wharton: Traveller in the Land of Letters* (New York: St. Martin's Press, 1990), 69–70. Treating Gilman as one of the "pioneers" who "studied the economics of marriage for women and . . . whose work helps set the stage for Wharton's treatment of the subject," Elizabeth Ammons observes that "her anatomy of the connection between marriage and femininity has much in common with Wharton's" and draws brief but suggestive parallels between Gilman's work and the dramatic situation in novels like *The Reef* (1912), *The Custom of the Country* (1913), and *The Age of Innocence* (1920); see *Edith Wharton's Argument with America* (Athens: University of Georgia Press, 1980), 27–28, 77–78, 100–101, 149.

35. Edith Wharton, *The Custom of the Country* (New York: Scribner's, 1913), 205. Hereafter referred to in the text as *C.*

Paper Mates: The Sisterhood of Charlotte Perkins Gilman and Edith Summers Kelley

CHARLOTTE MARGOLIS GOODMAN

SINCE THE INITIAL PUBLICATION OF CHARLOTTE PERKINS GILMAN'S "THE Yellow Wall-Paper" in 1892, Gilman has been compared, among other writers, to Edgar Allan Poe, Nathaniel Hawthorne, Charlotte Brontë, Olive Schreiner, Kate Chopin, Susan Glaspell, Edith Wharton, and Owen Wister. There is yet another writer with whom it is instructive to compare Gilman: Edith Summers Kelley, whose 1923 novel *Weeds,* about a poor Kentucky tobacco farmer's wife, was reissued by The Feminist Press, as was Gilman's chilling tale of female entrapment, "The Yellow Wall-Paper." Not only are there important biographical links between Gilman and Kelley but thematic ones as well. Moreover, a reconsideration of "The Yellow Wall-Paper" in light of Kelley's working-class novel can also serve to heighten the reader's awareness of significant issues concerning class that are implicit in Gilman's story.

Despite the growing reputation of *Weeds,* Kelley to date remains a far more obscure literary figure than Gilman. Born in Toronto in 1884, Kelley moved to New York City in 1903 after graduating from the University of Toronto. Hoping to establish herself as a writer, she settled in Greenwich Village, a milieu where the socialist and feminist ideas of such reformers as Crystal Eastman, Margaret Sanger, Mary Heaton Vorse, and Charlotte Perkins Gilman were then being debated by Village intellectuals. Subsequently, when Kelley was hired to serve as secretary to muckraking novelist Upton Sinclair, she had the opportunity to meet some of the celebrated thinkers of the day, particularly during 1905–6, when she joined Sinclair at the experimental cooperative community, Helicon Hall, which he had founded in New Jersey with the thirty thousand dollars he had earned from his novel, *The Jungle.* Among the more than forty members of Sinclair's community were a number of women writers. Sinclair credited the inspiration for this colony to a 1904 article by Charlotte Perkins Gilman in which she had advocated cooperative housing that included day nurseries and centralized kitchens.[1]

160

Pertinent to a discussion of the relationship between Gilman and Kelley is the fact that one of several reformers who lectured at Helicon Hall while Kelley was serving as Sinclair's secretary was Charlotte Perkins Gilman herself. An interesting connection between Gilman and Helicon Hall worth noting is that Gilman's subsequent description in her utopian novel *Moving the Mountain* of a group of apartments built for professional women bears a striking similarity to Helicon Hall, which was located on the premises of a former boys' boarding school. As Gilman notes in *Moving the Mountain,* in addition to providing day nurseries for children, the professional women's apartment buildings also had big rooms for meetings and parties, a billiard room, a bowling alley, and a swimming pool, all of which made this place resemble a well-appointed summer hotel.[2]

The short-lived Helicon Hall, unfortunately, was destroyed by fire on 14 March 1907. In a memoir Kelley wrote about her experience there, she lauded especially its communal kitchen and its nursery for the children, important features of Upton Sinclair's experimental community as well as of the communities Gilman advocated in her utopian fiction, *Women and Economics,* and her frequent public lectures. Kelley observed that because of its centralized kitchen and nursery, mothers at Helicon Hall could eat their meals in peace and converse freely with the adults, while their children enjoyed the company of other children and learned how to get along with their peers. "How many a harassed mother," she said, "has sighed in vain for just such an arrangement as that." Although she admitted that there was "not always perfect peace and harmony" at Helicon Hall, she nevertheless described Sinclair's community as "one of the beauty spots of the past" for her and for the others who had shared that experience.[3]

After the Helicon Hall fire, Edith Summers Kelley resumed her life in New York, began to publish short stories in women's magazines, married, and had two children. Following a divorce in 1913, she spent a brief period working on a Kentucky tobacco farm with C. Fred Kelley, the father of her third child and the man with whom she was to live for the remainder of her life. Kentucky later served as the setting for her novel *Weeds,* which she wrote when she moved with Kelley and her three children to California in 1920. There she and Kelley tried their hand first at farming and then at raising chickens. When these ventures proved unsuccessful, Fred Kelley took a job in a slaughterhouse while Edith tended to the house and the three children, sewed the family's clothing, milked the cow, raised and canned vegetables, and during the hours when the children were in school, completed the manuscript of *Weeds* and also a posthumously published second novel, *The Devil's Hand.* Her roles as wife, mother of three active children, and writer no doubt made her long for a more supportive environment like the one the writer-mothers had encountered at Helicon Hall. Seeking an advance from her publisher Alfred Harcourt to complete an essential revision of *Weeds,* Edith Summers Kelley explained to him that these funds would allow her husband to quit his job and "be near at hand to keep the children out of the way." The ordeal of writing her novel with three small children underfoot, she said, was "a supreme effort" she felt incapable of repeating.[4]

There is no direct evidence that Edith Summers Kelley read either Gilman's fiction or her poetry. However, despite the fact that Kelley's *Weeds* is set in a far different socioeconomic environment from Gilman's literary works, I believe a case can be made for Gilman's influence on Kelley's novel. The experience of encountering Gilman at Helicon Hall and the knowledge that Upton Sinclair had endorsed some of Gilman's ideas might well have inspired Kelley to read Gilman's works and to include a number of Gilman's key ideas in her own fiction as well. Moreover, when "The Yellow Wall-Paper" was reissued in 1920 in *The Great Modern American Stories,* edited by William Dean Howells, Kelley, an avid reader, would have had easy access to the story by the celebrated writer and speaker whom she had met in the past and who for some years also had lived in California.

As a number of critics have pointed out, what we now might term a feminist subtext initially was not apprehended by readers of Gilman's "The Yellow Wall-Paper," who linked this story generically with the Gothic tales of Poe. Male reviewers of Kelley's *Weeds,* too, did not appreciate Kelley's feminist subtext, positioning this novel instead within the predominantly male literary traditions of American realism and naturalism as defined by writers such as Theodore Dreiser and Frank Norris. This was true of Joseph Wood Krutch, who reviewed *Weeds* in *The Nation* in 1923. Although Krutch described Kelley's novel about a woman "disappointed by life" as a "story of all women," he failed to comment on the distinctions Kelley is at pains to draw between the lot of the women in her novel and that of her male characters.[5] Nor did Matthew J. Bruccoli, who was responsible for the rediscovery of *Weeds* and its publication in 1972 by Southern Illinois University Press, mention the feminist issues that Kelley addresses in her novel.[6] However, when I first read *Weeds* in the 1970s, I noted a number of feminist elements in it and was struck by the parallels between this novel and other works by women, including "The Yellow Wall-Paper" and *The Awakening,* which I also was reading at that time. As Annette Kolodny, Judith Fetterley, and Jean E. Kennard all have observed, feminist scholarship during the last three decades has enabled us not only to read many works by women that had been neglected or forgotten, but to read those texts in new ways and to limn connections among the works of various women writers.[7] This was true of me when I juxtaposed the work of Gilman with that of Kelley and considered the way both writers focus on gender roles, the adverse reactions of some women to motherhood, female entrapment, and female depression. Moreover, in "The Yellow Wall-Paper" and *Weeds,* Gilman and Kelley, alike, explore the unhappy plight of would-be artists, Gilman's a writer and Kelley's a person with artistic talents, female protagonists whose biological destiny and the gender roles a patriarchal society assigned them do not allow them to perfect their respective crafts.

Gender roles are a central focus in the work both of Gilman and Kelley. From personal experience, these two writers were painfully aware of the ways in which obligatory housekeeping too often relegates women, no matter what their intellectual or creative gifts, to domestic servitude. As Gilman observed about women's unpaid household labor,

> It has been amusing heretofore to see how this least desirable of labors has been so innocently held to be woman's natural duty. It is woman, the dainty, the beautiful, the beloved wife and revered mother, who has by common consent been expected to do the chamber-work and scullery work of the world.[8]

Reflecting her negative feelings about the consignment of housework to women, Gilman inserted into the front of her diary for 1882 the following oath of Charles Walter Stetson, the man she would marry two years later: "I hereby take my solemn oath that I shall never in future years expect of my wife any culinary or housekeeping proficiency. She shall never be required, whatever the emergency, to D U S T."[9] Kelley describes a similar prenuptial agreement in "The Old House," a posthumously published short story about a woman portrait painter who insists that the writer to whom she is engaged sign a prenuptial agreement to share the housework equally with her. The female protagonist of "The Old House," however, becomes increasingly disaffected after she marries and discovers that the housework has now become *her* work.[10]

Gilman's poem "The Mother's Charge" could serve as a fitting epigraph for Kelley's *Weeds.* In Gilman's poem, a dying mother instructs her daughter on how to perform the daily household chores, listing such tasks as ironing, washing potatoes, sewing, carpet-sweeping, quilting, cleaning windows, and gardening.[11] These are the kind of chores about which Mrs. Pippinger, mother of Kelley's female protagonist, Judith, also instructs her daughters. Mrs. Pippinger dies after catching cold while hanging the clothes outdoors on a bitterly windy February day, her destiny akin to that of the mother in Gilman's poem, about whom Gilman writes in the bitter concluding couplet:

> She died, as all her mothers died before.
> Her daughter died in turn, and made one more.

Kelley suggests that Judith's fate, too, will replicate that of her mother: although Judith insists that she much prefers to work outdoors along-side her father and her brother Craw, "men's work" and "women's work" are clearly differentiated in this rural community. Gilman's observation in *Women and Economics* that woman has been "compelled," traditionally, "to work with her own hands, for nothing, in direct body-service to her own family" applies to Kelley's protagonist Judith Pippinger, who is expected to clean up after her father and brother and, after she marries, to perform all the domestic chores for her husband and growing brood of children.[12]

What makes the description of Judith's domestic life seem so authentic to the reader is the way that Kelley enumerates in minute detail the tedious chores that consume the life of Judith and the rest of the women who dwell in the surrounding shanties:

> Families must be fed after some fashion or other and dishes washed three time a day, three hundred and sixty-five days in the year. Babies must be fed and washed and dressed and "changed" and rocked when they cried and watched and kept out of mischief and danger. The endless wrangles among older children must be arbitrated in some way or other, if only by cuffing the ears of both contestants; and the equally endless complaints stilled by threats, promises, whatever lies a harassed mother could invent to quiet the fretful clamor of discontented childhood. Fires must be lighted and kept going as needed for cooking, no matter how great the heat. Cows must be milked and cream skimmed and butter churned. Hens must be fed and eggs gathered and the filth shoveled out of henhouses. Diapers must be washed, and grimy little drawers and rompers and stiff overalls and sweaty work shirts and grease-bespattered dresses and kitchen aprons and filthy, sour-smelling towels and socks stinking with the putridity of unwashed feet and all the other articles that go to make up a farm woman's family wash. Floors must be swept and scrubbed and stoves cleaned and a never ending war waged against the constant encroaches of dust, grease, stable manure, flies, spiders, rats, mice, ants and all the other breeders of filth that are continually at work in country households. These activities . . . made up the life of the women, a life that was virtually the same every day of the year, except when their help was needed in the field to set the tobacco or shuck corn, or when fruit canning, hog killing, or house cleaning crowded the routine.[13]

Using the term "kitchen motherhood" to describe the role of women like Kelley's Judith Pippinger,[14] Gilman quotes the lament of one such woman in her poem "The Housewife":

Food and the serving of food—that is my daylong care;
What and when we shall eat, what and how we shall wear;
Soiling and cleaning of things—that is my task in the main—
Soil them and clean them and soil them—soil them and clean them again.[15]

Kelley does not fail to describe the back-breaking work of the men as well as the women in the farming community of *Weeds,* but she does emphasize, as Gilman did, that men have more choices available to them than women do. Early in the novel Judith Pippinger complains how unfair it is that her brother doesn't have to take a turn washing dishes; instead, Kelley writes, he sits rocking by the stove, "safe and aloof in his masculinity" (27). Nor is Judith's husband Jerry willing to do the housework, even when Judith is bedridden with influenza. Arising from her sick bed after four days have elapsed, she is furious to discover that everything is "in a dreadful mess." Far from being contrite when accosted by his angry wife, her husband merely shrugs his shoulders and remarks, "Well, I don't lay claim to be no expert pot wrastler ner wet nurse neither" (222). Obliged to help Jerry with *his* work on hog-killing day, she is angry that she has no say in what part of the job will be assigned to her. When she confronts the stinking tub full of steaming pig guts that he and his friend have set down before her, she thinks bitterly that the men have tried "to foist upon her the only part of the job that was tedious and hateful" (240).

The unequal financial rewards given to women for their work is another aspect of women's situation that Kelley as well as Gilman emphasizes. When Judith is old enough to earn some money, she gets a job as a hired hand at a neighboring farm. However, as soon as she realizes how tedious the work assigned to her is and decides to quit, Kelley notes that Judith's employer, Aunt Eppie, is bitter because "they would now have to pay a male hired man four times what they had been paying Judith" (82). Kelley again emphasizes the disadvantageous economic position of women in a scene in which Judith observes her neighbor Hat Wolf picking geese feathers that bring Hat's husband a good price in the market. Incensed because it is her husband, not she, who profits economically from her work with the geese, Hat complains to Judith:

"Las' time we sold feathers, Luke he got holt o' the money and that's the last I ever seen of it. An it was me that raised 'em an'fed 'em an picked 'em an done every durn thing." (144)

Motherhood, as Catherine Golden has noted, is another central issue that Charlotte Perkins Gilman deals with in both her literary works and her theoretical essays.[16] Motherhood—and the feelings of depression and entrapment that it generates—is a major focus in Kelley's *Weeds* as well. Like a number of Gilman's female protagonists, Kelley's Judith is considered by some to be an "unnatural mother" because she adapts so poorly to this role. Judith does not succumb to madness, as do both the narrator of Gilman's best known fictional work "The Yellow Wall-Paper" and a minor character in *Weeds* who is taken away to an insane asylum after she almost throws her baby into the flames of a bonfire. Kelley's protagonist, however, is profoundly depressed by the inexorable demands that motherhood makes on her. In her story called "The Unnatural Mother," Gilman criticizes those members of the community that use the word "unnatural" to describe a mother who puts the welfare of other children above the welfare of her own daughter, and in "The Yellow Wall-Paper," she implies that her depressed narrator is considered "unnatural" as well when she turns the care of her infant over to another woman in her household. As the following passage from *Weeds* reveals, Kelley also evokes empathy for a mother others might consider "unnatural," using this very word in connection with Judith. Of Judith, dismayed when she realizes she is pregnant for the second time, Kelley writes:

> She felt that she had neither the courage nor the strength to go through with it all again, and so soon after the last time. Her flesh cringed at the thought and her spirit faltered. And when the child was born it was only the beginning. She loathed the thought of having to bring up another baby. The women who liked caring for babies could call her *unnatural* (emphasis added) if they liked. She wanted to be unnatural. She was glad she was unnatural. Their nature was not her nature and she was glad of it. (240)

Both the female protagonist of "The Yellow Wall-Paper" and Kelley's Judith try to prevent another pregnancy, Gilman's narrator by insisting that she wants to occupy a downstairs bedroom though it is too small for a second bed and has "no near room" for John, and Judith, for a time, by arranging for herself a pallet on the floor in order to avoid sleeping in the bed she had formerly shared with her husband.[17] Alluding to her protagonist's anxiety about the inevitable consequence of sleeping in the same bed as Jerry, Kelley observes that after conceiving a second child so soon after the first one, Judith grows "to hate . . . that strong male vitality of which she was becoming the victim."[18]

For both Gilman and Kelley's entrapped female protagonists, the natural world outside their dwellings beckons invitingly. Looking longingly out the window, Gilman's narrator sees a "*delicious* garden" (25), Kelley's Judith an adjacent ridge that "seemed endless, as she imagined the ocean might be" (240). In contrast to an imagined freedom that the natural world represents to these two young women, however, images of imprisonment abound in the two works, whether expressed by the barred windows of the former nursery that Gilman's narrator occupies or the dark, almost windowless shanty of Judith Pippinger Blackford that looks from the outside "like a weathered packing case into which some one had sawed at random two or three small holes" (243).

Another significant parallel between "The Yellow Wall-Paper" and *Weeds* is that both are also portraits of would-be artists. Just as Gilman's narrator refers repeatedly to her own writing, so Kelley refers throughout the novel to Judith's drawing: pictures of human beings or animals, "usually comic, satirical, or derisive," that Judith draws in childhood "on her slate, the desk, the seat, the floor, the back of the pinafore of the girl in front, any available space within her reach" (25), and pictures the adult Judith draws of "the view from the little kitchen window as it appeared from every position in the room" (161). For both female protagonists, paper is important, whether it is the paper on which they write or the paper covering the walls of their house. As Elizabeth Ammons has observed, Kelley, echoing Gilman's narrator's preoccupation with the wallpaper on the bedroom wall, also depicts Judith examining the newspapers she has used to paper the walls of her shack, finding in the stains the rain had made on them "pictures that beguiled the eye and inspired the imagination."[19] Both would-be artists are discouraged from pursuing their craft: Gilman's narrator says that she is forced to be "sly" about her writing, "or else meet with heavy opposition" (25); likewise, Judith's pictures are judged to be "not nice" by her teacher (26), "ugly" by her sister (211). The work of neither protagonist reaches an audience during the course of these narratives: Gilman's narrator hastens to hide her diary when her husband approaches, remarking, "He hates to have me write a word" (26); and Kelley's Judith stows in the "bottom drawer of the dresser" the small number of crayon drawings she has made on scrap paper.[20]

Equally as significant as the links between the two writers, however, are the ways in which they differ. As John N. Duvall reminds us in his discussion of intertextual relationships between William Faulkner and Toni Morrison, just as the work of a literary successor may be profitably compared to that of a predecessor, so the reverse can also occur, allowing the reader to observe aspects of the earlier work that otherwise might have been overlooked.[21] Duvall's remarks certainly would apply to Gilman and Kelley: a consideration of the intertextual relationship between Kelley's naturalistic novel about the life of a poor woman in a rural farming community and Gilman's Gothic tale about a doctor's wife can prompt us to contrast the class issues that are evident in these two works. According to Elaine R. Hedges, in recent years some critics have objected to assigning Gilman's highly visible story the "privileged status" of "an exemplary text and a feminist critical touchstone." Instead, no matter how compelling such critics find Gilman's tale, they see it as a work that also reflects the biases and limited point of view of its privileged, white, middle-class creator.[22] Along with such critics, I would argue that Gilman's narrator is not a universal woman but a privileged white woman who sees her own reflection replicated in the wallpaper. I can imagine Kelley reading Gilman's story and then mentally comparing the lot of Gilman's middle-class protagonist to the lives of those poor rural women she had observed in Kentucky and would describe in *Weeds*.

Looking backward at Gilman's narrator through the lens of Kelley's *Weeds* can be instructive, for such a view underscores crucial class differences as well as similarities between Kelley's protagonist and Gilman's. Compare, for example, the house Gilman's narrator and John rent for the summer, which is variously described as "ancestral halls," "a colonial mansion," and a "hereditary estate" (24), to Judith's "three bare, box-like rooms" (242); Gilman's rose-filled piazza to Judith's "rickety back porch floored with boards many of which had rotted away from the nails that once held them" (242). Like those splintered shacks and their tubercular, toothless tenants in Walker Evans's Depression photographs, the successive shanties Judith Pippinger Blackford and her family occupy have no "downstairs" and "upstairs," no "nursery," no dining room or parlor, and old newspapers, rather than wallpaper, cover their walls. Compare, too, the food mentioned in Gilman's story to that described in *Weeds*: to keep her strength up, Gilman's narrator is given "lots of tonics and things, to say nothing of ale and wine and rare meat" (32), whereas the Blackfords' diet is extremely limited, especially during the winters, when there are "just four things in the pantry: coffee, corn meal, dried beans, and hog meat, with perhaps an occasional cabbage or squash that by some miracle had escaped the frost" (160). When the health of Gilman's protagonist fails to improve, a specialist, Weir Mitchell, is mentioned as a possible medical consultant, but when Judith and her husband both become ill with influenza, no doctor is summoned. Perhaps most important, Gilman's narrator is able to turn to a relative as well as to servants to care for her baby and the house when she is too depressed to fulfill her own domestic and maternal responsibilities, whereas Judith has no choice but to look after her children and her household, day after day, no matter how ill or depressed she feels. Finally, supporting the domestic economy in Gilman's story is the narrator's husband John, a successful physician, while Jerry Blackford's back-breaking work as a farmer barely produces enough money to sustain his wife and children. Gilman's point in her story that the seemingly beneficent middle-class patriarchal family arrangements can, nevertheless, be likened to a dictatorship is well taken, but one cannot help but contrast the concerned if patronizing remarks of Gilman's John with the drunken Jerry's beating of Judith after she, enraged by his sullen words, has hit him on the head with the stove lifter.

Critical opinion is divided about whether the ending of "The Yellow Wall-Paper" represents a triumph, a Pyrrhic victory, or a defeat for Gilman's narrator. In contrast, the ending of *Weeds* leaves no room for uncertainty. After the near-death of their young daughter, Judith and her husband reconcile. However, the death of an elderly male neighbor with whom she had felt a true spiritual and artistic kinship exacerbates Judith's depression; she sees her future stretching before her "through a sad, dead level of unrelieved monotony" (333). Convinced that there is absolutely no possibility of altering her fate, Judith thinks, "Like a dog tied by a strong chain, what had she to gain by continually pulling at the leash? What hope was there in rebellion for her or hers?" (330). Gilman and Kelley both appear to have believed in the Darwinian theory of evolution via natural selection.[23] Reflecting the negative implications of the application of this biological theory to human development, Kelley's naturalistic *Weeds* is profoundly pessimistic about the prospects of improving the lot of people like Judith. In contrast to Kelley, however, Gilman believed that biological imperatives could be shaped and controlled by purposeful human action focused on social reform.

In her fanciful short story called "If I Were a Man," Charlotte Perkins Gilman's female protagonist is suddenly transformed into a man, exchanging places with her husband. What wife *and* husband learn as a result of this transformation is how limiting rigid gender roles can be—particularly for women. That both women and men have the need to experience a world beyond the confines of the home is something that Kelley also emphasizes: When Judith's husband asks her why she is so determined to go to town, she replies angrily, "For the same reason you want go. . . . Because I'm sick o' doin' allus the same thing every day" (168). Charlotte Perkins Gilman and Edith Summers Kelley, alike, insisted that women should not be relegated exclusively to the domestic sphere. Believing that paper can serve a more important function than that of decorating the walls of one's house, Gilman and her successor, Kelley, used their fiction as a vehicle for protesting against the subjugation of women. Although Gilman was more sanguine than Kelley about the possibilities of ameliorating the lot of human beings, both writers dramatized in their writing the inequities of a patriarchal society that made women economically dependent on men, confined women to the home, and prevented them from participating in the larger world as fully as men did.

NOTES

1. See Upton Sinclair's *New Industrial Republic* (New York: Doubleday, 1907), 261. In her autobiography, Gilman maintained that Sinclair actually had misinterpreted her precepts when he had instituted "cooperative housekeeping" at Helicon Hall rather than hiring professionals to perform the housekeeping tasks, as she had recommended. "Upton Sinclair's ill-fated Helicon Hall experiment he attributed to my teachings, without the least justification," she observed in *The Living of Charlotte Perkins Gilman,* ed. Ann J. Lane (Madison: University of Wisconsin Press, 1990), 26.

2. See Charlotte Perkins Gilman, "Moving the Mountain," in *The Charlotte Perkins Gilman Reader,* ed. Ann J. Lane (New York: Pantheon, 1980), 178–88.

3. Edith Summers Kelley, "Helicon Hall: An Experiment in Living," ed. Mary Byrd David, *The Kentucky Review* 1 (Spring 1980): 32–40.

4. Edith Summers Kelley to Alfred Harcourt, 12 April 1923, courtesy of Patrick Kelley.

5. Joseph Wood Krutch, *The Nation* 118 (16 January 1924): 65.

6. See Edith Summers Kelley, *Weeds,* ed. Matthew J. Bruccoli (Carbondale: Southern Illinois University Press, 1972): 335–43. Alan Cheuse, in his review of Kelley's *The Devil's Hand,* a novel which also was reissued by Southern Illinois University Press, was the first critic to use the word "feminist" with respect to Kelley. See Alan Cheuse, *The Nation* 220 (26 April 1975): 536.

7. See Annette Kolodny, "A Map for Rereading: Or, Gender and the Interpretation of Literary Texts," in *The Captive Imagination: a Casebook on The Yellow Wallpaper,* ed. Catherine Golden (New York: The Feminist Press, 1992): 149–67; Judith Fetterley, "Reading about Reading: 'A Jury of Her Peers,' 'The Murders in the Rue Morgue,' and 'The Yellow Wallpaper,' " ibid., 253–60; Jean E. Kennard, "Convention Coverage or How to Read Your Own Life," ibid., 168–90.

8. Charlotte Perkins Gilman, *The Man-Made World* or, *Our Androcentric Culture* (New York: Charlton, 1911), 225. Quoted in Mary A. Hill, *A Journey From Within: The Love Letters of Charlotte Perkins Gilman, 1897–1900* (Lewisburg: Bucknell University Press, 1995), 20.

9. Quoted in *The Diaries of Charlotte Perkins Gilman,* vol. 2, ed. Denise D. Knight (Charlottesville: University Press of Virginia, 1994), 878.

10. See Edith Summers Kelley, "The Old House," *Women's Studies* 10 (1983): 66.

11. See Charlotte Perkins Gilman, "The Mother's Charge," in *The Norton Anthology of Literature by Women,* ed. Sandra Gilbert and Susan Gubar, 2d ed. (New York: W. W. Norton, 1985), 1132.

12. Charlotte Perkins Gilman, "Women and Economics," in *The Feminist Papers: From Adams to de Beauvoir,* ed. Alice S. Rossi (New York: Columbia University Press, 1973), 581.

13. Edith Summers Kelley, *Weeds* (New York: The Feminist Press, 1996), 195. All parenthetical citations from *Weeds* are from this text.

14. Charlotte Perkins Gilman, "Kitchen Women," *The Later Poetry of Charlotte Perkins Gilman,* ed. Denise D. Knight (Newark: University of Delaware Press, 1996), 72.

15. Charlotte Perkins Gilman, "The Housewife," ibid., 73.

16. Catherine Golden, "Light of the Home, Light of the World: The Presentation of Motherhood in Gilman's Short Fiction," *Modern Language Studies* 26 (Spring and Summer 1996): 135.

17. Charlotte Perkins Gilman, "The Yellow Wallpaper," in *The Captive Imagination,* 25. All parenthetical citations from "The Yellow Wall-Paper" are from this text.

18. Kelley, *Weeds,* 209. The graphic description by Kelley of the birth of Judith's first child, a section from her original manuscript of *Weeds* that her publisher insisted she omit because it would offend her readers, is included as an appendix to The Feminist Press edition of *Weeds,* 335–51.

19. Elizabeth Ammons, *Conflicting Stories: American Women Writers at the Turn Into the Twentieth Century* (New York: Oxford University Press, 1991), 178. The passage to which Ammons refers appears on p. 301 in *Weeds.*

20. Kelley, *Weeds,* 329. For a discussion of Judith as an *artiste manque* see Charlotte Goodman, "Portraits of the *Artiste Manque* by Three Women Novelists," *Frontiers* 5 (1980): 57–59.

21. John N. Duvall, "Toni Morrison and the Anxiety of Faulknerian Influence," in *Unflinching Gaze: Morrison and Faulkner Re-Envisioned,* ed. Carol A. Kolmerten, Stephen M. Ross, and Judith Bryant Wittenberg (Jackson: University Press of Mississippi, 1997), 4.

22. See Elaine R. Hedges, " 'Out at Last?' 'The Yellow Wallpaper' After Two Decades of Feminist Criticism," in *The Captive Imagination,* 319–33.

23. For a discussion of social Darwinism, see Robert C. Bannister, *Social Darwinism: Science & Myth* (Philadelphia: Temple University Press, 1989); and Richard Hofstadter, *Social Darwinism in American Thought* (Boston: Beacon Press, 1992). For a discussion of the Darwinian views of Charlotte Perkins Gilman, see Lois N. Magner, "Darwinism and the Woman Question: The Evolving Views of Charlotte Perkins Gilman," in *Critical Essays on Charlotte Perkins Gilman,* ed. Joanne B. Karpinski (New York: G. K. Hall, 1992), 115–28. For a discussion of the naturalistic elements in *Weeds,* see Charlotte Goodman, "Widening Perspectives, Narrowing Possibilities: The Trapped Woman in Edith Summers Kelley's *Weeds,*" in *Regionalism and the Female Imagination,* ed. Emily Toth (New York: Human Sciences Press, 1985), 93–96.

Part III
Re-Envisioning
"The Yellow Wall-Paper"

Overwriting Decadence: Charlotte Perkins Gilman, Oscar Wilde, and the Feminization of Art in "The Yellow Wall-Paper"

ANN HEILMANN

WHEN WILLIAM DEAN HOWELLS APPROACHED CHARLOTTE PERKINS Gilman about the inclusion of "The Yellow Wall-Paper" in his *Great American Short Stories,* she told him that it "was no more 'literature' than [her] other stuff, being definitely written 'with a purpose,' " adding that "[i]n [her] judgment it [was] a pretty poor thing to write . . . without a purpose."[1] Gilman's purpose in writing "The Yellow Wall-Paper" has been variously linked to a radical attack on the institutions of marriage and motherhood; to an indictment of patriarchal medicine and science; to a celebration of the subversiveness of the hysteric; to an interrogation of the relationship between the personal and the political, the autobiographical and the historical; and lastly, to a cultural critique of the literal as well as literary and linguistic, the material and the symbolic, problems faced by the woman who wants to survive as an artist in a male-dominated society.[2]

With "The Yellow Wall-Paper" today regarded as an almost unparalleled literary masterpiece which provides a brilliant exposition of the conditions of women's lives under patriarchy, the dichotomy between "literature" and "purpose," or "art" and "politics," which Gilman foregrounded in her comment to Howells, is not usually perceived as a problem. Neither was this dichotomy borne out by Gilman's life: after studying art at the Rhode Island School of Design, she earned her living as an art teacher and a decorative artist, painting flowers so perfectly that, as she tells us in her autobiography, if she had "give[n] [her]self to it" she could have made a name for herself (*Living* 46–47). Her first book, *In This Our World* (1893), was a collection of poems, the cover of which she devised herself, modeling it on *Dreams* (1890) by Olive Schreiner, another eminent turn-of-the-century feminist whose work combined art and politics (*Living* 168). In 1898, the year of her breakthrough as a feminist philosopher and author of *Women*

and Economics, she saw herself "[a]s poet—as author—as orator"—
the poet coming first, and the term author, like that of prophet or visionary, incorporating both aspects, the artist and the political
reformer. Even forty years later, at the age of seventy, after completing
her mystery novel, *Unpunished,* she was still planning for new work
which should form part of "Art, Service, Education, Religion."[3] Writing
as a form of art was clearly important to her, although this art was
always bound up with "service"—but here she had a famous role
model: Elizabeth Barrett Browning's *Aurora Leigh* (1857), an epic
novel-poem about a successful woman artist, a book Gilman read and
reread in the early years of her marriage to Walter Stetson, ends on the
message that "Art's a service," in other words, that art is a political
project for reforming the world as well as an aesthetic and philosophical endeavour.[4]

Even while considering herself a writer, and implying that she could
have been a notable artist, had she only wanted to, throughout her life,
Gilman qualified her artistic achievements by insisting that what she
had done was "perfect of its kind, but not 'art' "; that she was devoted
to "literature and lecturing," but that her writing was "not, in the artistic sense, 'literature' " (*Living* 46, 248; *Diaries* 2 : 846). Why this preoccupation with the dichotomy between art and purpose, and what
significance does it have for my reading of "The Yellow Wall-Paper?"
Conrad Shumaker and Sheryl Meyering have interpreted Gilman's dis-
avowal of her artistic self as a strategy common to women writers who
sought to defuse the threat they posed by emphasizing their own insig-
nificance[5]; however, this would be strangely at odds with the rest of her
work, which so manifestly sets out to challenge patriarchal values and
hierarchies. Another explanation might be found in the maternal inter-
diction of "brain-building" (day-dreaming), which may have caused
the thirteen-year-old girl to believe that purely pleasurable (aesthetic)
imaginative activity was selfish and immoral (not "work"), initiating a
life-long habit of checking her creative impulses if they were not directed toward a specific "purpose" (*Living* 23–24). However, in "The
Yellow Wall-Paper," such a narrow view of art is exposed as dangerous:
it is, after all, John's prohibition of writing, his utter incomprehension
of his wife's need for constructive creative expression, and his injunc-
tion to her not to "give way" to her "false and foolish" "fancies,"[6]
which propel the narrator on a journey to self-disintegration and madness.

While Gilman knew herself to be an artist in terms of her own *feminist* reconceptualization of art, I want to argue that she self-consciously
distanced herself from the contemporary conception of *"high"* art because she associated with it specific movements and a specific gender,

in other words, "masculine" art and an "androcentric" perspective—
the antithesis of everything she and her art stood for. The beginning
and end of her career saw her writing pitted against fin-de-siècle decadence and twentieth-century "high" modernism, predominantly or exclusively male-oriented movements whose most central aspects—"Art
for Art's Sake," privileging style and formal experimentation over content—clashed with her notion of "purposeful" art and explicitly political literature. "When Mrs. Gilman says, 'I am not an artist,' " an early
twentieth-century critic noted, "she is rebuking strictly esthetic expectations. . . . The whole effect of her work . . . is of . . . a seer's intentness,
a prophet's passion to say . . . she is making a case, she is translating a
vision."[7]

If "The Yellow Wall-Paper" was written to teach Silas Weir Mitchell
and, by implication, other wielders of patriarchal authority, "the error
of [their] ways" (*Living* 121), Gilman also responded to the dominant
artistic discourse of her time by "translating her vision" of political art.
In the context of the 1890s, the color and strange floral pattern of the
wallpaper literally and literarily take on a specific cultural meaning.
Why yellow? As Mary Jacobus and Susan Lanser have noted, yellow,
the "color of sickness," would at that time have been associated with
racial fears of national invasion (the "Yellow Peril") and with social
fears of the invasion of privacy (the sensationalist "Yellow Press").[8]
Most significantly, of course, it stood for the aesthetic and decadent
movement. Morris's fashionable designs in which, as Heather Kirk
Thomas points out in her contribution to this collection, yellow featured significantly, Van Gogh's sunflowers, Whistler's blue-and-yellow
room, the French yellowback novel, *The Yellow Book,* and indeed, the
Yellow Nineties. Above all, the color yellow evokes the image of Oscar
Wilde, self-styled "Professor of Aesthetics," carrying sunflowers and a
yellow silk handkerchief in lieu of aestheticism to the America of the
1880s, and responding to hostile newspaper reports by quipping, "If
you survive yellow journalism, you need not be afraid of yellow fever";
Wilde who put a novel bound in yellow, mistakenly thought to be *The
Yellow Book,* under his arm when he was arrested and whose *A Woman
of No Importance* (1893) features a young American woman with a purpose, teaching the higher morality to decadent English aristocrats in a
"Yellow Drawing-room."[9]

Wilde's poems "In the Gold Room: A Harmony" (1882), "Symphony in Yellow" (1889), "Remorse (A Study in Saffron)" (1889) and
"La Dame Jaune" (undated) established yellow as the color of decadence, conjuring up an atmosphere where the erotic connoted decay
and the rotting "flowers of evil" (falling hair in "Remorse" and "In the
Gold Room," falling clothes in "La Dame Jaune," falling leaves in

"Symphony in Yellow") (Wilde, *Complete Works* 862, 872–73; Ellmann, *Oscar Wilde* 196). Decadent eroticism was similarly visualized in painting, for instance in Albert Moore's "Yellow Marguerites" (ca. 1880), which encoded female "solitary vice" by depicting a languid young woman reclining on a sofa against a background of flowery yellow wallpaper.[10] Sexual perversion was made explicit in *The Yellow Room,* an anonymous sado-masochistic text published a year before "The Yellow Wall-Paper," in which the title room is the site of the heroine's flagellation by her uncle.[11]

By turning the two signifiers of aestheticism (the color yellow and the flower tapestry made so famous by William Morris) into the central metaphor of her story on women's sociocultural oppression, Gilman was visualizing her emerging feminist opposition to the "pointless pattern" of male thought and cultural production (31), juxtaposing these with a woman-centered politics and perspective, the central female consciousness of her text. Judging by a lecture she gave in 1894, "Art for Art's Sake" was, as she noted in her diary, bound to have "evil results" (*Diaries* 2: 583).[12] Like so many feminists of the time, in particular the British New Woman writers, Gilman constructed decadence not as subversion, but merely as a different expression of patriarchy. If, on a symbolic level, the yellow wallpaper denotes the phallocentric structures of science and the patriarchal family, it quite literally reflects contemporary male art and also, as Kirk Thomas illustrates in her essay, male consumer culture. Doctor, husband, artist, and interior decorator combine to enclose the female narrator in a prison of maleness, a *"delirium tremens"* of masculine frenzy, its "sprawling outlines run[ning] off in great slanting waves of optic horror" (31, emphasis in original), and pressing on the narrator "like a bad dream" (34). "Our androcentric culture," Gilman was to write two decades later in *The Man-Made World* (1911), "is ... a masculine culture in excess, and therefore undesirable."[13] In "The Yellow Wall-Paper," she suggested that this "excess of degeneracy," as Kirk Thomas calls it, was not only "undesirable," but also a health hazard.

In what sense does the biographical context throw further light on Gilman's critique of aestheticism? No record exists of any meeting between her and Wilde, but there is enough evidence to suggest that their paths crossed indirectly. In 1882, when Wilde toured America for a year, Gilman was twenty-two and teaching art and designing advertising cards in Providence. She might have heard about Wilde from her uncle Henry Ward Beecher, whom Wilde visited in July 1882. Wilde lectured in Rhode Island on three separate occasions, on 25 or 26 September in Gilman's home town. She neither attended nor made a note of Wilde in her diary, but she could hardly have avoided reports of the occasion in the local press and subsequent local gossip. As Wilde's lectures were transcribed almost verbatim by the newspapers, she would have had a good idea of what they were about. One can only speculate about the impact the media debate on Wilde had in terms of shaping her views on art and aestheticism. The *Woman's Journal,* for instance, which one year later accepted Gilman's poem "In Duty Bound" (1884), carried a heated diatribe against him on 4 February 1882 (*Diaries* 1 : 240; Ellmann, *Oscar Wilde* 174–75, 180–83). On the other hand, the poet Joacquin Miller, who was to become a friend some ten years later, was a passionate Wilde advocate, writing fiery open letters in his defense.[14] Since Wilde was in the habit of visiting art galleries and art schools of the cities in which he delivered lectures, he might have stopped at the Rhode Island School of Design or at the Providence Art Club (Ellmann, *Oscar Wilde* 175–76, 182). In any case, he did not conceal his disdain for "young ladies painting moonlights upon dinner plates and sunsets on soup plates"; "[t]here is one thing much worse than bad art," he said in his lecture on "The Decorative Arts," "and that is no art"—an attitude that would certainly have made Gilman feel ill at ease with her own flower painting, which, we remember, was "perfect of its kind," but (in the light of Wilde's comments?) "not 'art' " (*Living* 84; Wilde, *Complete Works* 932).

Richard Ellmann notes that, notwithstanding his bad press, Wilde's "opinion was constantly sought in connection with plans for new art schools and galleries, and young artists looked up to him . . . as a god" (*Oscar Wilde* 182); surely Gilman and Stetson must have discussed Wilde and aestheticism. It is possible that Gilman bowed to Stetson's "superior" judgment, at least outwardly, as she says she did in her autobiography: "Do it as you choose," she told him when they were furnishing their marital home, "I have no tastes and no desires. I shall like whatever you do" (*Living* 85).[15] Perhaps it was in this spirit that she dressed in yellow for an art reception of Stetson's in 1884, shortly before their wedding; her diary note of 4 March reads:

[D]ress for Walters [*sic*] reception. Carrie's black silk, white Spanish tie, ruching, & lace in sleeves, yellow ribbon, yellow beads, gold comb, amber bracelet; yellow breast on bonnet, yellow flowers. Many people there, all seemed pleased. (*Diaries* 1 : 262)

Two years later, after starting her course of reading on women, she was sufficiently confident to express divergent views on art; one wonders whether her disapproval of some of Stetson's paintings had anything to do with aestheticism. On one occasion she "criticize[d] his pictures, one so harshly from a moral point of view that he smashe[d] and burn[t] it" (*Diaries* 1 : 349). By the time she wrote "The Yellow Wall-Paper," she had established her artistic independence publicly, as a writer and also, as Kirk Thomas notes, as an interior decorator. If this independence took the form of anti-aestheticism, it was rooted in her personal experience, inextricably connected as it was with her sense of immurement in an artistic marriage which obstructed her (artistic) development.

Sensitive to the public prohibition of homosexuality despite her own love for two women, Gilman may have reacted negatively to Oscar Wilde's spectacular over-performance of a deviance she appears to have shared.[16] As Mary Hill notes (*Charlotte Perkins Gilman* 225), her sense of transgression—she had felt "queer" and "unfeminine," almost a "morbid, strange cold sort of monster" during her friendship with Martha Luther—indicates that she had "partially accepted the derogatory socially imposed attitudes towards [same-sex] love." Wilde's stance also alienated male homosexuals like Henry James who, after calling on him in Washington, concluded that " 'Hosscar' Wilde is a fatuous fool, tenth-rate cad" and an "unclean beast" (Ellmann, *Oscar Wilde* 171). With its "repellent, almost revolting," "lurid" and "smouldering unclean" color (26), associated, as the contemporary critic Holbrook Jackson wrote, "with all that was . . . queer in art and life,"[17] the wallpaper anticipates the discourse of the Wilde trial in 1895. Its unaccountably "inharmonious" (29) and unsavory aspects also recall the language of Robert Louis Stevenson's "Dr. Jekyll and Mr. Hyde" (1886), a story which, as Elaine Showalter has argued, encodes homosexuality. Both texts play on the word "queer," a word whose homosexual connotations were established in slang around the turn of the century.[18] On the very first page, Gilman's narrator informs us that "there is something queer" about the house (24), and in Stevenson's story one of the characters remarks in the first chapter that "the more it looks like Queer Street, the less I ask." Hyde and the wallpaper cause a similar feeling of nausea in the people exposed to them, and in each case this disgust defies any attempt at rational definition or explanation: the wallpaper has an "inexplicable look" and entirely indeterminable pattern (35, 31), and Stevenson's Utterson finds that he cannot give utterance to the unspeakable: "There *is* something more," he says, "if I could find a name for it."[19] Just as the wallpaper hides "a strange, provoking, formless sort of figure" behind its sub-pattern which, though "subdued" in the daytime, "is all the time trying to climb through" in the moonlight (30, 34, 38), Dr. Jekyll's house conceals a back street door from which Hyde emerges at night in pursuit of forbidden pleasure. The fact that Gilman read "Dr. Jekyll and Mr. Hyde" in January 1890, shortly before she wrote "The Yellow Wall-Paper," is significant in that it suggests that she deliberately drew on, and represented in her text, the "queer" register of contemporary male art.[20]

If the wallpaper denotes both aestheticism and sexual deviance, and therefore by implication Oscar Wilde, whose "extreme aesthetic[ism]" was "almost a euphemism" for homosexuality even in 1882 (Ellmann, *Oscar Wilde* 80), then Gilman "produce[d] [her] own etiology of the queer" when she "came out" as a feminist.[21] Using her story to pit her growing sense of a sociopolitical mission against what she would have perceived as decadent immorality, she contrasted a male politics of pleasure with the feminist agenda of "serious" social reform, implying that masculinized, androcentric culture would, and must, be transformed by the feminizing influence of the female artist. Combining the personal with the political, Gilman drew on her autobiographical knowledge of what it meant to be an artist's wife and medical patient to create a nameless narrator who stood for everywoman, at least in the white middle-class sphere.

With his notorious kneebreeches, lilies, dark velvet outfit, and "queer" sexuality, Wilde may not have been "dull enough to confuse the eye in following" (26), but his "defiance of law" (34) was certainly "pronounced enough to constantly irritate and provoke study," and like Gilman's wallpaper, his *bons mots,* witty repartees, and aphorisms were calculated to "plunge off at outrageous angles [and] destroy themselves in unheard of contradictions" (26). While Wilde, in his 1882 lecture on "The Decorative Arts," warned his American audience that nonaesthetic wallpaper would "lead a boy brought up under its influence to a career of crime" (*Complete Works* 934), Gilman argued ten years later that decadent wallpaper drove women mad. "Today more than ever the artist and a love of the beautiful are needed to temper and counteract the sordid materialism of the age," Wilde pronounced in "The House Beautiful" (1882), the second of his three American lectures; "the artist comes forward as a priest and prophet of nature to protest, and even to work against the prostitution of . . . what is lofty and noble in humanity" (*Complete Works* 925). Gilman, too, saw herself as a priest and prophet, engaged in uplifting humanity: "My business was to find out what ailed society, and how most easily and naturally to improve it," she wrote in her autobiography, "I [was] here to serve the world. As a perceiver and transmitter of truth and love" (*Living* 182; *Diaries* 2 : 849).

The overriding value Wilde attached to "beauty," Gilman placed on "truth." In her eyes, aestheticism did not reflect human existence "truthfully." Masculine art, she argued in *The Man-Made World,* was useless to society because it was based upon the premise of exclusionary practices. In a "properly developed" community, which furthered the artistic spirit in all its members irrespective of class or gender, we should enjoy "the pleasure of applied art in the making and using of everything we have." What was on offer in androcentric culture was "applied art at a very low level, small joy either for the maker or the user. Pure art, a fine-spun specialty, a process carried on by an elect few, who openly despise the unappreciative many" (*Man-Made World* 77-78). Just as Gilman juxtaposed "purpose" and "literature" in her comment to William Dean Howells, so she contrasted "applied art" and "pure art" in *The Man-Made World,* coming down firmly on the side of the former and condemning the latter as unnatural, artificial, and even antisocial. "It is sometimes said that our art is opposed to good morals," Wilde admitted in "The House Beautiful," but he took pains to emphasize that "on the contrary, it fosters morality" (*Complete Works* 925); to Gilman, on the other hand, the inevitable outcome of masculine cultural elitism was "a natural art wrested to unnatural ends, a noble art degraded to ignoble ends" (*Man-Made World* 81).

What were the parameters of this "noble art" Gilman saw degraded by the exclusion of women, and how did this affect her conception of "The Yellow Wall-Paper"? In "The House Beautiful," Wilde offered guidelines for creating the perfect aesthetic *ambience:* "in decorating a room," he urged, "one keynote of color should predominate." Whistler's painting, "Symphony in White," was proof of the fact that much could be achieved by restricting oneself to one single color. The true aesthetic mind avoided bright colors, choosing "toned or secondary," even "sombre" tones to set off the ceiling and walls against the ornaments and furniture. To enliven these more "gloomy colours," Wilde suggested selecting "joyous [wall]paper . . . full of flowers and pleasing designs," but warned against hanging "[t]wo pictures . . . side by side— they will either kill one another, or else commit artistic suicide"—this is of course precisely what the "lame uncertain curves" of the not so joyous flowers do on Gilman's wallpaper (26). To impress on his audience "what a great effect might be realised with a little and simple colour," Wilde gave a detailed description of Whistler's blue-and-yellow room:

> The walls are distempered in blue, the ceiling is a light and warm yellow; the floor is laid with a richly painted matting in light yellow, with a light line or leaf here and there of blue. The woodwork is all cane-yellow, and the shelves are filled with blue and white china; the curtains of white serge have a yellow border tastefully worked in, and hang in careless but graceful folds. When the breakfast-table is laid in this apartment, with its light cloth and its dainty blue and white china, with a cluster of red and yellow chrysanthemums in an old Nankin vase in the centre, it is a charming room, catching

all the warm light and taking on of all surrounding beauty, and giving to
the guest a sense of joyousness, comfort, and rest (*Complete Works* 916–17,
922)

No doubt this room, significantly also one singled out for providing
"rest," sounds incomparably more habitable and peaceful to the mind
than Gilman's nursery. In fact, Wilde stressed the importance of con-
gruence and symmetry, advising against compiling a "collection of a
great many things individually pretty but which do not combine to
make a harmonious whole" (*Complete Works* 915). In principle Gilman
shared Wilde's notion of beauty; in *The Man-Made World* she declared
the highest form of art, that is, "human" (as opposed to sex-specific)
art, to be characterized by "regularity, symmetry, repetition, and alter-
ation" (75)—the very opposite, that is, of her wallpaper, which, as she
notes in her story, is "not arranged on any laws of radiation, or alternation, or repetition, or symmetry" (31). The point that Gilman makes is
that "human" art and, therefore, true beauty and aesthetic expression
are not possible in an androcentric culture; as long as women are op-
pressed, Whistler's vision of peaceful symmetry must inevitably turn
into the nightmare of the nursery.

Taken by itself, or in conjunction with different furnishings and in a
more positive context, the wallpaper would not be as "horrid" as it
must appear to the narrator (32). What makes the nursery so disturbing
is the violent clash between the wallpaper's pretense to aestheticism
and the room's function as a prison. If, as Kirk Thomas points out,
Gilman's metaphor of the "yellow room," encoding male artistic taste
but also the callousness of an oppressive husband, was prefigured in
Henry James's *The Portrait of a Lady* (1881), it takes on even more
alarming dimensions in her story. The "rings and things in the wall"
(26), the nursery's sound-proof location at the top of the paradigmati-
cally patriarchal "colonial mansion" (24), separated from the rest of
the house with gates, the bars on the windows, the narrator pinned to
a "great heavy bed" which "looks as if it had been through the wars,"
nailed to a floor "scratched and gouged and splintered" (30, 31), the
strange, smelly, yellow stains all over her and her husband's clothes—
the sister-in-law who "wished we should be more careful" (35)—and
the "ravages" of the torn and "torturing" wallpaper which "slaps you
in the face, knocks you down, and tramples upon you" (29, 34), and
which reduces her to crawling; all of this hints at sexual assault. How
could harmony or peace of mind be conceivable against a background
of abuse? How could a male movement lay claim to creating beautiful
and enduring art while all the time witnessing and choosing to ignore,
the lives women had to endure? "This paper looks to me as if it *knew*

what a vicious influence it had!" the narrator writes, as if the "two bulbous eyes" of the male artist both watched and created the conditions for the subjection and disintegration of female identity (29, emphasis in original). What Gilman suggests, then, is that in patriarchy, art produced by the ruling sex (and class) serves to establish and consolidate the dominant power structures.

A society which suffers from an "excess of masculinity" and a concomitant "lack of femininity," Gilman argues in *The Man-Made World* (78), produces art that is defined by three features, which, conflating sex and gender, she sees as generic male characteristics: "desire, combat, [and] self-expression." These traits are written into the wallpaper. "I never saw so much expression in an inanimate thing before," the narrator tells us (29). In her futile attempt to define the pattern, she discovers that, while "each breadth stands alone," all breadths "connect diagonally . . . and . . . horizontally"; they seem to move toward "a common centre" but then "rush off in headlong plunges" (31). Read in terms of human society, this clash between centripetal and centrifugal presents us with an image of "isolated" combatants each competing for individual expression, unable to avoid interlinking and criss-crossing with others at times, but who, instead of cooperating (converging on a common objective), are continually in conflict. As a result, both the wallpaper and the society represented by it radiate antagonism, evoking the hatred of those subjected to its influence, women and children: "No wonder the children hated it!" (26). In addition, the wallpaper reflects an aggressive and frenzied sexual desire, an army of fetid "toadstool[s] in joints . . . budding and sprouting in endless convolutions" (34), steadily closing in on the narrator, whose only means of escape is through projecting her fear on to the sub-pattern, with the first sighting of the woman behind bars directly following this description of an ominous, terrifying, imperialist masculinity.

If male art has such dire consequences, what potential for change does Gilman see, and what solutions does she offer? "The true artist transcends his sex, or her sex," she argues in *The Man-Made World* (79); "Art is Human." But to achieve the conditions in which human art can be produced, art must first be feminized. Literature and fiction in particular need the feminizing influence of women artists because so far they have "not given any true picture of woman's life, very little of human life, and a disproportioned section of man's life." (102) Male writers, she claims, have in the main concentrated on two scripts, each foregrounding predatory masculinity: "the Story of Adventure, and the Love Story" (94). Neither has "touch[ed] on human processes, social processes" (95), in other words, shown a commitment to creating works of art that, while representing human psychology and social interaction truthfully, "lifted, taught, inspired [and] enlightened" the reader (123). To counteract this masculine influence, Gilman outlines the parameters of female and "feminine" fiction. This fiction is concerned with the real-life experiences of women, examining the problems and conflicts they have to contend with, and also exploring the great potential of female-to-female, and human, interaction and cooperation:

> The humanizing of woman . . . opens five distinctly fresh fields of fiction: First, the position of the young woman who is called upon to give up her "career"—her humanness—for marriage, and who objects to it. Second, the middle-aged woman who at last discovers that her discontent is social starvation—that it is not more love that she wants, but more business in life: Third, the inter-relation of women with women—a thing we could never write about before because we never had it before: . . . Fourth, the interaction between mothers and children; this not the eternal "mother and child," wherein the child is always a baby, but the long drama of personal relationship; the love and hope, the patience and power, the lasting joy and triumph, the slow eating disappointment which must never be owned to a living soul—. . . Fifth, the new attitude of the full-grown woman, who faces the demands of love with the high standards of conscious motherhood. (*Man-Made World* 104–5)

In "The Yellow Wall-Paper" Gilman turned her attention to the first of these new themes, describing with clinical precision and an acute psychological insight sharpened by her autobiographical experience what happens to the inner life of a young woman who, stifled by marriage and motherhood, is denied individual and professional growth. Gilman's story also addresses the other "feminizing" themes, but because she wanted to make a point about the sheer destructiveness of depriving women of careers and, therefore, of a human existence, they are developed in a negative sense. For instance, if we read between the lines of the narrator's story, we catch glimpses of Jennie, John's sister, the "perfect and enthusiastic housekeeper" who "hopes for no better profession" (30). Surely one of the tragedies of the text is the unexplored possibility of sisterhood, the failure of the two women to interrelate and thus to counteract the impact of the patriarchal alliance between husband, brother, and doctor. In a later short story with the same theme, "Making a Change" (1911), the older domestic and younger artistic woman get together behind the husband's back with the mother-in-law recovering her youth and sense of purpose when she turns infant-care into a lucrative business, opening a baby-park on the roof of their apartment block, while the wife resumes her career as a piano teacher, the housekeeping and cooking being taken over by a well-paid professional. What starts as a variant on "The Yellow Wall-Paper" (in her desperation the wife tries to gas herself) ends with domestic peace and happiness, aided by the substantial addition to the family economy.[22]

What Gilman suggests, then, is that woman-to-woman friendship is even more vitally important than a constructive female-to-male relationship; if Jennie identified with, and supported, her sister-in-law instead of acting as her jailer, the narrator would not have to seek for an imaginary "sister" in the mirror of the wallpaper. Instead of giving metaphorical birth to her Other self, a self that escapes out into the open road while she remains behind, tied to her umbilical cord (39, 41), she would, with Jennie's help, be able to set herself free in physical and material terms, too. As it is, she finds relief and some degree of mental liberty by crawling into the recesses of her mind, but even if, as she tells her husband, he can never "put [her] back" (42), she is, for the moment at least, a "captive imagination."

While the narrator herself remains suspended between absolute psychological freedom and physical confinement to a room in the "ancestral halls" of patriarchy (24), death (of her former self: the "Jane" she names on the last page) and rebirth (into a state unnamed and undefined by any man), the process of writing about the ripping of the wallpaper constitutes a metaphorical "overwriting" of the male patterns inscribed into the text: marriage, medicine, and art. Placed in the cultural context of the Yellow Nineties, the journey Gilman takes the reader on is thus one that leads from male aestheticism to the vision of a feminized future. As yet the Other self of the artist that the narrator has released is creeping, but she is creeping out in the open; she is moving fast, and has replaced the yellow of decadence and decay with the green color of life (41).

It is at this point that Gilman's story could be seen to move from the male-defined texts of patriarchy to a female artistic tradition. In Olive Schreiner's "Three Dreams in a Desert," an allegory highly prized by Gilman, a woman reaches the banks of a river which divides her from the land of Freedom. Before she can cross over, she must take off all her (patriarchally inscribed) clothes except one (Truth), and she also has to abandon her dream of Love (a male baby who bites her breast when she lays him on the ground). Not only does she feel *"utterly alone,"* but it is also unlikely that she will succeed in reaching the other side. All she can hope for is to "make a track to the water's edge" with her body, over which thousands of women, the sound of whose feet she can hear in the far distance, can walk into a new life.[23] In Gilman's story and Schreiner's allegory alike, the female protagonist must shed male coverings (wallpaper and clothes) and sacrifice herself to release other women into freedom (Gilman's creeping and Schreiner's marching women).

In a short memoir, Gilman's friend Harriet Howe describes the impact Gilman, and through her Schreiner's allegory, had on her:

[Mrs. Stetson] introduced me to [a] precious book, . . . "Three Dreams in a Desert," . . . And if I had been exulted before, over the poetry; here was vital truth, aspiration, reality for the whole human race, in so perfect a setting that no work of human hands could excel it. I cried incredulously, "And this book is in the world, and still the women are asleep? Then what use is it to try further, for this cannot be surpassed." In a reverent tone she answered me, in the very words of the book, "We make a path to the water's edge." And I wept, unashamed, while she walked away a little distance, I think to conceal her own eyes, but I am not sure. From that hour I was dedicated to the work of lifting humanity by awakening women to a knowledge of their power and their responsibility. It was a consecration.[24]

As the "art which gives humanity consciousness," Gilman wrote in *The Man-Made World* (93), literature was "the most powerful and necessary," "the most vital" of the arts. In "The Yellow Wall-Paper" she made "a track to the water's edge" of "human" art by mapping the transition from male aestheticism to a new female aesthetic.

NOTES

1. Charlotte Perkins Gilman, *The Living of Charlotte Perkins Gilman: An Autobiography,* introduction by Ann J. Lane (Madison: University of Wisconsin Press, 1990), 121.

2. For an overview of readings see Elaine Hedges, " 'Out at Last'? 'The Yellow Wallpaper' after Two Decades of Feminist Criticism," in Catherine Golden, ed., *The Captive Imagination: A Casebook on The Yellow Wallpaper* (New York: The Feminist Press, 1992), 319–33.

3. Charlotte Perkins Gilman, [from] "Thoughts and Figgerings," 18 January 1898 and 11 August 1930, in *The Diaries of Charlotte Perkins Gilman,* ed. Denise D. Knight, 2 vols. (Charlottesville: University Press of Virginia, 1994), 2 : 847, 854.

4. Elizabeth Barrett Browning, *Aurora Leigh* (London: Women's Press, 1982), bk. 9, l. 915.

5. Sheryl L. Meyering, "Introduction" to *Charlotte Perkins Gilman: The Woman and Her Work* (Ann Arbor: UMI Research Press, 1988), 2–10; Conrad Shumaker, " 'Too Terribly Good to Be Printed': Charlotte Perkins Gilman's 'The Yellow Wallpaper,' " ibid., 65–74.

6. Charlotte Perkins Gilman, "The Yellow Wallpaper" (1892), in Golden, *Captive Imagination,* 18, 34. Subsequent citations refer to this edition.

7. Alexander Black, "The Woman Who Saw It First" (1923), in Joanne B. Karpinski, ed., *Critical Essays on Charlotte Perkins Gilman* (New York: G. K. Hall, 1992), 64.

8. Jacobus, "An Unnecessary Maze of Sign-Reading," *Reading Woman: Essays in*

Feminist Criticism (London: Methuen, 1986), 234; Susan S. Lanser, "Feminist Criticism, 'The Yellow Wallpaper,' and the Politics of Color in America," in Thomas L. Erskine and Connie L. Richards, eds. *"The Yellow Wallpaper": Charlotte Perkins Gilman* (New Brunswick: Rutgers University Press, 1993), 225–56.

9. For references on Wilde see William Gaunt, *The Aesthetic Adventure* (London: Cape, 1945), 105; Martin Fido, *Oscar Wilde* (Leicester: Galley Press, 1988), 41; Richard Ellmann, *Oscar Wilde* (London: Penguin, 1987), 166, 168, 170; H. Montgomery Hyde, *Oscar Wilde* (London: Mandarin, 1990), 510; Fraser Harrison, "Introduction" to *The Yellow Book: An Anthology* (Woodbridge: Boydell Press, 1982), 10–11; Oscar Wilde, *A Woman of No Importance* (1893), in *The Complete Works of Oscar Wilde* (London: Harper Collins, 1996), 477.

10. Bram Dijkstra, *Idols of Perversity: Fantasies of Feminine Evil in Fin-de-Siècle Culture* (New York: Oxford University Press, 1986), 75.

11. Anon., *The New Epicurean and The Yellow Room* (Ware, Hertfordshire: Wordsworth Classics, 1996), 69–127.

12. As the lecture falls in the early stages of Gilman's career, it is likely that there was a written transcript; however, no such title appears in the 1894 file of Gilman's papers held by the Arthur and Elizabeth Schlesinger Library on the History of Women in America, Radcliffe College, Harvard University. I am obliged to Ellen M. Shea for checking the records.

13. Charlotte Perkins Gilman, *The Man-Made World or, Our Androcentric Culture* (New York: Johnson Reprint Corp., 1971), 22.

14. Mary A. Hill, *Charlotte Perkins Gilman: The Making of a Radical Feminist* (Philadelphia: Temple University Press, 1980), 210–26.

15. As Kirk Thomas points out, Gilman's diary entries present a different picture.

16. Gilman acknowledged her same-sex love for Martha Luther and Adeline Knapp in her autobiography (*Living* 78, 133) and was worried about the threat of public exposure after her relationship with Knapp collapsed; see Ann J. Lane, *To Herland and Beyond: The Life and Work of Charlotte Perkins Gilman* (New York: Meridian, 1991), 166–67.

17. Holbrook Jackson, *The Eighteen Nineties* (1913), cited in Stephanie Forward, "Charlotte Perkins Gilman's *Yellow Wallpaper*," *English Review* 7 (February 1997): 35.

18. Elaine Showalter, *Sexual Anarchy: Gender and Culture at the Fin de Siècle* (London: Bloomington, 1991), 105–26.

19. Robert Louis Stevenson, *The Strange Case of Dr. Jekyll and Mr. Hyde With Other Fables* (London: Longman's, 1914), 10, 23 (emphasis in original).

20. "The Yellow Wall-Paper" was written probably in July 1890 (*Diaries* 2 : 417, 905). I am obliged to Gary Scharnhorst for the information that Gilman read "Dr. Jekyll and Mr. Hyde" on 20 January 1890 (Second International Charlotte Perkins Gilman Conference, Skidmore College, Saratoga Springs, 26–28 June 1997).

21. Jonathan Crewe, "Queering *The Yellow Wallpaper?* Charlotte Perkins Gilman and the Politics of Form," *Tulsa Studies in Short Fiction* 14 (1995): 282.

22. Charlotte Perkins Gilman, "Making a Change" (1911), in *The Yellow Wall-Paper and Other Stories,* ed. Robert Shulman (Oxford: Oxford University Press, 1995), 182–90.

23. Olive Schreiner, "Three Dreams in a Desert," *Dreams* (London: Unwin, 1890), 81; reprint in Ann Heilmann, ed. *The Late-Victorian Marriage Question: A Collection of Key New Woman Texts* (London: Routledge/Thoemmes, 1998), vol. 4.

24. Harriet Howe, "Charlotte Perkins Gilman—As I Knew Her" (1936), in Karpinski, *Critical Essays,* 75–76.

"[A] kind of 'debased Romanesque' with *delirium tremens*": Late-Victorian Wall Coverings and Charlotte Perkins Gilman's "The Yellow Wall-Paper"

HEATHER KIRK THOMAS

I WOULD LIKE TO SUGGEST A REREADING OF "THE YELLOW WALL-PAPER" (1892), one that utilizes the medium of wallpaper in a markedly dissimilar manner from how scholars have traditionally interpreted this enigmatic signifier. Gilman, as we know, had a keen sense of irony regarding domestic matters and throughout her literary career displayed a penchant for subverting her culture's conventional advice to women. As Shelley Fisher Fishkin asserts, "One of Gilman's most fruitful strategies as a journalist involved revising and reclaiming familiar subjects in daringly new and unfamiliar ways."[1] For nineteenth-century upper- and middle-class women, wallpaper was a familiar subject. Indeed, illustrations accompanying wallpaper advertisements typically depict a solicitous male merchandiser serving an attractive and stylishly dressed female customer. Scholarly studies documenting the manufacture and marketing of nineteenth-century English and American wallpapers indicate, however, that the 1870s and 1880s marked a "major change in taste."[2] The brightly colored floral and scenic wall coverings favored in the first half of the century fell out of fashion following the publication of Charles Locke Eastlake's wildly successful decorating book, *Hints on Household Taste* (1868; American edition, 1872).[3] Eastlake's popular Gothic Revival décors in turn created a consequent demand for wallpapers designed by William Morris (1834–96), the most prominent spokesman for the English Arts and Crafts Movement.[4] "The Yellow Wall-Paper," I would argue, not only authentically delineates Morris's fashionable gilded olive, monochromatic yellow, and khaki Craftsman designs but also confronts wallpaper on other significant levels: (1) as a potential mental health hazard for women, children, and convalescents in restricted environments; (2) as an engineering medium in the late-nineteenth and early-twentieth centuries for inscribing gender in domestic spaces, a decorating strategy plausibly derived from fin-de-siècle ambivalence about home, family, and the advent of the New Woman; and (3) as evidence of the male take over and sequential androgynization of the decorative arts market, an aesthetic transformation that upset the female consumer's marketplace and domestic empowerment.

William Morris never visited America, but in late August 1896, when Gilman traveled to England for the International Socialist and Labor Congress, she met him one month before his death.[5] Fiona MacCarthy's biography of Morris contends that as a furniture and decorative arts designer, craftsman, artisan, poet, and utopian reformer, he was even more famous in the United States than in England, "a personal hero" to many Americans.[6] Thus, anyone interested in Morris's wallpaper patterns might have easily learned from contemporary journalists' accounts that his wife's name was Jane Burden Morris and their daughter's, Jane Alice Morris, although she was always called "Jenny." It appears to be more than coincidence that Gilman incorporates two female characters with the names Jane and Jennie in "The Yellow Wall-Paper," a narrative that explicitly depicts the psychological hazard of a Morris-style wallpaper pattern upon a depressed and forcibly housebound female convalescent.[7]

Gilman would have been attentive to new directions in the decorative arts, to designers like Eastlake and Morris, as she demonstrated an early love of and talent for art. By her mid-teens, as she recounts in her 1935 autobiography, *The Living of Charlotte Perkins Gilman,* she earned pocket money for her watercolors of flowers and for painting advertising cards for Kendall's Soap Company. Her autobiography modestly asserts she was "a skilled craftsman," not an "artist"; nonetheless Gilman always loved color and "beautiful things":[8]

> My passion for beauty dates far back; in picture books the one or two that were really beautiful; in the colors of the worsted mother used, loving some and hating others; in bits of silk and ribbon, buttons—children used to collect strings of buttons in those days; I keenly recall my delight in specially beautiful things. There was a little cloak of purple velvet, deep pansy-purple, made over from something of mother's, that enraptured my soul. (*Living* 17–18)

In her late teens in 1878–79, Gilman enrolled in Providence's newly opened Rhode Island School of Design, completing two years' of study in 1880 (Scharnhorst 3). The design school's explicit objectives were to train "artisans in drawing, painting, modeling, and designing so that they may successfully apply the principles of art to the requirements of trade and manufacture"; to educate instructors; and to advance "public art education by the collection and exhibition of works of art and by lectures and by other means of instruction in the fine arts." Evidently, "the Philadelphia Centennial Exposition of 1876 served as a catalyst for this endeavor," as it did for other design schools of the period, and commencing in 1879, the Rhode Island School of Design "held annual exhibitions of student work."[9] In 1883, Carol Kessler observes, one of Gilman's watercolors was chosen for a "juried exhibit" at the school.[10] Thus Gilman's studies included design instruction as well as studio classes, and she briefly entertained "some ambition to work as a political cartoonist," although a need to earn a satisfactory living might have been her chief motivation.[11] Nonetheless, it is interesting to ascertain that the stated mission of American industrial art schools launched during the 1880s to 1900 was "to offer training in the 'applied arts' to amateurs as well as to professional or commercial designers."[12] In commingling an aesthetic education with practical manufacturing and production skills, these schools paralleled the rise of large corporate design firms, such as Morris and Co., in merchandising art in the age of mechanical reproduction. In fact, Morris was only one of the successful industrial Arts and Crafts figures who benefited. Other male artists and craftsmen whose influential design and manufacturing firms came to dominate the American interior design market included Louis Comfort Tiffany, Walter Crane, Henry Hobson Richardson, Gustave and Christian Herter, Gustav Stickley, and Frank Lloyd Wright.[13]

After completing at the Rhode Island School of Design what Gilman later termed her "art school experience," she taught drawing in a private school and subsequently gave private art lessons for more than a decade (*Living* 47). Perhaps her love of art influenced her decision in 1884 to marry painter Charles Walter Stetson. Her diary maintains that she admired her husband's aesthetic taste in all things, but as Mary A. Hill notes, when the Stetsons decorated their first apartment, the bride did not hesitate to offer her own opinions about "rugs and wallpaper, ordering fixtures and 'lovely curtain stuffs.' "[14] *The Living of Charlotte Perkins Gilman* mentions that Gilman continued painting floral watercolors previous to and following her daughter Katharine's birth in 1885, a birth that plunged Gilman into her well-documented postpartum depression (95). When she left her husband in 1888, she and Katharine spent time in Pasadena, California, during which time Gilman immersed herself in painting, lecturing, gardening, and writing, completing in 1890 approximately "thirty-three short articles, and twenty-three poems" (*Living* 111), and a number of short stories, including "The Yellow Wall-Paper." More significant to my argument, she was invited to serve as interior decorator for the new Pasadena Opera

House, a major decorating commission. Thus during the same interval that she wrote "The Yellow Wall-Paper," her autobiography chronicles that she was selecting textiles, "seat-coverings, curtains, etc.," for the Opera House (*Living* 112).

Throughout her career Gilman championed tasteful interior design as well as pleasant, functional, and healthy domestic spaces, most markedly in *Women and Economics* (1898), *The Home: its Work and Influence* (1903), and *Herland* (1915), in addition to editorials in the *Forerunner* and sardonic stories like "The Cottagette" (1910) and "Making a Change" (1911). Clearly feminist, these works also attack the era's decorating excesses. Gilman's concerns about slavish imitation in fashion and the decorative arts, moreover, were echoed by literary figures like Edith Wharton. Published five years after "The Yellow Wall-Paper," Wharton's first book *The Decoration of Houses* (1897), a decorating manual co-written with Ogden Codman, Jr., was an immediate best seller, notwithstanding its attack on Victorian society's pretentious, dysfunctional, and overdecorated rooms crammed, as Wharton put it in her autobiography, "with curtains, lambrequins, jardinières of artificial plants, wobbly velvet-covered tables littered with silver gew-gaws, and festoons of lace on mantelpieces and dressing-tables."[15] Jackson Lears's cultural history of American advertising, *Fables of Abundance,* contends that 1890s popular women's magazines similarly condemned "the bric-a-brac habit," a term Gilman also banters about in *Women and Economics.*[16]

In the 1870s and 1880s, Charles Eastlake's Gothic Revival style papers, superciliously discussed and colorfully illustrated in *Hints on Household Taste,* as well as Morris and Co.'s Arts and Crafts patterns were the rage. Subsuming Eastlake's Gothic vaults, arches, and geometric repeats by imbricating a serpentine, or arabesque design, Morris and Co.'s papers anticipate Art Nouveau's "undulating line" (Hapgood 93). In the opinion of art historian Marilyn Hapgood, Morris's designs constitute mysterious, " 'complex' texts" that respond to nature on one level but on another level provoke the viewer's "imagination, even fantasy." His studied chimerical effects—imposing "a primary pattern" upon "a secondary pattern"—ensure that "the eye does not see everything in the pattern at once" (Hapgood 65–66). In the early 1870s, Morris and Co. Craftsman style papers were available in Boston, Philadelphia, and New York (Hoskins 148), but following Philadelphia's 1876 Centennial Exhibition, where millions of visitors viewed the latest trends in wall coverings, these English patterns were widely copied. In 1884 the New York magazine *Carpentry and Building* boasted that "[t]here was a time when if one wanted a good paper for his wall he must pay the enormous prices asked by William Morris and Co. of

London. Now he can find quite as good designs as Morris ever made by looking over the stock of any first-class American papers at not more than one-third the price" (quoted in Lynn 384).

It is no stretch of the imagination to suggest that Dr. S. Weir Mitchell, who lived and practiced his rest cure for neurasthenia in Philadelphia, might have attended the 1876 Centennial Fair and observed the latest Morris fashions in wallpaper design. By the time he treated Charlotte Stetson in April 1887, as Ann Lane remarks, Mitchell "had an international reputation" and "an enormously affluent medical practice. He was adored by hundreds of women patients who traveled from all over the world to undergo his treatment."[17] Wealthy women might well expect a society doctor, research scientist, and successful novelist to decorate his residence and offices in the latest style. Apparently, literary lion William Dean Howells, who tried to help Gilman place the manuscript of "The Yellow Wall-Paper," was a Morris and Co. customer.[18] In 1873 Howells wrote to Henry James, "We have done some aesthetic wall-papering, thanks to Wm. Morris whose wall-papers are so much better than his poems." Still, Howells's admiration for Morris's wallpaper was short-lived. In reviewing a new Morris poetry collection in 1875, Howells compared the volume to "a modern house . . . hung with Mr. Morris' own admirable wall-papers; it is all very pretty indeed; charming; but . . . it is so well aware of its quaintness, that on the whole, one would rather not live in it."[19]

The narrator in "The Yellow Wall-Paper" claims to know the underlying aesthetic principles governing interior design: "I knew a little of the principle of design," she modestly divulges, "and I know this thing [the wallpaper] was not arranged on any laws of radiation, or alternation, or repetition, or symmetry, or anything else *that I ever heard of.*"[20] Her statement also replicates in nearly exact language a passage from the editor's preface to the Sixth American Edition of Eastlake's *Hints on Household Taste* (1878), which evaluates as an aesthetic barometer "[t]he opinion of one who has studied the essential principles of beauty, such as harmony, balance of parts, symmetry, and radiation."[21] Be that as it may, the narrator's caveat—"that I ever heard of"— implies that she has probably decorated her own home, discussed wallpaper selection with merchants, or read about wall covering styles in women's magazines or decorating books, perhaps even in Eastlake's famous volume. Although she is an affluent doctor's wife, the industrial revolution and increasingly sophisticated machinery and printing techniques during the Gilded Age brought paper wall coverings within financial reach of many households, and Morris's androgynous Craftsman styles, touted on the women's page and in magazine advertising, in short course influenced evolving popular tastes. I use the term "androgynous" because Morris's Gothic Revival-influenced arabesques meld masculine angles and feminine curves, unlike the stereotypically feminine florals or landscape murals hung in early nineteenth-century homes.

Clarence Cook's decorating manual, *What Shall We Do With Our Walls?*, published in 1880 in New York, applauds "the courage it would take to own that one liked an old-fashioned landscape-paper in a hallway or in a dining room" when those designs marked an antiquated, passé taste (quoted in Lynn 227). When Gilman's narrator arrives at the rented estate, she, nonetheless, self-confidently declares her preference for the "pretty old-fashioned" (26) first-floor bedroom's feminine, flowery chintz. Yet despite her preference, her physician-husband installs her in a horrid attic room she dislikes on sight. Gilman's caustic description of the wallpaper's "particularly irritating . . . sub-pattern" (648) clearly parodies and simultaneously reviews the era's adulation of Morris's serpentine designs. The narrator condescendingly lampoons the wallpaper's "bloated curves and flourishes—a kind of 'debased Romanesque' with *delirium tremens*—[which] go waddling up and down in isolated columns of fatuity" (31). The term "Romanesque"—an architectural style developed before 1100 in Italy and western Europe between the Roman and Gothic styles and subsequently characterized in building construction by arches and vaults—was associated in late-nineteenth-century wall covering and textile design with profuse or arabesque ornamentation. The narrator's accompanying terms of derision for the Romanesque pattern—she calls it a "debased" facsimile of "*delirium tremens*"—intensify its ethos of degeneracy. Gilman's artistically precise delineation of the wallpaper seems a clever strategy conceived to ensure that her contemporary reader would imaginatively associate Morris's popular arabesque designs with the attic bedroom's sinuous pattern, bilious color, and nightmarish aquarium effect, which the narrator describes in one light as "great slanting waves of optic horror, like a lot of wallowing seaweeds in full chase" (31) and in another, as "a florid arabesque, reminding one of a fungus" or "a toadstool in joints, an interminable string of toadstools, budding and sprouting in endless convolutions" (34).

Elaine Hedges has suggested that Gilman felt "trapped by the role assigned the wife within the conventional nineteenth-century marriage."[22] Exposed day after day to the wallpaper's eye-popping repetitions, the story's narrator likewise gradually becomes convinced not only that her husband has entrapped her in the attic but also that the wallpaper contains other trapped women whom she must rescue. A common dilemma in hanging boldly repetitive and large-scaled patterns, Hapgood contends, is that "the wallpaper viewer is in an enclosed space. If a wallpaper repeat is too insistent, the viewer may feel trapped" (10). Thus in a Gothic story in the "madwoman in the attic" literary tradition, to borrow Gilbert and Gubar's phrase, Gilman adroitly multiplies the operative irony in reproducing one of Morris's Pre-Raphaelite, Gothic Revival-inspired wallpapers to reinforce the narrative's medieval aura of female entrapment. A concomitant, if un-discernible, contextual irony is that Morris, who designed at least "forty-one wallpapers and five ceiling papers" for other people's homes, only "rarely" hung wallpaper in his own.[23]

Although the narrator dislikes the wallpaper's convoluted pattern, its saffron color also makes her queasy: "It is the strangest yellow, that wall-paper! It makes me think of all the yellow things I ever saw—not beautiful ones like buttercups, but old foul, bad yellow things" (37). Ann Heilmann's essay in this collection, "Overwriting Decadence: Charlotte Perkins Gilman, Oscar Wilde and the Feminization of Art in 'The Yellow Wall-Paper,'" establishes that the color yellow was widely associated at the turn-of-the-century with the Aesthetic Movement and its most flamboyant literary celebrity, the out-of-the-closet homosex-ual, Oscar Wilde, and moreover that Gilman asutely utilized this color-charged subtext of decadence in her story. Walter Kidney further main-tains that aestheticism's sway "was to change American architecture, particularly the architecture of the home, dramatically."[24] The aesthetic movement's adoption of Eastern objects as domestic accessories and its craze for Orientalism in the decorative arts affected wallpaper pat-terns as well. The most highly desired colors for Gothic Revival wallpa-pers were tone-on-tone, and monochromatic combinations of cream, khaki, and shades of yellow, often overlaid with gold in imitation of Japanese leather stenciled papers, were exceptionally popular. Accord-ing to Catherine Lynn's encyclopedic study, *Wallpaper in America,* Charles Eastlake's preference for "very light drab or green (not emer-ald)" perhaps accounted in the 1880s for "the predominance of olive shades in commercially produced wallpapers" accented with "metallic gold" (429). But consumers also associated William Morris with the late-nineteenth-century rage for greenish-yellow tones in home decora-tion, so much so that in 1882 he published a staunch denial that he favored the color. In *Making the Best of It* (1882), Morris cautioned cus-tomers never to "fall into the trap of a dingy bilious looking yellow-green, a colour to which I have special and personal hatred, because (if you will excuse my mentioning personal matters) I have been supposed to have somewhat brought it into vogue. I assure you I am not really responsible for it" (quoted in Wilhide 94). In making this statement, he plausibly wished to disassociate himself from Wilde and other "devi-ant" artists who wore and were currently associated with the signifying color yellow. An additional nuance of what Gilman's narrator calls the wallpaper's "smouldering unclean yellow" (26) appears in Eastlake's decorating manual *Hints on Household Taste;* in an intriguing footnote to his discussion of "[v]ery light drab or green (not emerald), and silver-gray" tinted wallpapers, he warns readers that olive drab or greenish wallpapers often contain perilous arsenic levels:

> We cannot allow the word "green" to pass in this connection without a word of caution. Not all, but many green wall-papers owe their tint to the arsenite of copper, and on this account are poisonous. Numerous and well-attested cases of their deleterious effects are given in the Third Annual Report of the State Board of Health of Massachusetts, pp. 33–57, January, 1872. . . . The writer of the Report, Dr. T. W. Draper, states that "the cases of poisoning by this means constitute a mass of evidence which cannot well be refuted."—ED. (119–20)

Whether Gilman's narrator absorbed or ingested hazardous levels of arsenic from the wallpaper or, more likely, its distasteful design and color affronted her postpartum despondency, the bed chamber's yellow sinuosities encapsulate one of Gilman's chronic concerns—that women and children entrapped in domestic spaces, in comparison to men who work elsewhere, require extraordinarily satisfying personal environments. In recent research funded by the Xerox Corporation, Ellen Hoadley, a professor of business and management, substantiates that even 1990s social scientists know relatively little about the effects of color and its role in human information processing.[25] Nonetheless, the color yellow—a commonplace androgynous choice in today's infant apparel and nursery furnishings—might not assuage universal tastes. In chapter 37 of Henry James's 1881 novel *The Portrait of a Lady,* Isabel Archer Osmond's Roman palazzo features a "yellow room" decorated by her husband, Gilbert Osmond, conceivably literature's most nefarious interior designer. Isabel avoids the room whenever possible; her stepdaughter, Pansy, and Pansy's suitor, Ned Rosier, both consider the locale "ugly" and "cold." Nonetheless, Pansy feels compelled to defend the room's yellow-upholstered walls and French Empire furnishings: "It's papa's taste," she loyally upholds, "he has so much."[26]

Further complicating Gilman's story, the narrator, herself a new mother, speculates at several points whether the attic bedroom had formerly been a nursery. But special wallpaper patterns for nurseries came into vogue in the Gilded Age during the 1870s, particularly among the wealthy. "The needs of children were not a preoccupation of society before the last half of the nineteenth century," Hapgood maintains, and previously "nursery papers were virtually unknown" (246). When Samuel and Olivia Clemens built their Hartford mansion in 1874, she chose a fashionable children's pattern for the nursery called "Miss Mouse at Home," created by English artist, Walter Crane, a reproduction of which hangs in the Clemens nursery today (Hapgood 237). William Morris's more diminutive patterns—"Daisy" or "Willow Boughs," for example—were sometimes hung in children's rooms, but juvenile book illustrators like Crane, Kate Greenaway, Ralph Caldecott, Beatrix Potter, and others later designed or sold their designs for nursery papers.[27] Thus when the narrator questions if her attic bedroom was once a nursery, it is arguable; since she claims some knowledge of the decorative arts, her statement is meant sardonically, and any fashionable woman of her class would recognize it was never decorated for children. If the narrator disguises her misgivings in her secret writings about the room's former use, it offers further evidence that she does not trust her husband, John, and suspects he misrepresented the rented mansion's history when he told her initially that "the place has been empty for years" (25). She evidently has grounds to be skeptical when the attic of the rented residence sports a stylish, if shabby, Morris or Morris-inspired wallpaper pattern, yet the first-floor bedroom remains un-renovated from its out-of-date floral chintz. Gilman might even have expected an *au courant* reader to detect this decorating subtlety. Be that as it may, the narrator's acquaintance with interior design might inevitably lead her to the chilling conclusion that the attic had been decorated within the past decade for another purpose, perhaps to house her husband's or another doctor's female patients.

In *Women and Economics* Gilman attests that "[t]o be surrounded by beautiful things has much influence upon the human creature" (66). By the turn of the century, according to Rae Beth Gordon, "scientific inquiry" had established "the link between interior decoration and morbid pathology."[28] Typical of turn-of-the-century reformers concerned with sanitation, Edith Wharton in her 1897 decorating manual, *The Decoration of Houses,* called wallpaper "objectionable on sanitary grounds" and "inferior as a wall-decoration," pronouncing it "well for the future of house-decoration when medical science declared itself against the use of wall-papers."[29] In "The Yellow Wall-Paper" the attic room's crawling women, barred windows, and odoriferous yellow wallpaper collaboratively symbolize the physiological and emotional womb-to-tomb domestic restriction of nineteenth-century women; Gilman also believed that the "isolation of a private nursery" injured children (Lane 259). Her story anticipates an early twentieth-century decorating manual's cautionary note to mothers that some wallpaper patterns are unsuitable for children or invalids: "The secret worlds in the wallpaper can be very entertaining for the sick-a-bed but they can be maddening when they haunt the rooms day after day" (quoted in Ackerman 123). The story's narrator is consoled that her own "baby is well and happy, and does not have to occupy this nursery with the horrid wallpaper. . . . Why, I wouldn't have a child of mine, an impressionable little thing, live in such a room for worlds" (32). Forty years earlier, Eastlake's decorating manual also validated calm and healthful sleeping environments. "A room intended for repose ought to contain nothing which can fatigue the eye by complexity," he advised. "How many an unfortunate invalid has lain helpless on his bed, condemned to puzzle out the pattern of the hangings over his head, or stare at a wall which he feels instinctively obliged to map out into grass-plots, gravelpaths, and summer-houses, like an involuntary landscape gardener!" (*Hints* 211). Most readers will notice the uncanny resemblance between Eastlake's description of "an unfortunate invalid," who, in imagining in the wallpaper "grass-plots, gravel-paths, and summer-houses," assumes the role of "an involuntary landscape gardener" and Gilman's narrator, who, comparably, surveys from her barred windows a landscape arranged in "hedges and walls and gates that lock, and lots of separate little houses for the gardeners and people" (25).

Gilman additionally treats domestic environments in *Women and Economics,* arguing that "[t]he progressive individuation of human beings requires a personal home, one room at least for each person" (258). In "The Yellow Wall-Paper" and despite the narrator's illness, her physician-husband refuses to occupy separate quarters and allow her some privacy. He also denies his wife the distinctly feminine firstfloor bedroom she prefers. Initially he promises to repaper the attic, then refuses because, as he reasons, "after the wall-paper was changed it would be the heavy bedstead, and then the barred windows, and then that gate at the head of the stairs, and so on" (28). On the one hand, John's illogical rationalization substantiates that he sees his spouse as a consummate consumer; on the other hand, it reveals that he sees himself as the man of the house, a forceful, if tender, fiscal comptroller. Gilman parodied gender-specific economic roles throughout her career, perhaps most comically in the story "If I Were a Man."[30] Still, although the narrator's attic bedroom and its furnishings suggest in aesthetic terms a "boys' school" (26), she is not allowed to move downstairs to the pretty floral room she prefers. Apparently the attic room's color and serpentine pattern appeal more to her husband, another implication that Morris's androgynous patterns complement male sensibilities more than female.

Helen Damon-Moore's study of nineteenth-century periodicals and gender, *Magazines for the Millions,* notes that in the 1890s *The Ladies' Home Journal*'s advice to married couples with "troubled" domestic lives was increasingly to involve the husbands in domestic matters. While the *Journal* continued advocating traditional domestic roles for women, it encouraged men to "spend more time at home" and "be more attentive to their wives and children." The problem with championing "masculine domesticity," Damon-Moore contends, is that while men were advised to spend more quality time at home, women were urged not to leave home except as consumers.[31] But "[i]n the early 1890s," William Leach notes in *Land of Desire,* "most buyers in the U.S. fashion business, as in merchandising generally, were men."[32] Anticipating that 1890s business and professional men might be persuaded to carve out more time for home and domestic matters, male manufacturers of wallpaper and related decorative products quickly responded to masculine tastes. Furthermore, when the public began to think of interior designs as a "profession," typically men entered, and then dominated, the decorative arts market and related retail merchandising.

Wealthy businessmen, in particular, were attracted as new consumers to interior design during the Gilded Age. According to an American furniture historian, "The business of interior decorating was fostered by the nouveaux riches"—industrial and railroad magnates like Cornelius Vanderbilt, Jay Gould, and J. Pierpont Morgan, for example—yet, among their wives, Frances Tracy Morgan, J. Pierpont's wife, evidently furnished "[t]he only specific documentation of a wife who assumed the decorating responsibility" for her New York City mansion (Frelinghuysen 81, 86). For the majority of the financial titans who constructed Gilded Age villas, "both finishing and furnishing of the interior were left to an interior decoration firm" (Platt 17). These self-made men typically selected the architect, then collaborated with a decorating firm to oversee the residence's furnishings and decor. As a result, Sarah Burns contends, "the buyer, who is usually a keen business man, not unnaturally says, 'I must have value for my money.'" When the values and standards of male commerce infiltrated the art market, there was a resultant "shift to surface values, intrinsically identified with commercialism" (59, 62). As wealthy male patrons and the male-headed design firms they hired appropriated the interior design marketplace, they effectively "colonized" female domestic space, and women lost ground. In this sense, Burns remarks, the notion of separate spheres was "very much a one-way affair. Women invaded male territory at the peril of becoming unnatural, unsexed, repellent, barren, and offensive. Men, by contrast, could travel freely into the female preserve, appropriating what they found there and adding it to their 'natural' endowments to achieve the complete and perfect, most highly evolved form of genius" (Burns 168). Juliet Kinchin establishes that earlier in the nineteenth century, bedrooms and drawing rooms were considered feminine spaces, decorated and furnished in light colors and styles, but by the turn of the century there was a "blurring of the boundaries, a trend towards greater integration between the sexes. The hall and library, for example, were now increasingly furnished as family 'living rooms,' and more open planning was leading to greater continuity between adjacent interiors."[33] Male business considerations and workplace stress were newly and thoughtfully weighed in interior decoration. In the opinion of one 1890s male architect and designer, for example, surface design and pattern were more likely to present a soothing backdrop than framed art work to "the tired man of business returning to his suburban home in the evening," since "it can hardly be supposed that he will be in a position to make the special mental effort involved in inspecting his pictures."[34]

If, as Ann Heilmann argues, Oscar Wilde's deviant sexuality was synonymous in 1880s America with the English aesthetes, then American corporate design firms run by creative but solid businessmen and catering to the tastes of heterosexual male consumers with a demonstrated Yankee work ethic might obliterate the decadent taint from marketing art for profit. With the 1890s proliferation of the Newport, Rhode Island, mansions, Wendell Garrett claims, "The age of the architect-decorator had arrived."[35] The gradual effacement of the narrator in "The Yellow Wall-Paper" within her de-feminized androgynous environment—a literal absorption among and identification with the wallpaper's camouflaged women—recalls Martha Banta's ironic statement in *Imaging Women* that when women lose control over their environments, they sometimes "do best by learning to blend with the scene."[36] Yet, if the rage for Eastlake and Morris's androgynous designs in home furnishings pervasively masculinized formerly feminine spaces, it did nothing to free women from traditional domestic and marital duties, Gilman's story imparts, nor to ease their entry into the public sphere. In *Women and Economics* she protests that

> freedom of expression has been more restricted in women than the freedom of impression, if that be possible. Something of the world she lived in she has seen from her barred windows. Some air has come through the purdah's folds, some knowledge has filtered to her eager ears from the talk of men. Desdemona learned somewhat of Othello. Had she known more, she might have lived longer. (66)

"The nineteenth century," Wilhide observes, "saw an increasing separation of activities in the home, with different rooms being assigned to different uses in a manner that would have been unthought of a century previously" (41). If, on the one hand, the Victorian "cult of the child" was responsible for creating unique wallpapers for nurseries—in effect, as Leach argues, for "abstracting" children as "*individual* consumers out of the family"[37]—and, on the other hand, wealthy businessmen's agendas transformed the interior design market, the affordability of mechanically reproduced wallpapers created an innovative means with which to inscribe gender or otherwise territorialize domestic space. A circa 1899–1902 English wallpaper intended for a gentleman's study or bed chamber, for example, reprints battle scenes from the Boer War pirated from the pages of the *Illustrated London News,* and an 1889 pattern, no doubt slated for a young man's library, depicts a disheveled sprawl of "popular books" with discernible text and illustrations (Hoskins 170, 178). Suitable for a bachelor's flat, a 1902 wallpaper features an eye-boggling repeat of the disembodied heads of hundreds of illustrator Charles Dana Gibson's elaborately coiffed "Gibson Girls" (Hapgood 93). And the national post-World War I rhetoric to displace women from jobs traditionally held by men and return them to their homes not surprisingly marked a sudden demand for colorful kitchen wallpapers (Ackerman 236).

If the late-nineteenth-century's increasing inclination to masculinize, androgynize, or infantalize interiors displaced women's domestic empowerment, that trend continues today. A review of Arlie Russell Hochschild's recent book *The Time Bind* emphasizes that women's "increased presence" in the workplace "has led to a mild feminization of work, with more emphasis placed on cooperation and support, but also to a pronounced masculinization of home."[38] Gilman, a trained artist with an auxiliary platform for domestic reform, understood that pleasant, feminine oases within the home could create for women, at least symbolically, what Virginia Woolf advocated: "a room of one's own." In contrast, the ornamental demarcation of residential interiors as male- or children-only spaces illustrates a documentable erosion of female territory within woman's traditional sphere. In this sense Gilman's wallpaper "codes" function in the story to critique her era's increasing exercise of the decorative arts in domestic spaces spatially to define, and consequently further to confine, women's lives. In the tradition of Susan S. Lanser's suggestive essay "Feminist Criticism, 'The Yellow Wallpaper,' and the Politics of Color in America," which investigates Gilman's story in light of late-nineteenth-century constructs of and prejudices against yellow-skinned people, contextualizing "The Yellow Wall-Paper" from the perspective of the turn-of-the-century decorative arts and design market enhances our understanding of evolving economic, social, familial, and sexual roles.[39] A comprehension of late-nineteenth-century society's new proclivity to inscribe, indeed to prescribe gender or otherwise territorialize private space vis-à-vis home decoration, exposes an additional layer of Gilman's palimpsestic text.

Ultimately, whatever Gilman's contemporary readers knew of or might agree upon matters of postpartum depression, masculine domesticity, androgynous home decoration, or female consumerism in a patriarchal market economy, they doubtless shared a common conclusion about the sanity of Gilman's first-person narrator. In January 1892 when "The Yellow Wall-Paper" first appeared in *New England Magazine,* three pen-and-ink illustrations accompanied the story (27, 36, 41).[40] Two show no wallpaper at all on the attic bedroom's walls. The third demands a keen eye to detect a faint serpentine pattern on the shadowed wall behind the housemaid, Jennie, who in protectively shielding the wallpaper from the narrator's eyes also cannily obscures it from the reader's.[41] More recently, a 1977 cinematic adaptation of Gilman's story features a pale yellow striped paper with a benign floral repeat in the narrator's bedroom, while the paperback cover of the 1996 revised second Feminist Press edition of *The Yellow Wall-Paper* utilizes a similarly innocuous pale yellow floral with intermittent stripes.[42] In selecting conservative designs and pleasing tones to represent the wallpaper in Gilman's story, both the twentieth-century cinematic adaptation and the newly revised textual edition, analogous to the original 1892 illustrations, antithetically underscore the narrator's mental illness and her weakness in surrendering herself to the paper's power. Alternatively, in realistically portraying the narrator's paranoia that her ugly, unhealthy surroundings constitute a malignant influence upon her sanity, Gilman accents the woman's strength. Although "The Yellow Wall-Paper" offers many readings and addresses countless material concerns, it can be profitably read as both a parody of and cautionary tale against the era's veneration of mercantile artists like William Morris, whose Arts and Crafts designs understandably attracted wealthy male patrons and sparked the genesis of other prestigious, male-headed interior design firms but also transformed "feminine" rooms within the domestic sphere and eroded women's authority in the home and marketplace.

Most readers are shocked at the conclusion of "The Yellow Wall-Paper" to discover that the narrator has control of, indeed, has always controlled the key to her attic room. She was essentially free at any time to walk out the door and down the stairs, to stroll in the garden and savor the fresh air. This terminating plot twist seems designed as a symbolic shock treatment to Gilman's female contemporaries, admonishing them to grow up, stop blaming men for their troubles, and take responsibility for their own lives. Unlike the story's narrator, Gilman quit Dr. S. Weir Mitchell's treatment of her own volition and subsequently spent her literary career advocating changes to make domestic space less injurious to women's and children's mental and physical health. Her reiterative call for efficient kitchen layout, for windows freed of heavy draperies to admit air and light, and for congenial spaces suitable for reading, conversation, and musical endeavors represents not only a feminist statement but an outcry against her era's egregious decorating excesses. If Gilman's more radical ideas like communal kitchens and child care centers were ahead of their time, her concerns about slavish imitation in women's fashions and the decorative arts were not. An inveterate cultural observer, Gilman cast a disparaging eye at the nineteenth-century "Art for Art's Sake" decorative arts movement, an aesthetic renaissance which metamorphosed into a business enterprise targeted at and merchandised for wealthy Gilded Age businessmen and their wives. Overall, as Elaine Hedges observes, "The Yellow Wall-Paper" illuminates ways in which "women as a group must still contend with male power in medicine, marriage, and indeed most, if not all, of culture."[43] Paralleling the narrator's aggressive assault on the wallpaper, the story attacks the tyranny of the patriarchal marketplace; at the same time, it cautions readers to resist the allure of fashion, advertising, and the superficially chic. If the century's "New Women" are to partake in a sophisticated market economy increasingly directed at regulating and transforming the home, Gilman forewarns, they are obligated to become informed, outspoken, and, above all, influential consumers.

NOTES

1. Shelley Fisher Fishkin, " 'Making a Change': Strategies of Subversion in Gilman's Journalism and Short Fiction," *Critical Essays on Charlotte Perkins Gilman,* ed. Joanne B. Karpinski (New York: G. K. Hall, 1992), 237.

2. Catherine Lynn, *Wallpaper in America: From the Seventeenth Century to World War I* (New York: Norton, 1980), 367. For wallpaper history, see also Marilyn Oliver Hapgood, *Wallpaper and the Artist: From Dürer to Warhol* (New York: Abbeville Press, 1992); Lesley Hoskins, ed., *The Papered Wall: History, Pattern, Technique* (New York: Harry N. Abrams, 1994); Jean Hamilton and Charles C. Oman, *Wallpapers: An International History and Illustrated Survey from the Victoria and Albert Museum* (New York: Harry N. Abrams, 1982); Brenda Greysmith, *Wallpaper* (New York: Macmillan, 1976); E. A. Entwisle, *Wallpapers of the Victorian Era* (Brighton, England: Dolphin Press, 1964); and Phyllis Ackerman, *Wallpaper: Its History, Design and Use* (New York: Tudor, 1923).

3. Charles L. Eastlake, *Hints on Household Taste in Furniture, Upholstery, and Other Details* (Boston: James R. Osgood, 1872; ed. Charles C. Perkins, 6th ed., Boston: James R. Osgood, 1878).

4. Morris, educated at Exeter College and later articled to architect G. E. Street, was heavily influenced in the late 1840s and 1850s by artist and writer Dante Gabriel

Rossetti and the members of the Pre-Raphaelite Brotherhood, a coterie that rejected regnant conventionality in the arts and called for a return to the simplicity and natural devotion inherent in Italian painting Pre-Raphael. Pre-Raphaelite poetry demonstrates sensuousness, metrical experimentation, intricate symbolism, and a partiality for the medieval and supernatural. Morris's most effective narrative poetry appeared in *The Defence of Guenevere* (1858); his passion for Gothic architecture and medievally inspired home furnishings led in 1861 to the establishment of Morris, Marshall, Faulkener and Co., manufacturer of handcrafted furniture, textiles, tapestries, stained glass, and wallpaper. Edward Bourne-Jones, Ford Madox Brown, D. G. Rossetti, and other Pre-Raphaelite artists also participated in the firm.

5. See Gary Scharnhorst, *Charlotte Perkins Gilman* (Boston: Twayne, 1985), 49, and Denise D. Knight, ed., *The Diaries of Charlotte Perkins Gilman*, 2 vols. (Charlottesville: University Press of Virginia, 1994), 2 : 636.

6. Fiona MacCarthy, *William Morris: A Life for Our Time* (London: Faber & Faber, 1994), 604.

7. See MacCarthy, *William Morris,* for additional information about the lives of Jane and Jenny Morris. Another circumstantial irony: Jenny Morris (1861–1935) and Charlotte Perkins Gilman (1860–1935) were born about six months apart, and both died in the same year. "The Yellow Wall-Paper" refers in the next-to-the-last paragraph to a character named "Jane" (42), a name most critics attribute to the narrator; for the character "Jennie," see endnote 41.

8. Charlotte Perkins Gilman, *The Living of Charlotte Perkins Gilman: An Autobiography* (New York: D. Appleton-Century, 1935; reprint, New York: Arno Press, 1972), 46, 47.

9. Biographical entry on Helen Metcalf (1831–1895), founder of the Rhode Island School of Design, in Doreen Bolder Burke, et al., *In Pursuit of Beauty: Americans and the Aesthetic Movement* (New York: Metropolitan Museum of Art and Rizzoli, 1986), 453–54, discusses the school's curriculum and goals. See also John S. Gilkeson, Jr., *Middle-Class Providence, 1820–1940* (Princeton, NJ: Princeton University Press, 1986), 88, who discusses the founding of Rhode Island School of Design "by women whose interest in the decorative arts had been piqued by the Centennial Exposition at Philadelphia," and John R. Frazier, *A History of Rhode Island School of Design* (Providence: Rhode Island School of Design, 1961).

10. Carol Farley Kessler, *Charlotte Perkins Gilman: Her Progress Toward Utopia with Selected Writings* (Syracuse, NY: Syracuse University Press, 1995), 19.

11. Polly Wynn Allen, *Building Domestic Liberty: Charlotte Perkins Gilman's Architectural Feminism* (Amherst: The University of Massachusetts Press, 1988), 34.

12. David Howard Dickason, *The Daring Young Men: The Story of the American Pre-Raphaelites* (Bloomington: Indiana University Press, 1953), 164.

13. On prominent American arts and crafts firms which designed for domestic spaces, see exhibition catalogue, *The Quest for Unity: American Art Between World's Fairs, 1876–1893* (Chicago: Detroit Institute of Arts and Rohner Printing Co., 1983); Sarah Burns, *Inventing the Modern Artist: Art and Culture in Gilded Age America* (New Haven: Yale University Press, 1996); Alice Cooney Frelinghuysen, "Patronage and the Artistic Interior," *Herter Brothers: Furniture and Interiors for a Gilded Age* (New York: Harry N. Abrams, 1994); and Frederick Platt, *America's Gilded Age: Its Architecture and Decoration* (South Brunswick, NJ, and New York: A. S. Barnes, 1976).

14. Quoted in Mary A. Hill, *Charlotte Perkins Gilman: The Making of a Radical Feminist, 1860–1896* (Philadelphia: Temple University Press, 1980), 118.

15. Edith Wharton's lampoon appears in her autobiography, *A Backward Glance* (New York: D. Appleton-Century, 1934), 106.

16. Jackson Lears, *Fables of Abundance: A Cultural History of Advertising in America* (New York: Basic Books, 1994), 381; Charlotte Perkins Gilman, *Women and Economics: A Study of the Economic Relation between Men and Women As a Factory in Social Evolution* (Boston: Small, Maynard & Co., 1898; 5th ed., Boston: Small, Maynard & Co., 1911), 257.

17. Ann J. Lane, *To "Herland" and Beyond: The Life and Work of Charlotte Perkins Gilman* (New York: Random House, 1990), 113.

18. See Julie Bates Dock, *Charlotte Perkins Gilman's "The Yellow Wall-paper" and the History of Its Publication and Reception* (University Park: The Pennsylvania State University Press, 1998), 11–16, for facts and myths associated with the publication of Gilman's short story. In October 1890, Howells sent Gilman's short story to Horace Elisha Scudder, then editor of the *Atlantic Monthly,* who rejected it as "too terribly good to be printed," 11.

19. Quoted in Catherine Lynn, "Surface Ornament: Wallpapers, Carpets, Textiles, and Embroidery," *In Pursuit of Beauty: Americans and the Aesthetic Movement,* ed. Doreen Bolder Burke, et al. (New York: Metropolitan Museum of Art and Rizzoli, 1986), 69–72. Lynn reports that at the 1876 Philadelphia Centennial Exposition, Jeffrey and Company served as agents for William Morris, 69; she also catalogues American merchandisers for Morris papers during the 1870s–1880s, all firms owned and managed by men, 106n32.

20. Charlotte Perkins Gilman, "The Yellow Wallpaper," *The Captive Imagination: A Casebook on "The Yellow Wallpaper,"* ed. Catherine Golden (New York: The Feminist Press, 1992), 31, emphasis added. All quotations are from this edition and henceforth appear parenthetically in the text.

21. The passage from editor Charles C. Perkins's preface to Eastlake's *Hints on Household Taste* reads as follows: "The opinion of one who has studied the essential principles of beauty, such as harmony, balance of parts, symmetry, and radiation, and thus acquired the knowledge necessary to enable him to separate the good from the bad, or in other words the fit from the unfit (for this is the determining-point in selection), ought to be of the same weight upon matters of taste as that of any man upon subjects which he has taken pains to master. But, unfortunately, it is not," viii.

22. Elaine B. Hedges, ed., afterword to *"The Yellow Wall-Paper,"* by Charlotte Perkins Gilman, rev. ed. (New York: Feminist Press, 1996), 45.

23. Elizabeth Wilhide, *William Morris: Decor and Design* (New York: H. N. Abrams, 1991), 71, 98.

24. Walter C. Kidney, *The Architecture of Choice: Eclecticism in America, 1880–1930* (New York: George Braziller, 1974), 5.

25. Ellen Hoadley, "Investigating the Effects of Color," *Communications of the ACM* 33 (February 1990): 120–25, 139.

26. Henry James, *The Portrait of a Lady,* ed. Leon Edel (Boston: Houghton Mifflin, 1963), 305–6.

27. Hapgood notes that "Crane's rivals in the nursery were Kate Greenaway and Ralph Caldecott" (239), although the latter two sold their illustrations to manufacturers rather than designed wallpapers (240, 243). By the twentieth century, Cecil Aldin, John Hassall, Beatrix Potter, and Mabel Lucie Attwell, who drew the cherubs in Charles Kingsley's book, *Water Babies,* likewise "had been translated into wallpaper" (Hamilton and Oman 67).

28. Rae Beth Gordon, "Interior Decoration in Poe and Gilman," *LIT: Literature, Interpretation, Theory* 3 (1991): 93.

29. Edith Wharton and Ogden Codman, Jr., *The Decoration of Houses* (New York: Charles Scribner's Sons, 1897; New York: Norton, 1978), 44.

30. In Gilman's "If I Were a Man," a married woman dresses up as a man and rides the train into the city with her husband's associates. During the trip she "learned and learned" that males equated purchasing power with enterprise, entrepreneurialism, and pecuniary exchange, whereas in men's eyes women were thoughtless consumers. *The Charlotte Perkins Gilman Reader: "The Yellow Wallpaper" and Other Fiction,* ed. Ann J. Lane (New York: Pantheon, 1980), 36.

31. Helen Damon-Moore, *Magazines for the Millions: Gender and Commerce in the "Ladies Home Journal" and the "Saturday Evening Post"* (Albany: State University of New York, 1994), 98.

32. William Leach, *Land of Desire: Merchants, Power, and the Rise of a New American Culture* (New York: Pantheon, 1993), 95.

33. Juliet Kinchin, "Interiors: Nineteenth-Century Essays on the 'Masculine' and the 'Feminine' Room," *The Gendered Object,* ed. Pat Kirkham (Manchester and New York: Manchester University Press, 1996), 23, 25.

34. Architect Baillie Scott, quoted in Nicholas Cooper, *The Opulent Eye: Late Victorian and Edwardian Taste in Interior Design* (New York: Whitney Library and Watson-Guptill Publications, 1977), 12.

35. Wendell D. Garrett, et al., *The Arts in America: The Nineteenth Century* (New York: Charles Scribner's Sons, 1969), 377.

36. Martha Banta, *Imaging American Women: Idea and Ideals in Cultural History* (New York: Columbia University Press, 1987), 232. See Banta's discussion of nineteenth-century camouflage techniques in art and literature (Wharton's *The Age of Innocence* and *The Custom of the Country,* Chopin's *The Awakening,* and Dreiser's *Sister Carrie,* for example) for representations of women who variously stand out from or are absorbed into their cultural backgrounds, 232–38. See also Thorstein Veblen's classic treatment of "conspicuous consumption" and women as chattel in *The Theory of the Leisure Class* (1899).

37. Leach, *Land of Desire,* 38, who furthermore notes that with the rise of the mega-department store during the 1880s, "children's departments with carnival atmospheres (especially toy departments) began to appear in retail stores, symptomatic of an emerging child world, quite separate from the adult world, that had never existed before in the United States," 72.

38. Review of Arlie Russell Hochschild, *The Time Bind: When Work Becomes Home and Home Becomes Work* (New York: Metropolitan Books, 1997), by Nicholas Lemann, "Honey, I'm Not Home," *The New York Times Book Review* (11 May 1997), 8. Hochschild also wrote *The Second Shift: Working Parents and the Revolution at Home* (New York: Viking, 1989), a startling comparison of gender equity in the home and workplace as illustrated in two-career families.

39. Susan S. Lanser, "Feminist Criticism, 'The Yellow Wallpaper,' and the Politics of Color in America," *Feminist Studies* 15 (Fall 1989): 415–41.

40. Golden, *The Captive Imagination,* identifies the illustrator as "Jo. H. Hatfield," 4–5. The illustrations are also included in the 1992 Feminist Press edition of Gilman's story.

41. Literary critics have disagreed upon the identity of Jennie as variously the narrator's sister-in-law or the housekeeper. An endnote to Elaine Hedges's "Afterword" in the recent Feminist Press edition, however, identifies Jennie as "the housekeeper," a "guardian/imprisoner for the heroine," *"The Yellow Wall-Paper,"* 62n19.

42. Marie Ashton, dir. and screenplay, *The Yellow Wallpaper* (New York: Women Make Movies, 1978); Elaine Hedges edited the 1996 revised Feminist Press edition of *"The Yellow Wall-Paper"* and wrote the afterword, 37–59.

43. Elaine R. Hedges, untitled bibliographic essay on "The Yellow Wall-Paper," *Charlotte Perkins Gilman: A Study of the Short Fiction,* ed. Denise D. Knight (New York: Twayne, 1997), 152.

Part IV
Late Gilman: The Mixed Legacy

Reading Gilman in the Twenty-First Century

SHELLEY FISHER FISHKIN

W HEN CONSTANCE COINER TOOK A JOB AS AN ASSISTANT PROFESSOR AT SUNY-Binghamton, she tells us that she

> went immediately to the public elementary school, where the principal told me that the kindergarten Ana would attend ended at 10:30 A.M. Having had my expectations affected by 16 years in what *Sixty Minutes* dubbed the People's Republic of Santa Monica, California, I asked, "And what provisions are made for children after 10:30?" "Oh, their mothers come and pick them up," he offered with a shrug. "What about *parents* who work outside the home?" I said, emphasizing "parents" through gritted teeth. "Oh, they get babysitters," he replied.[1]

It was much more than a purely "academic" exercise, then, when Constance required her students that semester—most of whom were pre-law or pre-med or pre-graduate school—to read, as a companion piece to Charlotte Perkins Gilman's "The Yellow Wall-Paper," the epilogue to Sylvia Ann Hewlett's *A Lesser Life: The Myth of Women's Liberation in America.* Coiner writes that

> The epilogue describes a reunion that Hewlett organized in 1984 for the female students she had known as a teacher at Barnard from 1974 to 1981. "The first topic the women gravitated toward," Hewlett reports, "was how to combine careers with children." These economically privileged, highly educated, and professionally successful women, who "at eighteen and twenty . . . truly felt the world was at their feet," expressed despair in the face of overwhelming family-work conflict.
>
> Depending on their gender, my students respond to the epilogue in dramatically different ways: the females—many struck for the first time that combining their career aspirations with parenting might be at best difficult, at worst impossible—echo the anxiety expressed by the women at the reunion. But almost unanimously, males consider this a "women's issue."[2]

For Constance Coiner, as for Charlotte Perkins Gilman, these issues were human issues—not women's issues. And nothing less than the fate of society lay in the balance.

These passages come from Constance Coiner's essay titled "Silent Parenting in the Academy" that appears in the book *Listening to Silences*. Constance Coiner lost her life on TWA Flight 800 in the summer of 1996, as did her daughter Ana. Many of us mourn the loss of a friend. All of us are poorer for the loss of an eloquent and imaginative feminist voice—a voice which gave us, most recently, the remarkable book, *Writing Red: The Writing and Resistance of Tillie Olsen and Meridel LeSueur*. My remarks honor both the passion and the wry sense of humor that Constance brought to everything she did. The passion and the humor she brought to her work—and the passion with which she addressed the challenge of both doing meaningful world-work, as Gilman would have put it, and raising a child—continue to inspire and empower those who knew her.

* * *

How will our students read Gilman in the next millennium? Will they read her at all? Will she strike them as hopelessly dated, a curious memento of a bygone era? Or will she strike them as having things to say to them that they need to hear? What, in short, will last? Perhaps that question might best be approached by a quick look at what will not last.

A generation reared under Title IX is one likely to take working out as an entitlement. Gilman's pioneering campaign to give women access to a gym will interest them—since it will underline how relatively recently such access could not be taken for granted—but it will not impress them. Neither will they be impressed by Gilman's arguments in favor of suffrage: they were born, after all, with the right to vote. Gilman's assertion, in "The Humanness of Women," that "the functions of democratic government may be wisely and safely shared between men and women" will produce a yawn.[3] Votes for women, like physical fitness for women, no longer sparks controversy. Equally dated will be Gilman's idea that world-work could be rewarding for women as well as men. The steady move of women into higher education and the work force has made this idea, as well, incontrovertible—although managing the demands of home and work remain highly challenging, as Arlie Hochschild's newest book, *The Time Bind: When Work Becomes Home and Home Becomes Work* painfully demonstrates.[4] Some of Gilman's improvised anthropology and social theory do not wear well; neither do her racism, her ethnocentrism, her anti-Semitism, her homophobia, her xenophobia, and her simplistic faith in evolutionary progress. And no young women of this generation or the next would consider for a moment eating food that had been kept hot in asbestos-lined containers!

Nonetheless, as Ann Lane comments in *To Herland and Beyond,* Gilman

> offered perspectives on major issues of gender with which we still grapple: the origins of women's subjugation, the struggle to achieve both autonomy and intimacy in human relationships; the central role of work as a definition of self; new strategies for rearing and educating future generations to create a humane and nurturing environment.[5]

Since 1973 when Elaine Hedges first drew our attention to the gender issues it illuminated, *The Yellow Wall-Paper* has come into its own in the American literature classroom and the American studies classroom, as well as in the women's studies classroom, and in scholarly journals. I believe that as long as the social structures for running homes and raising children continue to be improvised and often chaotic, as long as every woman must invent her own strategies for meeting the challenge of melding motherhood and work, then it is likely that students will be able to relate to a pattern that is "dull enough to confuse the eye in following, pronounced enough constantly to irritate and provoke study."[6] And I believe that as long as double standards continue to confine women's horizons of expectations and achievement in the world, they will see the patterns shaping too many of their lives reflected in the yellow wallpaper's "lame uncertain curves [that] . . . plunge off at outrageous angles, [and] destroy themselves in unheard-of contradictions" (13).This small masterpiece is likely to continue to spark stimulating discussions in the years to come.

Women and Economics also continues to be taught in American studies, women's studies, and sociology classrooms and still prompts impassioned debates in academic journals like the *Review of Social Economy.* And if a recent thread of discussion on H-AMSTDY, the American studies electronic discussion group on the Internet, is any indication, *Herland* is likely to remain in classrooms as well as in courses in feminist theory, women's studies, and utopian visions, despite the fact that in December 1996 the publication *Christianity Today* declared that it was "neither a good book nor an influential one." But some less familiar works, as well, engage today's and probably tomorrow's students in surprising and powerful ways.

Gilman's list of "Reasonable Resolutions" published in a *Forerunner* issue of January 1910 never fails to surprise my students. "Let us collectively resolve," Gilman wrote,

> That we will stop wasting our soil and our forests and our labor!
> That we will stop poisoning and clogging our rivers and harbors.

That we will stop building combustible houses.

That we will now—this year—begin in good earnest to prevent all preventable diseases.

That we will do our duty by our children and young people, as a wise Society should, and cut off the crop of criminals by not making them.[7]

My students often observe that these ideas are as reasonable today as they were eighty-eight years ago—and as honored in their breach.

What of Gilman's analysis of "Masculine Literature" in "Our Androcentric Culture"? Gilman writes that while men can do all sorts of things in fiction, women are relegated to "the Love Story",

the story of the pre-marital struggle. It is the Adventures of Him in Pursuit of Her—and it stops when he gets her![8]

Gilman's own stories, of course, broke this mold; but is it still the norm? Other plots seem to be available to women today, my students note. But a few choice excerpts from Joanna Russ's hilarious experiment in gender reversals, "What Can a Heroine Do?" quickly set off not only peals of laughter but clicks of recognition: maybe, they realize, things haven't changed that much after all. Can a woman heroine star in a made-for-TV movie without a love interest? Several students try to come up with examples. Others point out the man waiting in wings, an actual or potential love interest—a minor character, perhaps, in some cases, but one whose presence reinscribes Gilman's archetypal female plot.

What about Gilman's comments on dress? Consider Molly Mathewson's paean to *pockets* in Gilman's story, "If I Were a Man":

These pockets came as a revelation. Of course she had known they were there, had counted them, made fun of them, mended them, even envied them; but she never had dreamed of how it *felt* to have pockets.[9]

Will the unisex dressing of today's teenagers make Molly Mathewson's elation incomprehensible to them? Maybe not. Whenever I teach this story, I conduct my annual "pocket survey." I ask each student to count the pockets in his or her clothing (excluding coats and jackets) and have a census taker record the number in two columns, male and female. Even in classrooms where virtually everyone is dressed in jeans, the differences are striking. The average number of pockets the men have is always significantly higher than the average number of pockets the women have. Women students chime in about fake pockets and half pockets and women's suit jackets having none of the hidden real pockets mens' jackets have. Some even confess to buying their clothes in the

men's department just for the pockets. Men are puzzled by the dispar-
ity. But eventually an underlying principle becomes apparent: the design of women's clothing—even sportswear—still puts form over
function, silhouette over utility, while men's clothing puts utility first.
The discussion inevitably broadens—as Gilman no doubt hoped it
would—to the resonances of these gendered differences and where
those differences come from. The number of women who have had
their purses snatched always dwarfs the number of men who have had
their pockets picked, providing, if you will, a gender-based index of vul-
nerability that is as thought-provoking as Gilman's story itself.

Gilman may not be generally known for her press criticism. But at
least one sagacious column she wrote entitled "Do We Get The News?"
has earned her my respect in this field, and the respect of my students.
Here Gilman wrote,

> These clamorous papers, justifying all sins by their mission as press-ven-
> dors, give us from day to day great masses of "facts" in no sense news, and
> other masses of "facts," new indeed, but of no earthly importance. Mean-
> while, the vital incidents of the day—the era-making events, are sometimes
> passed over and sometimes so buried in unimportant details as to com-
> mand no attention.[10]

This rather lacerating picture of newspapers of her day—filled with
"great masses of 'facts' in no sense news, and other masses of 'facts,'
new indeed, but of no earthly importance"—strikes my students as no
less true of the papers of our day than of hers. What era-making events
are today's paper missing? they ask. What kinds of massive, incremen-
tal changes pass below the radar of contemporary newsbeats and editorial strategies? A couple of years ago the editor of the *Daily Texan*
turned up in my seminar. He was so impressed by the challenge Gilman
posed to the press that he made "Do We Get The News?" required
reading for his entire editorial board.

As for a piece by Gilman that works in the upper elementary school
classroom and that might remain of interest to children in the future, I
nominate "The Unnatural Mother." I taught it a few years ago to an
enrichment class for fifth graders, and they understood the story and
its implications about as well as my college students have.

Might there be approaches to Gilman and her work that are not yet
salient but that may be useful to students and teachers in the near future? Let me briefly suggest three such contexts.

First, Gilman's views on architecture are likely to be reexamined with
interest by contemporary advocates of co-housing, an increasingly
popular strategy for building and structuring communities. [I always

tell my students that if I hadn't lived in housing much like that which Gilman describes, my first book would have come out years after it did: I was a resident fellow in a Yale College during the first twelve years of my marriage, and my husband and children and I ate many pleasant meals in the college dining hall. The book got written in large part during the hours I would have spent shopping for, preparing, and cooking food.]

Second, Gilman's life and writings may well come to play a larger role in our growing understanding of the contours of romantic friendships among women in the nineteenth century. Her relationships with women including Martha Luther, Adeline Knapp, and others might help illuminate the spectrum of attachments between women that we are just beginning to explore as scholars. Might it be possible that some future scholar might read "The Yellow Wall-Paper" as a parable of thwarted lesbian desire? Will this scholar read it as an expressionistic fable about one woman's separation from another, a reading reinforced by Gilman's traumatic separation from Martha Luther by the latter's marriage?

Third, Gilman may have value to future generations of scholars interested in the challenge of how someone who is progressive and enlightened on issues of gender can be so myopic and unenlightened on issues of race and ethnicity. How these blind spots endure—how someone can decry discrimination against one group while tolerating it, even engaging in it, against another—is something we need to understand more fully in the present as well as the past. Unfortunately, Gilman can be "exhibit A" in our investigations of the phenomenon.

In a *Forerunner* piece entitled "Mind Cleaning," Gilman writes,

> When we are housecleaning we should clear out and destroy, give or sell if we can, bury in the wholesome earth or consume with clean fire, as much old stuff as possible. Old papers, old bottles, old rags, old junk of all sorts—out it must go, if we are to have a clean house
> When we are mind-cleaning we should clear out and cast away the moldy heaps of old ideas, still to be found in the dark corners of the mind . . .[11]

We might as well face it: some of Gilman's own ideas belong in those moldy heaps we need to discard. But others—indeed, others like the very notion of tossing out worn and useless ideas as readily as we toss out a threadbare garment—are likely to remain fresh and vital for generations to come.

How would Gilman read "us" in 1997? What would this writer who fashioned herself as the consummate archeologist of the present say if she took a stroll to the newsstand today and perused such publications as *Teen, Woman's World, McCalls, Glamour, Cosmopolitan, Vogue, Seventeen, Self, Ebony, Essence, New Woman,* and *Ladies Home Journal,* among others?[12]

The Gilman who wrote, "For the health and beauty of the body it must have full exercise"[13] would be pleased by the focus on women's fitness in these magazines—by a sportswear ad, for example, featuring a stunning, muscular woman athlete. The headline, "Sports Are Giving Women a Strong, Sexy, Smart, Female Bravado" would please the Gilman who wrote, "Men have filled the world with games and sports, from the noble contests of the Olympic plain to the brain and body training sports of to-day, good, bad, and indifferent. Through all the ages the men have played; and the women have looked on, when they were asked."[14] She would be intrigued by an article entitled "How I Got Stronger—and Happier" about one woman's participation in a study of whether women were capable of physical tasks traditionally thought to be beyond them. An ad for clothes that "move the way you do" and another for comfortable shoes would please the author of "If I Were a Man." The "shocking answer" promised in an article on "How Different Are Men from Women" would not shock Gilman at all. The article's conclusions—that "The scientific evidence on sex differences is really quite paltry," and that "barriers between the sexes are more prejudiced than reasoned"—are things that Gilman knew all along. It's about time, she might sniff. She would probably approve of an article challenging teenage girls to judge whether they were thinking about boys too much ("Do You Have Boys on the Brain?"). And she would be pleased by articles entitled, "Why It's Better Not to Be Perfect," "Protect Your Family from Food Poisoning," and "Are You Too Good a Wife?" Ads and articles featuring women doing work in the world as entrepreneurs and professionals would please her, too, as would a story in *Teen* about a girl named Molly who is a whiz in shop.

But Gilman's pleasure in Molly's story would be offset a bit by other aspects of the June 1997 *Teen Magazine* that undercut this image of strong, competent American girlhood. In 1894 under the heading, "Woman's Exchange," Gilman wrote in *The Impress:*

> It was asked of the editor, eagerly, if *The Impress* could be written to about matters of special interest of women and women's clubs; if it was to be a medium for exchange of thought on such subjects. That is one of the things The Impress is for. Letters should be short, very short, and only those dealing with matters of real importance will be answered.
>
> No inquiries as to what is good to remove freckles, and whether a lady should take a gentleman's arm or he hers, or what color goes with what kind of dress you want to make over will be answered here.[15]

What would the Gilman who refused to answer inquiries about what is good to remove freckles make of the pressing questions considered here: "What's the hottest look for toenails this summer?" and "What's the best way to remove glitter nail polish?" Or how would she read a similar column in a magazine pitched to the teenager's mother that deals with how to conceal a beauty mark? And what would she make of the cover of *Teen Magazine,* which features, alongside an article on "How to Show Your Hair Who's Boss," a "true story" titled, "My Mom Killed Herself"? Or of an ad featuring a girl who changes her nail polish every time she calls a boy and hangs up?

Gilman's pleasure in ads for clothes that move as you do and comfortable women's shoes would be diluted by the opposing images of what women should wear that appear alongside them. Omnipresent ads for spike heels would prompt her to repeat a comment she made in her essay, "Why Women Do Not Reform Their Dress": "The present style of dress means, with varying limits, backache, sideache, headache, and many other aches; corns, lame, tender or swollen feet, weak, clumsy and useless compared to what they should be; . . . with a thousand attendant . . . restrictions and unnatural distortions amounting to hideousness."[16] As she wrote in a poem entitled "The Cripple," "There are such things as hoofs, sub-human hoofs, / High-heeled sharp anomalies; / Small and pinching, hard and black, / Shiny as a beetle's back, / Cloven, clattering on the track, / These are hoofs, sub-human hoofs . . ."[17] Some of the more *outré* concoctions in the fashion pages might prompt her to repeat the observation that women tend to put upon their bodies "without criticism or objection every excess, distortion, discord, and contradiction that can be sewed together" (*The Home* 55). And she would be disheartened by the piece entitled "Guy Spy" featuring a young man who opines that comfortable shoes and clothing look "ridiculous" on a girl.

The Gilman who wrote—probably with things liked cinched waists in mind—that "physical suffering has so been so long considered an integral part of a woman's nature, and is still so generally borne, that a little more or less is no great matter"[18] might, nonetheless, be shocked at the physical suffering today's women voluntarily undergo in the name of beauty (not that Gilman was against reconstructive plastic surgery for accident victims, as her novel *Unpunished* demonstrates).

Regarding the vibrant young women enjoying themselves ecstatically in the ubiquitous cigarette ads that target women, Gilman would likely repeat a comment she had made in a letter to Katharine: "The mass of women are the same old fools they always were. . . . I have small patience with them—painted, powdered, high-heeled, cigarette-smoking idiot. To deliberately take up an extra vice—or bad habit—just to show off—imbecile."[19]

In these magazines, ads for romance novel book clubs, provocative, steamy ads for perfume, and ads for china sculptures featuring Clark Gable scooping Scarlet O'Hara up in his arms would give Gilman ample reason to assume that the "love story" plot was no less prevalent in our day than in hers.

An ad for crystal candles and porcelain collectibles which asks, "What do women want?" and answers, "Beautiful things," would leave Gilman muttering to herself,

> To consume food, to consume clothes, to consume houses and furniture and decorations and ornaments and amusements, to take and take and take forever,—from one man if they are virtuous, from many if they are vicious, but always to take and never to think of giving anything in return except their womanhood—this is the enforced condition of the mothers of the race. (*Women and Economics* 118–19)

Gilman would sigh at the level of meaningless consumption of an ad that urged women to change the sheets on their beds every night.

She would be intrigued by the labor-saving devices for the home that she would see advertised in these magazines—washing machines and dishwashers that would revolutionize housework. But Gilman would soon recognize that these machines were being marketed for private kitchens in private homes, and her old anger would rise.

> We have to pay severally for all these stoves and dishes, tools and utensils, which, if properly supplied in one proper place instead of twenty, would cost far less to begin with; and, in the hands of skilled professionals, would not be under the tremendous charge for breakage and ruinous misuse which now weighs heavily on the householder. Then there is the waste in fuel for these nineteen unnecessary kitchens, and lastly the largest of any item except labour, the waste in food.
> First the waste in purchasing in the smallest retail quantities; then the waste involved in separate catering, the "left overs" which the ingenious housewife spends her life in trying to "use up"; and also the waste caused by carelessness and ignorance in a great majority of cases. . . .
> Count as you will, there could hardly be devised a more wasteful way of doing necessary work than this domestic way. (*The Home* 118–19)

A washing machine ad that asserted, "Washing clothes is a job with no end in sight. But now it can be a cleaner, quicker, easier job with no end in sight," would make it clear to Gilman that not that much had changed. She would fume,

The bottled discord of the woman's daily occupations is quite sufficient to account for the explosions of discord on her wall and floors. She continually has to do utterly inharmonious things, she lives in incessant effort to perform all at once and in the same place the most irreconcilable processes.

She has to adjust, disadjust, and readjust her mental focus a thousand times a day; not only to things, but to actions; not only to actions, but to persons; and so, to live at all, she must develop a kind of mind that *does not object to discord.* Unity, harmony, simplicity, truth, restraint—these are not applicable in a patchwork life, however hallowed by high devotion and tender love. (*The Home* 151–52)

But what in the array of publications on the newsstands today would *really* ignite Gilman's ire? And what figure on the publishing scene today would make her sputter with frustration and rage? Her *bette noire,* I suggest, the "Darth Vader" against whom she would willingly do battle, would be none other than the self-anointed queen of the home herself, Martha Stewart.

Gilman anatomized the isolation of the single-family home, the psychic pain that that isolation inflicted on the wife and mother, and the waste of human energy and fossil fuel in its maintenance; she devoted much of her life to trying to transform it. Gilman would be appalled by Martha Stewart's efforts to make that home even *more* demanding and more time-consuming than it already was. "The free woman," Gilman wrote,

having room for full individual expression in her economic activities and in her social relations, will not be forced to pour out her soul in tidies and photograph holders. The home will be her place of rest, not of uneasy activity; and she will learn to love simplicity at last. (*Women and Economics* 257)

While Gilman bemoaned the hours women felt obligated to spend fashioning useless antimacassars, Stewart would have us stitch our own upholstery. While Gilman urged families to abandon the single-family kitchen for more efficient communal dining, Stewart would have the housewife become adept in the fine art of crafting crystallized sugar flowers. " 'Fancy cookery,' " Gilman writes, is "a thing as far removed from true artistic development as a swinging ice-pitcher from a Greek vase. . . . neither pure food nor pleasure, but an artificial performance, to be appreciated only by the virtuoso" (*Women and Economics* 232). Gilman might be impressed by the multiplicity of media through which Martha Stewart pushes her message—magazines, cookbooks, decorating books, television programs, even a line of household paints. But she would mince no words about what is wrong with the ideals Stewart is projecting and glorifying:

For each man to have one whole woman to cook for and wait upon him is a poor education for democracy. The boy with a servile mother, the man with a servile wife, cannot reach the sense of equal rights we need today. Too constant consideration of the master's tastes make the master selfish; and the assault upon his heart direct, or through that proverbial side-avenue, the stomach, which the dependent woman needs must make when she wants anything, is bad for the man, as well as for her."[20]

The "kitchen mind," Gilman wrote,

> focused continually upon close personal concerns, limited in time, in means, in capacity, and in mechanical convenience, can consider only; a, what the family likes; b, what the family can afford; and c, what the cook can accomplish. ("Kitchen-Mindedness" 10)

What gets neglected, in Gilman's view, is "matters of real importance" with which women, as well as men, need to concern themselves not just for their own good, but for the good of the world.

Gilman also wrote,

> What sort of citizens do we need for the best city—the best state—the best country—the best world? We need men and women who are sufficiently large-minded to see and feel a common need, to work for a common good, to rejoice in the advance of all, and to know as the merest platitude that their private advantage is to be assured *only* by the common weal. That kind of mind is not bred in the kitchen. (*The Home* 318)

"The home," Gilman wrote,

> is one thing, the family another; and when the home takes all one's time, the family gets little. So we find both husband and wife overtaxed and worried in keeping up the institution according to tradition; both father and mother too much occupied in home-making to do much toward child-training, man-making! (*The Home* 71)

In her tour of today's magazines for women, then, Gilman would find the same perplexing mixed messages that we ourselves encounter daily: be strong and athletic, but make sure you know the right way to make crystallized sugar flowers; seek out comfortable clothes that move as you do, but also be prepared to torture your feet in the time-honored tradition of spike heels; go out into the world as a professional, but welcome the romance plot lurking in the wings, be sure you consume your quota of beautiful things, and if you feel like being creative and productive, go for it: wrap your wine bottle in five festive ways.

Gilman would take a deep breath. Then she would sigh. Then

maybe—just maybe—she would smile and recall the old saying that the good part of working for social change is that at least you know you've got steady work.

For better or worse, much of Gilman's writing is nowhere close to being obsolete. There is still much cultural work left for her to do.

Who else, after all, has the guts to take on Martha Stewart where she lives?

NOTES

1. Constance Coiner, "Silent Parenting in the Academy," in *Listening to Silences: New Essays in Feminist Criticism,* ed. Elaine Hedges and Shelley Fisher Fishkin (New York: Oxford University Press, 1994), 198.

2. Ibid., 218.

3. Charlotte Perkins Gilman, "The Humanness of Women," *Forerunner* 1 (January 1910): 13.

4. See also Arlie R. Hochschild, "A Work Issue That Won't Go Away," *The New York Times,* 7 September 1998, A17.

5. Ann J. Lane, *To Herland and Beyond: The Life and Work of Charlotte Perkins Gilman* (New York: Pantheon, 1990), 3–4.

6. Charlotte Perkins Gilman, *The Yellow Wall-paper,* ed. with afterword by Elaine Hedges (New York: The Feminist Press, 1973). 13.

7. Charlotte Perkins Gilman, "Reasonable Resolutions," *Forerunner* 1 (January 1910): 1.

8. Charlotte Perkins Gilman, "Masculine Literature" [part 5 of serialized version of "Our Androcentric Culture: or, The Man-Made World"] *Forerunner* 1 (March 1910): 18.

9. Charlotte Perkins Gilman, "If I Were a Man," in *Charlotte Perkins Gilman Reader,* ed. Ann J. Lane (New York: Pantheon, 1980), 33.

10. Charlotte Perkins Gilman, "Do We Get 'The News'?" *Impress,* 20 October 1894, 2.

11. Charlotte Perkins Gilman, "Mind Cleaning" *Forerunner* 3 (January 1910): 5–6.

12. All of the advertisements cited here appeared in the May or June 1997 issues of *Teen, Woman's World, McCalls, Glamour, Cosmopolitan, Vogue, Seventeen, Self, Ebony, Essence, New Woman,* and *Ladies Home Journal.* The ads were part of national advertising campaigns, running in multiple publications. When this essay was originally presented as the closing plenary talk of the Second International Charlotte Perkins Gilman Conference at Skidmore College in June 1997, it was accompanied by slides of all the advertisements and articles from *Teen, Woman's World, McCalls, Glamour, Cosmopolitan, Vogue, Seventeen, Self, Ebony, Essence, New Woman,* and *Ladies Home Journal.*

13. Charlotte Perkins Gilman, *The Home, Its Work and Influence* (Urbana: University of Illinois Press, 1972), 261.

14. Charlotte Perkins Gilman, *Women and Economics* (New York: Harper & Row, 1966), 308.

15. "The Woman's Exchange," *Impress,* 6 October 1894, 4.

16. Charlotte Perkins Gilman, "Why Women Do Not Reform Their Dress," *Woman's Journal,* (23 October 1886): 338.

17. Charlotte Perkins Gilman, "The Cripple," *Forerunner* 1 (March 1910): 26.

18. Charlotte Perkins Gilman, "Why Women," 338.

19. Gilman's letter to Katharine quoted in Lane, *To Herland and Beyond,* 342.

20. Gilman, "Kitchen-Mindedness," *Forerunner* 1 (February 1910): 9.

Select Bibliography

By Charlotte Perkins Gilman

Benigna Machiavelli. Serialized in *Forerunner* 5 (1914). Reprint, Santa Barbara: Bandanna Books, 1993.

Charlotte Perkins Gilman Papers, Schlesinger Library, Radcliffe College, Cambridge, MA.

Charlotte Perkins Gilman Reader. Edited with an introduction by Ann J. Lane, New York: Pantheon, 1990.

Concerning Children. Boston: Small, Maynard & Co., 1900.

The Diaries of Charlotte Perkins Gilman. 2 vols. Edited with an introduction by Denise D. Knight, Charlottesville: University Press of Virginia, 1994.

Forerunner. Vols. 1–7 (1909–16). Reprint, with an introduction by Madeleine B. Stern, New York: Greenwood, 1968.

Herland. Serialized in *Forerunner* 6 (1915). Reprint, with an introduction by Ann J. Lane, New York: Pantheon, 1979.

His Religion and Hers: A Study of the Faith of Our Fathers and the Work of Our Mothers. New York and London: Century Co., 1923. Reprint, London: T. Fisher Unwin, 1924. Reprint Westport, Conn.: Hyperion Press, 1976.

The Home: Its Work and Influence. New York: McClure, Philips & Co., 1903. Reprint, New York: Source Book Press, 1970.

In This Our World. Oakland: McCombs & Vaughn, 1893, 3d. ed. Boston: Small, Maynard & Co., 1898. Reprint, New York: Arno, 1974.

"Kitchen-Mindedness." *Forerunner* 1 (February 1910): 7–11.

The Later Poetry of Charlotte Perkins Gilman. Edited with an introduction by Denise D. Knight, Newark: University of Delaware Press, 1996.

The Living of Charlotte Perkins Gilman: An Autobiography. Foreword by Zona Gale. New York: Appleton-Century, 1935. Reprint, with an introduction by Ann J. Lane, Madison: University of Wisconsin Press, 1990.

The Man-Made World or, Our Androcentric Culture. Serialized in *Forerunner* 1 (1909–10). Reprint, New York: Charlton Co., 1911.

"Mind Cleaning." *Forerunner* 3 (January 1912): 5–6.

"Moving the Mountain." Serialized in *Forerunner* 2 (1911). Reprint, New York: Charlton Co., 1911.

"The New Motherhood." *Forerunner* 1 (December 1910): 17–18.

"The New Mothers of a New World." *Forerunner* 4 (June 1913): 145–49.

Unpunished. Edited with an afterword by Catherine J. Golden and Denise D. Knight. New York: The Feminist Press, 1997.

What Diantha Did. Serialized in *Forerunner* 1 (1909–10). Reprint, New York: Charlton Co., 1910.

With Her in Ourland. Serialized in *Forerunner* 7 (1914).

Women and Economics: A Study of the Economic Relation Between Men and Women as a Factor in Social Evolution. Boston: Small, Maynard & Co., 1898. Reprint, edited with introduction by Carl N. Degler, New York: Harper & Row, 1966.

"The Yellow Wall-Paper." *New England Magazine* (January 1892): 647–56. Reprint, with an afterword by Elaine R. Hedges, Old Westbury: The Feminist Press, 1973. Revised ed. 1996.

The Yellow Wallpaper. Boston: Small, Maynard & Co., 1899.

"The Yellow Wall-Paper" and Selected Stories of Charlotte Perkins Gilman. Edited with an introduction by Denise D. Knight. Newark: University of Delaware Press, 1994.

SECONDARY READINGS

Ceplair, Larry, ed. *Charlotte Perkins Gilman: A Nonfiction Reader.* New York: Columbia University Press, 1992.

Golden, Catherine, ed. *The Captive Imagination: A Casebook on "The Yellow Wallpaper."* New York: The Feminist Press, 1992.

Hill, Mary. *Charlotte Perkins Gilman: The Emergence of a Radical Feminist, 1860–1896.* Philadelphia: Temple University Press, 1980.

———. *The Journey from Within: The Love Letters of Charlotte Perkins Gilman, 1897–1900.* Lewisburg, PA: Bucknell University Press, 1995.

Karpinski, Joanne, ed. *Critical Essays on Charlotte Perkins Gilman.* New York: G. K. Hall, 1992. (Includes critical essays by Catherine Golden, Elaine Hedges, Mary Hill, Shelley Fisher Fishkin, Joanne Karpinski, and Gary Scharnhorst.)

Kessler, Carol Farley. *Charlotte Perkins Gilman: Her Progress Toward Utopia, with Selected Writings.* Syracuse: University of Syracuse Press, 1995.

Knight, Denise D. *Charlotte Perkins Gilman: A Study of the Short Fiction.* New York: Twayne Publishers, 1997.

Kolmerten, Carol A. "Texts and Contexts: American Women Envision Utopia, 1890–1920." In *Utopians and Science Fiction by Women,* edited by Jane A. Donawerth and Carol A. Kolmerten. Syracuse: Syracuse University Press, 1994.

Lane, Ann J. *To "Herland" and Beyond: The Life and Work of Charlotte Perkins Gilman.* New York: Pantheon, 1990.

Lanser, Susan. "Feminist Criticism, 'The Yellow Wallpaper,' and the Politics of Color in America." *Feminist Studies* 15, no. 3 (Fall 1989): 415–41.

Meyering, Sheryl L., ed. *Charlotte Perkins Gilman: The Woman and Her Work.* Ann Arbor, MI: University Microfilms International, 1989.

Robinson, Lillian S. "Killing Patriarchy: Charlotte Perkins Gilman, the Murder Mystery, and Post-Feminist Propaganda." *Tulsa Studies in Women's Literature* 10, no. 2 (Fall 1991): 273–85.

Rudd, Jill and Val Gough, eds. *Charlotte Perkins Gilman: Optimist Reformer.* Iowa City: University of Iowa Press, 1999. Forthcoming.

———. *Charlotte Perkins Gilman: A Very Different Story.* Liverpool: University of Liverpool Press, 1998.

Scharnhorst, Gary. *Charlotte Perkins Gilman.* Boston: Twayne Publishers, 1985.

List of Contributors

SHELLEY FISHER FISHKIN is Professor of American Studies and English at the University of Texas. She is the author of *Lighting Out for the Territory: Reflections on Mark Twain and American Culture* (1996); *Was Huck Black? Mark Twain and African American Voices* (1993); *From Fact to Fiction: Journalism and Imaginative Writing in America* (1985), and editor of *The Oxford Mark Twain* (1996). She co-edited with Elaine Hedges *Listening to Silences: New Essays in Feminist Criticism* (1994), and with Jeffrey Rubin-Dorsky, *People of the Book: Thirty Scholars Reflect on Their Jewish Identity* (1996). She co-founded the Charlotte Perkins Gilman Society with Elaine Hedges and served as its first Executive Director from 1990–1998.

CATHERINE J. GOLDEN is Associate Professor of English at Skidmore College, where she specializes in Victorian Literature and American and British women writers. She is co-editor with Denise D. Knight of Gilman's *Unpunished* (1997), and editor of *The Captive Imagination: A Casebook on "The Yellow Wallpaper"* (1992). Her work on Gilman has appeared in *Studies in American Fiction, Modern Language Studies,* and several books. She is Executive Director of the Charlotte Perkins Gilman Society. In addition, she is the author of many essays and reviews on Victorian literature and book illustration, published in *Victorian Poetry, Victorian Studies, Victorian Periodicals Review, CEA Critic,* and *Profession 95.*

CHARLOTTE MARGOLIS GOODMAN is Professor of English at Skidmore College. She is the author of numerous articles on American writers, wrote the critical and biographical Afterword for the Feminist Press editions of Edith Summers Kelley's *Weeds* (1982, 1996), and is author of a feminist biography of Jean Stafford: *Jean Stafford: The Savage Heart* (1990). Her article, "The Lost Brother/The Twin: Women Novelists and the Male-Female Double Bildungsroman," was awarded Honorable Mention in the Florence Howe Award for Feminist Scholarship in 1982.

ANN HEILMANN is Lecturer in English at Manchester Metropolitan University, UK, where she teaches nineteenth- and twentieth-century literature, women's writing, and feminist theory. Her most recent publication is an anthology, *The Late-Victorian Marriage Question: A Collection of Key New Woman Texts* (1998), and she is currently writing two monographs on New Woman fiction. Another anthology, *Sex, Social Purity and Sarah Grand* (co-edited with Stephanie Forward), is forthcoming.

MARY A. HILL is Presidential Professor of History and Women's Studies at Bucknell University. She has received National Endowment for the Humanities grants (1980–81, 1986–87) and was a Fellow at the National Humanities Center (1981–82) and at the University of Washington for the American Council of Education (1991–92). Her publications include: *Charlotte Perkins Gilman: The Emergence of a Radical Feminist, 1869–1896* (1980); *Endure: The Diaries of Charles Walter Stetson* (1985); *The Journey From Within: The Love Letters of Charlotte Perkins Gilman, 1897–1900* (1995).

JOANNE B. KARPINSKI is Professor and Chair of English at Regis University, Denver, Colorado. She is editor of *Critical Essays on Charlotte Perkins Gilman* (1992); "When the Marriage of Two Minds Admits Impediments: Charlotte Perkins Gilman and William Dean Howells," in Shirley Marchalonis, ed., *Patrons and Protégées: Gender, Friendship and Writing in Nineteenth Century America* (1989), and several review essays about Gilman's work.

CAROL FARLEY KESSLER is Professor of English, American Studies, and Women's Studies at the Delaware County Campus of the Pennsylvania State University. Her publications include: *Daring to Dream: Utopian Fiction by United States Women Before 1950* (revised second edition, 1995), *Charlotte Perkins Gilman: Her Progress Toward Utopia, with Selected Writings* (1995); and *Elizabeth Stuart Phelps* (1982).

DENISE D. KNIGHT is Professor of English at the State University of New York College at Cortland, where she specializes in nineteenth-century American literature. She is author of *Charlotte Perkins Gilman: A Study of the Short Fiction* (1997) and editor of *The Diaries of Charlotte Perkins Gilman* (1994); *The Yellow Wall-Paper and Selected Stories of Charlotte Perkins Gilman* (1994); *The Later Poetry of Charlotte Perkins Gilman* (1996); and *Nineteenth Century American Women Writers: A Bio-Bibliographical Critical Sourcebook* (1997). She is President of the Charlotte Perkins Gilman Society.

ANN J. LANE is Professor of History and Director of Women's Studies at the University of Virginia, Charlottesville. She is author of *The Char-*

lotte Perkins Gilman Reader, new edition (1999); *To 'Herland' and Beyond: The Life and Work of Charlotte Perkins Gilman* (1997); *The Charlotte Perkins Gilman Reader* (1980); *Herland: A Lost Feminist Utopian Novel* (1979); *The Living of Charlotte Perkins Gilman* (introduction to new edition, 1991), and articles on Gilman.

JILL RUDD is Lecturer in English at the University of Liverpool, where she teaches medieval literature and women's writing courses. Her publications include *Managing Language in "Piers Plowman"* (1994) and, with Val Gough, two edited collections of essays on the work of Charlotte Perkins Gilman: *A Very Different Story* (1998) and *Charlotte Perkins Gilman: Optimist Reformer* (forthcoming).

GARY SCHARNHORST is Professor of English at the University of New Mexico. He is editor of *American Literary Realism* and editor in alternating years of *American Literary Scholarship.* He is the author of *Charlotte Perkins Gilman* (1985), *Charlotte Perkins Gilman: A Bibliography* (1985), and books on Thoreau, Bret Harte, and W. D. Howells.

HEATHER KIRK THOMAS is Associate Professor of American Literature at Loyola College, Baltimore. She has published essays on Emily Dickinson, Mary Wilkins Freeman, and Kate Chopin in *American Literature, Studies in the Novel, Studies in American Fiction,* and *American Literary Realism.* She is co-editor with William Rossi of Henry David Thoreau's *Journal 6: 1853* (forthcoming).

JENNIFER S. TUTTLE teaches in the Department of Women's Studies at San Diego State University. She is the editor of *The Charlotte Perkins Gilman Newsletter* and the author of "Liminality in Women's History-Mystery: The Case of Anne Perry" (forthcoming in *Popular Culture Review,* Fall 1999). Her writing on Gilman forms part of her manuscript "Contested Territories: Healing Identities in California and the West, 1880–1910."

FREDERICK WEGENER is Assistant Professor of English at California State University, Long Beach. He is the editor of *Edith Wharton: The Uncollected Critical Writings* (1999), and his work has appeared in such journals as *Modern Language Studies, Texas Studies in Literature and Language,* and *Tulsa Studies in Women's Literature.* His essay on women doctors in Gilman's life and writing will appear in *Charlotte Perkins Gilman: Optimist Reformer* (forthcoming).

Index

dence in marriage, 13; similarities with
African American contemporaries, 42;
on social reform, 11, 12–13, 16, 34, 58,
148; social motherhood and, 67–68;
Social Purity movement and, 70; on *St.
Katharine by the Tower* (Walter Besant),
59; on stereopticon show, 60–61; suffrage movement and, 12, 42–43, 210;
on theories of S. Weir Mitchell, 103;
Thomas Perkins and, 40, 41, 93–94; on
Titus Andronicus (William Shakespeare), 59; on unpaid household
labor, 163; utopian fiction by, 18, 19,
30, 65, 79, 80, 82, 89, 90–91, 92, 95, 99,
115, 122, 125, 143, 161; West Cure,
107, 110, 111, 112, 114–15; Western
immigration of, 18; on *Wizard of Oz*
play, 62; on *Woman in the Nineteenth
Century* (Margaret Fuller), 60; on
Womankind (Charlotte Yonge), 60; on
women's sphere, 13, 70, 71, 203,
217–18; work ethic, 47; Zona Gale and,
152
Gilman, George Houghton, 18, 30, 90,
96–97; correspondence with, 16, 35, 47,
49, 83, 94, 97, 98, 99
Glaspell, Susan, 130
Golden, Catherine J., 14, 18–19, 99, 115,
117, 166, 223
Goodman, Charlotte Margolis, 14, 19,
125, 223
Gordon, Linda, 41
Gordon, Rae Beth, 197
Gothic fiction, 168, 195
Great Modern American Stories, The (Wil-
liam Dean Howells, ed.), 162
Griffes's funeral, 56–57
Gynecocentricism, 122, 123–24; in *Her-
land*, 95

Hale, Edward Everett, 38, 91
Hapgood, Marilyn, 192
Harcourt, Alfred, 162
Harper's Bazar, 65
Harris, Susan K., 98
Hayden, Dolores, 71
Hedges, Elaine R., 9–10, 90, 125, 194,
203, 211; as author of "Afterword" for
reprinting of "The Yellow Wall-Paper,"
9, 11; dedication of Gilman essays to,
10

Heilbrun, Carolyn, 94
Heilmann, Ann, 20, 195, 223–24
Helicon Hall, 160, 161
Herland (Charlotte Perkins Gilman), 18,
28, 68, 90, 91, 93, 95, 96, 97, 98, 99,
115, 124–25, 131, 192, 211; gynecocen-
tricism in, 95; literary style of, 96; *Look-
ing Backward* (Edward Bellamy) as
inspiration for, 65; patriarch in, 131;
utopian themes in, 18, 89, 95
Hill, Mary A., 15, 16, 31, 34, 45, 53, 67,
224
Hints on Household Taste (Charles Locke
Eastlake), 189, 192–93, 196
*His Religion and Hers: A Study of the Faith
of Our Fathers and the Work of Our
Mothers* (Charlotte Perkins Gilman),
33–34
Hochschild, Arlie Russell, 201
Home, The: Its Work and Influences
(Charlotte Perkins Gilman), 39, 71,
144, 146, 192, 219
"Housewife, The" (Charlotte Perkins Gil-
man), 165
Howe, Florence: "The Yellow Wall-
Paper" reprinting and, 9
Howe, Harriet, 38, 187
Howells, William Dean, 40, 139, 162, 175,
193
"Human Nature" (Charlotte Perkins Gil-
man), 80
Human Work, 39

"If I Were a Man" (Charlotte Perkins Gil-
man), 169, 198, 212
Imaging Women (Martha Banta), 200
Impress, 14, 38, 39, 40, 66, 114, 116, 135,
215
"In Duty Bound" (Charlotte Perkins Gil-
man), 179
"In the Gold Room: A Harmony" (Oscar
Wilde), 177
In This Our World (Charlotte Perkins Gil-
man), 11, 67, 139, 175
International Socialist and Labor Con-
gress, 56, 190
"Is America Too Hospitable?" (Charlotte
Perkins Gilman), 69
Ishtar. *See* Ashtoreth

Jacobi, Mary Putnam, 43–44
Jacobus, Mary, 177